STATES OF LIBERALIZATION

SUNY SERIES IN GLOBAL POLITICS

James N. Rosenau, editor

A complete listing of books in this series can be found at the end of this volume.

STATES OF LIBERALIZATION

Redefining the Public Sector in Integrated Europe

MITCHELL P. SMITH

STATE UNIVERSITY OF NEW YORK PRESS

Published by
State University of New York Press, Albany

Printed in the United States of America

For information, address State University of New York Press,
194 Washington Avenue, Suite 305, Albany, NY 12210-2384

Production by Kelli Williams
Marketing by Anne M. Valentine

Library of Congress Cataloging-in-Publication Data
Smith, Mitchell P., 1960–
States of liberalization: redefining the public sector in integrated Europe / Mitchell P. Smith.
p. cm.—(SUNY series in global politics)
Includes bibliographical references and index.
ISBN 0-7914-6543-8 (alk. paper)-ISBN 0-7914-6544-6 (pbk.: alk. paper)
1. Europe—Economic integration. 2. Competition—European Union countries. 3. European Union countries—Social policy. 4. European Union countries—Politics and government. I. Title. II. Series.

HC241.S555 2005
337.1'42—dc22 2004066246

10 9 8 7 6 5 4 3 2 1

CONTENTS

TABLES

ACKNOWLEDGMENTS

This project has developed over the course of several years, and was possible only with the support of numerous institutions and individuals. Early portions of the research were supported by a European Union Fulbright Fellowship of the Council for International Educational Exchange. I am grateful to the Centre for European Policy Studies in Brussels for hosting me during this period, and for providing infrastructural support, a dynamic place to work in the heart of Brussels, and a valuable opportunity to interact with policy makers from EU institutions. Dan Kelemen offered important insights during several discussions of the ideas behind the project.

I benefited greatly from participation in the 2000–01 European Forum, "Between Europe and the Nation-State," at the Robert Schuman Centre for Advanced Studies of the European University Institute. The directors of the Forum, Stefano Bartolini, Thomas Risse, and Bo Stråth, lent a robust intellectual energy to the program. Lisa Conant provided trenchant comments as discussant of an early presentation of the argument in the European Forum seminar series. I gained from interaction with the other participants, including Daniele Caramani, Simona Piattoni, Frans Van Waarden, Thomas Vesting, and Carolyn Warner. The intellectually fertile environment of the Centre fostered tremendous progress on the manuscript, despite the stunning views from the Villa la Fonte that at times threatened to lure me into a blissful Tuscan trance.

I am grateful to the University of Oklahoma for financial support that made it possible to spend seven months in Florence. Support from the President's International Travel Fellowships funded a highly productive research visit to Brussels and Düsseldorf in spring 2001. During this visit, along with several others, officials of the institutions of the EU, including members of Commissioners' cabinets; officials of the Permanent Representations to the Council of Germany, of France, and of the Netherlands; and especially members of the European Commission's DGs for Competition and Internal Market, gave their time and knowledge. I deeply appreciate their willingness to share their understanding of the European integration process. Representatives of the Westdeutsche Landesbank also were very generous in answering questions and providing documentation concerning the WestLB dispute with the European Commission. I also thank Cees Wittebrood and Yolanda Lok. During several visits to Brussels, they provided a superbly comfortable place for me to conquer jet lag and hosted meals that were truly memorable both for the cuisine and the company. Thanks to Casper and Douwe for welcoming me into their home with smiles.

For steadfast intellectual support, encouragement, and camaraderie throughout this project, I thank Tom Banchoff. Vivien Schmidt contributed to the project through her scholarly example and thoughtful comments on portions of the work. Two anonymous reviewers for SUNY Press provided insightful and constructive comments which helped me improve the manuscript.

The Political Science Department at the University of Oklahoma has provided a congenial working environment. Like the European Union, the department thrives on unity in diversity. To sustain a high level of collegiality among faculty with such diverse interests and approaches to pursuing them is an impressive achievement from which I have benefited greatly.

Throughout the numerous iterations and tribulations of this project, one thing has been constant: the support of Lynn Lewis. Lynn's faith in my work broke me free of the repeating loop of revisions of the introduction and gave me the confidence to forge ahead. Without her loving support, I would not have completed the book.

My children, Micah and Megan, have matured so much during the course of this project. From a source of gleeful distraction at the outset, they have become supporters who have taken an interest in the project. I cherish and admire them; they are a source of infinite pride. I thank my mom, Cynthia Rosen, who is certain every project I undertake is wonderful. Finally, I thank my father, Murray Smith, for teaching me the inherent value of the pursuit of knowledge, and so much more. This book is dedicated to his memory.

1

INTRODUCTION

In June 2000, a German Socialist member of the European Parliament (MEP) criticized the European Commission's relentless push to extend liberalization of public services in successive steps. "Salami tactics are all very well," commented the MEP, "but we want to know how long the sausage is."[1] The MEP's concern mirrors the scholarly debate taking place in comparative political economy: what are the limits to processes of economic liberalization that have continued to spread across West European countries for two decades? What does the paring away of slices of political regulation and public sector functions suggest about the ultimate impact of the liberalization process? Governments operate in an international environment in which the free flow of capital generates conditions highly conducive to economic liberalization. European integration has intensified these pressures for EU member states. As competition spreads to encompass areas formerly monopolized by public services, to what extent do governments lose discretion over their use of the public sector to achieve political objectives?

From the perspective of many policy makers, the fluidity of global capital and intensity of international competition have created conditions in which economic growth can be secured only by relaxing political constraints on the operation of markets. This process affects all of the regulatory structures of national political economies, including social insurance systems; structures of industrial relations and corporate governance; and the operation of public services such as transportation, telecommunications, and energy supply and distribution. Evidence of reforms across these policy regimes in West European political economies ultimately invokes the current debate in comparative political economy between those who see an ineluctable process of convergence between national economic policies and institutions and those who believe in sustained diversity. Assessments of the relative degree of convergence and diversity vary with convictions about the sources of the most critical forces shaping national political economies. Are these forces internal or external to national systems? To the extent that forces outside the national system drive policy and institutional restructuring, markets overwhelm politics and there is only limited latitude for continued political regulation of markets. Where internal factors bear more causal weight, political regulation may be more resistant to market forces and therefore more stubborn and enduring.

The first approach, which may be termed a "globalization" perspective, indicates that the forces shaping national political economies increasingly are external rather than internal. Adherents of this globalization perspective believe that global economic forces have produced a market liberalization process that leaves little discretion to national political economies (Cerny, 1997; Strange, 1996). Summing up this approach, Alberta Sbragia points out that "the underpinnings of comparative politics which assumed that domestic politics was the crucial variable in explaining policy change are being challenged as never before" (Sbragia, 1998a: 2). The globalization perspective asserts that the potency of international economic factors, especially intensified competition for markets and the mobility of financial capital, undermines the effectiveness of government efforts to determine the contours of the national economy. National systems are punished for sustaining policies or institutional arrangements that are unattractive to investors; national systems of economic regulation compete, inducing emulation of best practice; and the liberalization of international trade increasingly exposes domestic arrangements for economic policy making to pressures for reform from trade partners and multilateral institutions. International integration of markets and the unrestricted mobility of financial capital severely constrain domestic policy choice and foster convergence of policies and institutional forms.

The globalization perspective reflects what Linda Weiss terms "state denial"—the notion that states have been displaced as powerful actors both in domestic and international politics. Taking a critical perspective on that position, Weiss argues that external economic pressures are mediated by domestic factors; the strength of these factors determine the relative intensity with which external pressures are felt.[2] From this domestic institutionalist standpoint, the ability of external forces to foster redesign of domestic policy regimes is severely restricted.[3] National political economies are highly functional interlocking systems of formal and informal institutions rather than simply efficient solutions to economic problems that may be reconfigured in response to market signals. The path-dependence of institutional arrangements and the policies they generate constrain, if not determine, future choices. The factors that determine the degree of liberalization undertaken by national systems therefore are predominantly internal, and national governments retain substantial capacities to shape domestic economic outcomes (Wade, 1996). Mediated by national institutional structures, exogenous forces for fundamental change are likely to be muted, mutated, and resisted. Confronted with common external shocks, national political economies respond in different ways.[4] Moreover, forms of economic governance are not easily transferable from one political economy to another, so that "best practice" does not diffuse readily across systems. This perspective explicitly rejects the notion that institutional arrangements emerge through market selection (Hollingsworth, 1997; Hollingsworth and Boyer, 1997: 49–54).

This study enters the debate by exploring the impact of forces of economic liberalization in western Europe on public sector activities. The book examines how the focus of European economic integration on deepening competition encroaches on the ability of governments to use public sector resources to achieve political objectives. What is the significance of the transformative impact of these forces on the public sector?

To begin with, European Union member countries, though varying considerably in their institutional configurations, are politically regulated market economies with wide-ranging public sector activities. Even in the first decade of the twenty-first century, the defining feature of the political economies of western Europe—of the "European model" of society—remains widespread, if varied, political regulation of the market economy. For several decades, public resources have been used to achieve a range of objectives by West European governments, from protecting jobs (most West European countries) to securing ties between government ministries and critical segments of the business sector (France), to undergirding federalism (Germany), to fostering redistribution of economic resources across regions (Italy). These functions are the product of deeply embedded institutions and norms not given to easy or rapid change. Moreover, as Fritz Scharpf reminds us, the "market-correcting" policies pursued by West European governments in the postwar era have been anchored by popular support as well as a belief that the ends sought through these measures represent legitimate policy goals of national governments (Scharpf, 1999).

Therefore constraints imposed on these policies by the single market process at the center of European integration may "reduc(e) the capacity of national political systems to pursue democratically legitimized political goals" (Scharpf, 1999: 49).

Moreover, like systems of social welfare and industrial relations that are considered defining components of national models of political economy, public services are vital to national conceptions of the state and of economic management. French republicanism, with its ethic of *service publique*—the notion that the equal access of all citizens to quality public services is a vital component of the republican tradition—is but the most immediate illustration of this point. The application of European Union competition rules to Germany's public law banks, the subject of chapter 7, powerfully illustrates this point. The case demonstrates the critical role of European Union institutions in altering domestic political relationships. It also reveals the significance of resulting constraints on the ability of governments to pursue policy objectives through the public sector.

The system of public law banks—which dates to the nineteenth century—was reestablished as a core element of Germany's federal structure after World War II. Also conceptualized as a central component of the social market economy, the state Landesbanken and local Sparkassen (savings banks) were charged with a series of public service functions, including regional economic development and support for small and medium enterprises—Germany's vital *Mittelstand.* As a consequence, the public sector banks have developed close political linkages with local and state-level political party organizations. Throughout the postwar era, the public sector banks have been an integral part of the social market economy, recipients of extensive support from state and municipal governments that value their role as promoters of regional economic development. The public law financial institutions came under the scrutiny of the European Commission beginning in the early 1990s when Germany's private sector banks raised questions about the impact on competition of the financial support accorded the public law banks by the state and municipal governments that own them. Because this financial support affects competitive conditions within Europe's unified internal market, it falls within the jurisdiction of European Community competition law.

By the end of 2001, this process culminated in fundamental reform of the public law banking system marked by dissipation of the financial privileges from which they had benefited for more than a half-century. Only the gradual extension of European Community competition law to the public sector, a process traced in chapter 4, made this change possible. Attesting to the significance of the European Commission's role in the reform of the Landesbanken and Sparkassen in the face of powerful domestic political opposition, one representative of Germany's commercial banking federation asserted that "without Brussels, we would have achieved nothing here in Germany."[5]

But why does such restructuring of a public sector regime matter? In the case of Germany's public law banks, the impact is potentially dramatic for German federalism, the social market economy, Germany's overall economic performance, and public sector institutions throughout European Union member countries. The German federation of public savings banks (DSGV) has warned that the European Commission's application of Community competition rules to the public law banks in effect establishes minimal capital return requirements—and not only for public sector banks, but for public law institutions generally. This endangers the provision of public services by shifting the focus of these institutions toward profit maximization. Dramatizing the perceived threat to the public sector posed by the progressive extension of competition law to additional sectors by the European Commission, Germany's largest public law bank warns that "the Commission puts in jeopardy the future viability of all public-sector enterprises throughout Europe."[6] If this is true, such an approach to competition policy promises to fundamentally recast the European social model, characterized by the extensive and varied use of the public sector to sustain social cohesion.

European Community[7] competition policy can impinge on modes of national economic management and redefine the tools available to governments in their pursuit of prosperity. The public law banks, for example, also make a substantial contribution to the constitutional obligation of the German government to equalize living conditions across regions. By inhibiting the regional development functions of the public sector banks, the Commission's application of Community competition law potentially undermines this federal principle of equality of economic opportunity for all regions [German Savings Bank and Giro Association (DSGV) and Federal Association of Public Banks (VOeB): 13; and German Savings Bank and Giro Association (2000): 11]. Furthermore, public savings banks are the primary bankers for Germany's *Mittelstand,* and finance a large share of business start-ups. To the extent that compliance with Community competition law diminishes the ability of the public law savings banks to perform this public service function, the single market imposes substantial constraints on a crucial dimension of the German strategy for promoting economic growth and employment (German Savings Bank and Giro Association and Federal Association of Public Banks: 5).

When the European Commission ruled in July 1999 that Westdeutsche Landesbank (WestLB), the largest of Germany's public sector banks, would have to repay a very substantial sum to the state of Nordrhein-Westfalen because it had not paid a market rate of return on assets transferred to WestLB by the state (Land) government, WestLB promptly challenged the Commission's decision in the European Courts. Justifying its action, WestLB asserted that "it is imperative that the Commission's decision be tested in the courts, given that it has far-reaching implications for any economic activity performed by the public sector" (Westdeutsche Landesbank: 1). Speaking in the German Bundesrat the day following the Commission's decision, the Economics Minister of Nordrhein-Westfalen proposed that the Commission's decision could have dire implications for the public sector: "in the future every investment—literally every investment—by the public sector on behalf of public-law enterprises could be declared to be unlawful aid."[8] Explaining the robust political defense of Germany's public law banks from a scholarly perspective, Richard Deeg writes that "the historical coalitions supporting this model of banking remain firmly committed to it, for its undoing would shock the very institutional core of the German political economy" (Deeg, 1999: 33).

The conflict between the European Community and Germany's public law banking system therefore underscores the core question of this study: If the competition rules embedded in the single European market can bring about fundamental reform of such purposefully designed, politically entrenched, and staunchly defended public sector institutions in the most powerful EU member state, are there any limits to the transformation of the public sector wrought by Europe's single market process? Considering the concerns of the German Member of the European Parliament, just how much of the public sector "salami" will be kept from the knife of economic liberalization?

The robust debate in comparative political economy about convergence and diversity in capitalist democracy in recent years has been closely related to analyses of the changing role of the state in the economy. Much of the scholarship in this genre has focused on either of two aspects of the state's role: privatization of public enterprises and reform and retrenchment of social welfare policy. The privatization literature has explored the impact of privatization on the role of the state—how does a reduction in state ownership alter the state's control over the marketplace? In general, the literature suggests that privatization does not simply imply a retreat of the state, but represents a shift in the way states exercise control over markets.[9] In the study of social welfare policy, scholars debate the extent to which reforms that have taken place in West European political economies over the past decade or two represent a fundamental departure from the postwar social welfare model—that is, welfare state retrenchment—or simply a quantitative change in social welfare benefits in the face of severe fiscal pressures that in fact indicates relative welfare state resilience.[10]

Both literatures focus on questions of change in public sector objectives and the relative autonomy with which states choose policy tools. Though less studied in the political economy literature than issues of privatization and welfare state reform, examination of the relationship between states and public services complements the way privatization and welfare state studies approach the changing relationship between state and market by asking whether states exhibit a reduced capacity to use public resources to pursue economic, political, and social objectives. Like shifting forms of state control over enterprises and changing social welfare policies, the recasting of how states use public services is a crucial measure of continuity and change of national patterns of political economy. To the extent that governments must establish competition as the guiding principle for the activities of the public sector, they relinquish opportunities to use the public sector to sustain networks of political elites or party-constituency ties, secure jobs, reduce inequality, or promote regional redistribution. The result may or may not be a more efficient, more meritocratic, more transparent, or more democratic system, but it certainly is a different one, with significant implications for the distribution of economic and political opportunities and resources.

The Emerging Focus on "Europeanization"

A central emerging focus of European Union studies concerns the impact of European integration on domestic policies and institutions. Among others,

Simon Hix and Klaus Goetz suggest this debate is overdue, its emergence retarded by the long immersion of EU scholarship in efforts to explain the dynamics of the integration process.[11] Domestic politics have long served as an explanatory factor in accounts of the integration process, but only recently have they been viewed as a dependent variable.[12] Efforts to assess the relationship between the construction of Europe and domestic political change in the states and societies that constitute the European Union are in their infancy. As Markus Haverland notes, "the shaping forces and dynamics of national adaptation to European legislation are still poorly understood" (Haverland, 2000: 84).

In a sense, the study of Europeanization constitutes a microcosm of the debate over globalization and its impact on national political economies. A crucial difference—and one that makes European integration a productive laboratory for studying the impact of external forces for domestic political adaptation—is that the forces promoting domestic adaptation appear to be much more direct and "concentrated" in the EU. This is so for two reasons. First, for the countries of the European Union, economic integration represents a conscious attempt to foster increased competition within Europe's internal market in order to promote prosperity. Second, to accomplish this, Europe's single market process embodies a potent set of market-making mechanisms. The single market, in short, may be conceptualized as an efficient mechanism for transmitting forces of economic liberalization.

The theoretical approaches that have dominated efforts to explain European integration (i.e., integration as the dependent variable) offer conflicting answers to the question of limits to domestic political transformation wrought by the integration process. Liberal intergovernmentalism, which views integration as a sequential process involving first preference formation at the national level and then bargaining between governments, implies that national preferences represent firm limits to the transformational capacities of European-level policies. National executives may embrace European policies as a means of achieving desired political adjustments at diminished domestic political cost. However, if the adjustment costs imposed on a government exceed the benefits generated by the existence of institutionalized arenas that lower the transaction costs of bargaining with other governments, the government will reject efforts to impose adjustment, and may eventually reject the bargaining forum itself. Aware of this danger, the European Commission, which nominally sets the policy agenda for European integration, will be careful not to put forward proposals that may impose excessively costly adjustments on states.

Neofunctionalism represents the principal alternative to liberal intergovernmentalism as an explanation of European integration. While neofunctionalism experienced a revival with the renewal of European integration beginning in the mid-1980s, it was vulnerable to criticism for failing to provide an explanation for the preceding period of stagnation. In other words, neofunctionalism provides an insightful account of the mechanisms that foster integration. However, it is less useful for establishing limits to the process. Approaches to the dynamics of integration that build on neofunctionalist theory emphasize the growing autonomy of the supranational institutions of the EU—especially the European Commission and Court of Justice. From this perspective, the capacity of European integration to transform domestic political economies is defined by the limitations of supranational entrepreneurship. Policy networks effectively organized by the European Commission or in response to the activities of EU institutions can have a dramatic impact on domestic preferences, policies, and even institutions. However, as the empirical material presented in this book makes clear, it is not difficult to find pairs of cases in which similar levels of Commission entrepreneurship produced very different results. This is true, for example, of frustrated efforts to liberalize European postal services in the late 1990s, in contrast with successful liberalization of telecommunications services earlier in the decade, as demonstrated in chapter 6. Such a comparison suggests that while supranational entrepreneurship may at times contribute to the transformation of a sector, it is not necessarily a decisive independent variable in the explanation of outcomes.

European economic integration may be seen in part as a reaction by policy makers against the deeply entrenched defense of political regulation of public services by its beneficiaries—a way to transcend the multiple veto points that block institutional change. The initial impetus behind economic integration may be understood in terms set forth by liberal intergovernmentalist theory: integration serves as a means through which national executives can oversee an orderly process of economic liberalization (Moravcsik, 1994; 1998). Governments gain leverage to implement desired economic reforms while keeping the social and political costs of liberalization within acceptable margins. This reveals why economic integration accelerated after national executives in West European states converged in the mid-1980s on a general preference for fiscal and monetary prudence and liberalization of markets for goods and services: European integration enabled them to lower the political risks of pursuing these ends by locking in commitments to liberalization and neutralizing domestic political opposition. This made it possible for national executives to "harden" their states, rendering them less susceptible to rent-seeking by particularistic interests.[13] European economic integration therefore can be expected to constrain public sector activity because the single market has been consciously embraced by governments of EU countries; it is not simply an exogenous shock to national political economies.

But just how high is the price for this commitment? To what extent have governments bought added discretion to harden the state by ceding control over the scope of domestic political regulation? Embedded in the institutional apparatus developed to implement and regulate Europe's internal market is a competition policy regime with strict provisions for the regulation of government subsidies to industry. Moreover, the internal market and competition policy units (DGs, or Directorates General) of the Community's administrative bureaucracy, the European Commission, are firmly committed to market liberalization as a means to deepen European integration, and therefore are anxious to exploit opportunities to broaden the applicability of the competition rules to new cases or sectors. As Susanne Schmidt puts this, "the Commission has the potential to seriously interfere with those parts of the national economies that are *not* predominantly *structured by market principles*" (Schmidt, 2000: 45). In other words, economic integration produces substantial pressures on domestic political structures to adapt—sometimes in ways unforeseen in the original bargain that set the single market process in motion. Pressures for change in the scope of the public sector represent one such consequence.

Chapter 4 depicts the process through which the institutions of the European Union, particularly the European Commission and the European Court of Justice, but also the European Council representing heads of state and government of member countries, gradually brought the public sector within the remit of the single market program. As this occurred, competition rules governing state aid to industry were extended to public enterprises, and government restrictions on competition designed to protect public sector services providing for the "general economic interest" progressively became incompatible with single market competition law. As a consequence of these developments, the European integration process represents fertile territory for probing political limits to economic liberalization and constraints on the ability of governments to continue to define the scope and purpose of the public sector.

The Political Significance of Competition Policy

The book explores the complex fate of economic liberalization in European Union countries by examining attempts to constrain the use of public sector resources to achieve political objectives in three areas: markets for the procurement of goods and services by public authorities; sectoral liberalization of postal services; and government aid to public enterprises, with a particular focus on a single national case in which the form of aid is deeply institutionalized and the public service function broadly supported—Germany's system of public sector banks. All three areas are highly politicized because, from the perspective of domestic politics, they represent areas of high political sensitivity that justify political regulation, while from a European Union perspective, they comprise protected sectors that undermine the economic objectives of Europe's single market.

The importance of this goal to the integration project can not be overstated. The European Union's effort to construct a single market for goods, services, capital (and, in theory, labor) has focused on breaking down barriers to free competition. The ongoing pursuit of the tantalizing end of a single market—to which Europe can draw ever closer but never entirely achieve—has been the core objective of the European integration project for two decades. The duration of this project, along with its force and pervasiveness have, as in the case of the governing institutions shaping twentieth-century British industrial policy studied by Peter Hall in *Governing the Economy* (1986), "imparted a consistent bias to policy" in the institutions of the EU and, in many instances, in domestic institutions of member states as well. It is unsurprising that the consuming occupation of the past twenty years of European integration has had crucial institutional consequences. Following its mid-1980s launch, the single market project elevated components of the EC institutions responsible for pursuing the completion of the single market to a privileged position in the policy making machinery, rendering the competition and internal market segments of the institutional apparatus *primus inter pares*. From the late 1980s, competition within Europe's internal market took on hegemonic status within EU institutions as the most effective means of promoting competitiveness of

European industry. As a result, the expanse of Community competition policy increased and mechanisms of enforcing competition rules became increasingly robust.

As explained in more detail in chapter 2, the expanded application of EC competition policy associated with implementation of the single market fostered and in turn has been reinforced by four developments. The first is the institutional bias toward liberalism previously described. Second is the Community's penchant for regulatory governance. The significance of the European Commission, the EU's administrative bureaucracy and executive branch, resides in its role as a neutral arbiter and enforcer of rules rather than as an initiator of major spending programs (Majone, 1994). Employing this comparative advantage in regulatory governance, the Commission has elaborated a series of rules for the application of competition policy. These rules were designed to bind other actors, such as national governments and state-owned enterprises; over time, articulation of rules also increasingly has bound the Commission itself. Even where the European Commission hoped to exercise political discretion in the application of rules governing competition, other actors—especially existing and potential private sector competitors of public enterprises—relied on the rules to demand their consistent application by the Commission. In other words, there was significant private sector mobilization on behalf of competition policy goals. Thus, the third development undergirding the strengthening of competition policy is the emergence and growth of a constituency for enhanced competition. Private sector actors seeking opportunities to step outside the confines of domestic politics in order to challenge the market dominance of public sector monopolies and national government subisidies to industry, including both private sector competitors and public enterprises, increasingly became constituents of the Commission—but constituents who at times demanded stricter application of competition rules than the Commission itself was prepared to undertake.

Finally, policy entrepreneurs in national governments seized on the opportunity provided by Community competition policy to firm up their resistance to demands from particularistic interests and strengthen their position relative to patrons of subsidized public enterprises (Smith, 1997). This fourth development may be described as "state hardening," in which governing institutions become "less permeable to penetration from interests and demands emanating from civil society" (Della Sala, 1997: 15).

Hardening is characterized by a depoliticization of policy making that reduces opportunities for rent-seeking.

These developments provide the context for the rising political significance of struggles between protection and competition in the areas of industrial aid, government procurement, and public services such as telecommunications, electricity, and postal services. Industrial aid takes many forms, from direct subsidies to tax exemptions to loan guarantees, and has been pervasive across western Europe for several decades as a means of protecting jobs, promoting industrial restructuring, and selecting national champions. Similarly, purchases of goods and services represent vast expenditures of resources by public authorities (an estimated 15 percent of European Union GDP), constituting a core function of all levels of government. While economic efficiency is an essential guiding principle of such expenditures, public procurement also has served as an important instrument of social, industrial, and regional policies. Finally, the political sensitivity of postal services—an 80 billion euro market (equal to 1.4 percent of GDP for the older EU 15)—derives from both the central economic role of postal communications and the social role of postal networks, which often provide services extending beyond mail delivery, especially in rural areas. These range from the payment of old age pensions to the doorstep delivery of basic provisions to providing a venue (the local post office) for a municipal council meeting. In the postal services sector as in each of these policy areas, European economic integration has brought powerful market-making forces to bear, and the cause of competition has advanced as a consequence of Europe's single market project.

The focus on competition policy is not intended to be representative of European Union policy making. Indeed, the powers of the European Commission in competition policy are unique. These powers include authority to regulate assistance to industry, which has the potential to distort competition within the European market, as well as jurisdiction to review potential abuses of market position. The original EC Treaty acknowledged the disjuncture between individual and collective national economic interests, and accordingly vested substantial authority to regulate competition in the supranational European Commission. This disjuncture made it inappropriate for national governments to regulate a European market. Accordingly, the methodological advantage of a focus on the application of EU competition policy is precisely the significant role of supranational institutions and processes in policy making. Nonetheless, with a few exceptions (Cini and McGowan, 1998; McGowan and Wilks, 1996; Scharpf, 1999), the political implications of Community competition policy have been neglected in the political science literature. Instead, the subject has been dominated by legal scholars who analyze changing interpretations of the meaning and scope of competition law (Gardner, 1995; Gerber, 1994; Goyder, 1998; Hancher, 1993; Page, 1982; Pappalardo, 1991).

One aspect of the development of competition policy most carefully studied by legal scholars—but understudied by political scientists interested in the changing role of the state in capitalist democracies—concerns the gradual extension of competition rules to the public sector. In the early evolution of the European Community, participants widely assumed that application of the competition rules was confined to the private sector. But the inception of the single market project ushered in a new era in the relationship between national governments and EU institutions, especially the European Commission and Court of Justice. The European Commission became much more ambitious in its pursuit of economic integration; both bodies figured prominently in the increasingly active application of competition rules to relations between governments and public enterprises. Moreover, as the European Commission began to apply its Treaty powers in the area of competition policy to public enterprises, successive decisions of the European Court of Justice narrowed the scope of exclusions from Treaty rules for undertakings charged with providing public services. This empowered the European Commission to attack public sector practices that restricted competition, and raised the prospect that European Community competition law could impose liberalization across the public sector landscape in EU member states. Subsequent developments also have raised the question of the limits to that process.

Organization and Argument

Given the treatment of competition policy in the EC Treaty, we should expect Community-level mechanisms to play a formative role in the expansion of competition. To put this in the language of recent studies of "Europeanization," defined as the impact of emergent European level governance on domestic political structures (Cowles, Caporaso, and Risse, 2001), the pressures for domestic adaptation to European governance, though they vary across countries, generally are intense. Indeed, the examination of Europe's extensive market-making mechanisms presented in chapter 2 creates a strong prima facie case for expectations of convergence around free market outcomes with depoliticized regulation.

However, the central puzzle explored in the book concerns the existence of powerful forces of liberalization alongside the uneven, incomplete, and sometimes halting nature of liberalization actually attained. Table 1.1 provides an overview of the state of liberalization in the sectors analyzed in this book. It details the timing of steps toward liberalization at the European Community level, the substance of the liberalization regime proposed, and the actual extent of competition in the sector. As the table illustrates, the gap in time between initial efforts to expand competition and the achievement of a competitive environment, and the distance between aspirations and scope of competition realized vary across sectors.

In the public procurement sector, the extent of competition has fallen far short of bold aspirations for an open, competitive, European market dating back more than a decade. Competition has been introduced into postal services markets in EU member states, but its scope will remain quite limited even two decades after the inception of the liberalization debate. Finally, in the case of Germany's public sector banks, protectionist practices have been overturned, but only through a protracted process spanning well over a decade. The ensuing discussion offers an overview of each sector as discussed in the empirical chapters.

Through the case studies, the book analyzes empirical evidence of the gains and constraints of competition in the public procurement, state aid, and postal services regimes. The powerful drive toward liberalization or "market-making" built into the integration process is the focus of chapter 2. As the chapter asserts, Europe's single market project efficiently transmits forces of economic liberalization to the EU member state governments and other economic actors. Chapter 3 sets out the logic of alternative hypotheses concerning the impact of Europe's forces of liberalization on the public sectors of EU countries. How extensively are public sector arrangements remolded by pressures for economic liberalization? What is the impact on protected public sector monopolies of private sector actors using European Union law as a fulcrum for the introduction of greater competition? To what extent are outcomes determined by these private actors; to what extent by public sector managers or national regulators that may wish to control the expansion of competition?

TABLE 1.1: **States of Liberalization**

Sector	Inception of Substantial Liberalization Process at European Level	Scope of Early Proposed Market Opening	State of Liberalization
Public Procurement	First legislation dates to 1970 Major ECJ cases in mid-1980s Updated liberalization legislation completed in 1993	Contracts offered by public authorities at all levels to be awarded based on value for price; no discrimination in favor of regional or national firms	Relatively little cross-national market penetration; only limited evidence of price convergence across markets
Postal Services	First discussions of a European-level regulatory regime in 1989 First liberalization measure agreed in 1997; effective February 1999 Second liberalization measured adopted in May 2002; took effect in 2003	Proposals ranged from marginal opening to competition (3% of market) to full sectoral liberalization	Letter delivery services representing three-quarters of revenues still reserved to national postal services operators even after second legislated phase of liberalization in 2006; no date established for full liberalization of postal services market
Public Sector Banks (Germany)	1992: Complaint by German Banking Federation to European Commission concerning transfer of housing funds to Westdeutsche Landesbank 1999: European Banking Federation complaint to Commission concerning state guarantees	Elimination of competitive distortions, initially by restricting public sector banks' use of capital provided by state governments; later by ending state guarantees	State governments were required to phase out by 2005 existing liability guarantees extended to public sector banks; newly created liabilities may be guaranteed until 2015

Chapter 4 analyzes the political process through which the European Community's competition policy regime progressively became extended to the public sector in the 1980s and 1990s. Beginning from the premise that the EU's commitment to a liberal economic order is firmly grounded in the 1957 Rome Treaty, the chapter points out that the Community began to fulfill this commitment as national and European level factors coalesced around the 1986 Single European Act that set in motion Europe's single market project. In addition, the chapter examines several cases that came before the Court of Justice that established legal precedents important to efforts to broaden the scope of competition. Yet the chapter also demonstrates that legal outcomes, however favorable to the cause of sectoral liberalization, were by themselves insufficient to infuse with competition markets served by the public sector.

Beginning the empirical section of the book, chapter 5 explores the frustrated efforts of the Commission of the European Communities to create a single market in public procurement. In this sector, a full-fledged competition regime has been legislated at the European level. Nonetheless, restrictive practices persist at national and regional levels, so that the share of public sector contracts awarded across borders remains small. The ineffectiveness of efforts to broaden competition appears overdetermined. On the one hand, the public authorities expected to follow single market procurement rules view the regime as antithetical to their interests, explaining their inclination to skirt the rules. On the other hand, prospective beneficiaries of competition perceive weak incentives to lodge complaints with the European Commission, undermining the prospects for enforcement of the competition regime. The chapter therefore reinforces and extends the lesson of chapter 4, demonstrating that Community legislation by itself can not enhance competition in sectors served or governed by the public sector.

Chapter 6 analyzes the European Commission's efforts to advance postal services liberalization within the EU, and places this case in comparative context with liberalization of the telecommunications and electricity sectors. The chapter demonstrates that telecommunications liberalization was a product not only of Commission leadership, but also of the receptiveness to liberalization of actors in entrenched market and political positions in the member states that supported the liberalization program. Electricity provides an interesting comparison with postal services; until 1996, critical actors in domestic political economies had not yet redefined their interests in ways compatible with sectoral reform, and electricity liberalization was stalled despite long and intense efforts by the European Commission to promote collective action. Postal services in 2001 were in precisely the position of the electricity sector in 1996; stalled, but with the prospect of an advance of liberalization contigent on a shift in the domestic regulatory environment in a member state whose support would be pivotal to the advance of sectoral liberalization at the Community level (Britain in postal services; France in the case of the electricity sector). Illustrating the dynamics of Europeanization, this took place in 2001–2002 as a consequence of changes in Britain's national regulatory structure for postal services that followed directly from the Community's initial steps toward sectoral liberalization. The altered regulatory environment in Britain changed the dynamics of interest articulation, shifting the British position in favor of increased competition in the postal services sector; agreement at the European level on a further modest step toward liberalization ensued.

Chapter 7 examines the development of the European Commission's regime of control of state aid to public enterprises. The chapter focuses on the case of Germany's public sector banks. In this case, public sector activities egregiously violated state aid rules; in such instances European Community competition law places powerful mechanisms for resolving the conflict at the Commission's disposal. Nonetheless, in the instance of Germany's public sector banks these mechanisms led only gradually and indirectly to a reduction in public sector privileges and the introduction of fairer competition. Institutionally and politically dominant domestic actors also brought substantial resources to bear on the struggle to determine how the sector was to be governed. Only after pressure from EU institutions that mounted over the course of a decade, and, critically, a significant shift over time in domestic political alignments, did Germany's public law banks lose their protected status. This shift took place as the application of EC competition policy made it possible for private sector competitors of the public sector banks first to enter, then to carry added weight in, the making of the regulatory regime for the sector. This occurred as national and then regional political elites in Germany acknowledged that the sector was subject to European-level jurisdiction, and as private sector competitors exploited opportunities to pursue their interest in market opening by invoking the provisions of Community competition law.

Drawing on the evidence presented in chapters 5 through 7, chapter 8 returns to the questions posed at the outset. This concluding chapter sets out more systematically how European-level and domestic factors interact to determine the contours of change and continuity in the public sector across countries and market sectors. The analysis establishes that while European economic integration certainly has infused competition into several sectors previously controlled by state-owned monopolies, the process has been more modest and deliberate than a simple reading of Europe's market-making mechanisms would predict.

The chapter outlines the central findings that the timing and scope of liberalization in a sector depend on three factors. The first factor focuses on the stimulus for public sector reform induced by the increased scope of Community competition law. This factor concerns the extent to which the reach of EC competition rules into a public sector activity fosters formal complaints by competitors and potential competitors of protected public service providers. Since the administrative units of the European Commission do not have the capacity to police extensively each sector across EU member states, complaints from third parties typically are required to invoke Community enforcement mechanisms. However, in some sectors there may be few potential market entrants, or willing competitors may be discouraged from complaining to EC authorities because enforcement proceedings are cumbersome, and competitors therefore are unlikely to capture substantial direct benefits. A second question deals with the consequences when there are sufficient complaints to trigger the enforcement process. In some instances, public sector monopolists will adopt a strategy of reform and preparation for intensified competition in anticipation of, or in response to, real or threatened competition law enforcement proceedings. In other cases, public operators in dominant market positions may respond by battling Community institutions.

The second factor accounting for liberalization outcomes is the degree to which entrenched public sector monopolists and protectionist governments revise their assessments of the relative costs and benefits of liberalization. For example, protected public sector operators may promote sectoral liberalization in response to market opportunities, such as the chance to garner market share following the opening of a previously monopolized public service market in another country within Europe's single market. Conversely, concerns about asymmetries across member states in the opening of markets may raise the anticipated costs of liberalization, as public service providers fear foreign penetration of national markets without corresponding opportunities to expand market share abroad.

Finally, outcomes vary with the extent to which domestic political interaction with European-level policies and institutions fosters a reduction in the weight of public sector monopolists in national policy formulation. This shift in the relative weight of domestic political actors comes about as new actors enter the policy making process or the weights of existing actors are redistributed in response to the broadening of the political arena to the European level. This phenomenon is described as "participation expansion," a concept borrowed from the wider literature on international pressures and domestic political change, particularly the work of Leonard Schoppa on international trade and U.S. demands for economic reform in Japan (Schoppa, 1993).

While participation expansion is a critical element of the process of liberalization, the injection of broader competition into markets served by the public sector may be constrained—both in scope and timing—even where participation expansion occurs. Even as the construction of Europe's single market has drawn in additional private sector interests previously on the fringes of policy formulation, and has strengthened opponents of restrictive practices for these sectors, steps to introduce greater competition typically have had to accommodate the interests of public sector monopolists and their domestic political protectors.

In sum, this work shares common concerns with recent work in comparative political economy that addresses the impact of forces demanding adaptation of social welfare systems, systems of industrial relations, patterns of corporate governance, and national models of capitalist democracies generally.[14] Foremost among these is a focus on the nuanced interaction between international forces of change and domestic forces—some of which resist, and others that resonate with and are mobilized by the thrust of outside pressures. In analyzing the outcomes of this interaction, the study finds that the Europeanization process is indeed a clear determinant of far-reaching changes in the relationship between states and markets. Nonetheless, while we should not underestimate the potency of external forces such as globalization and Europeanization in provoking change, this book adds to our understanding of how reform, including its scope and timing, follows a path shaped largely by actors in dominant market positions and by existing institutional arrangements.

2

EUROPEAN INTEGRATION AS MARKET-MAKING

This chapter establishes the baseline, prima facie case for expecting sweeping liberalization of public service sectors across EU member states. The case is based on defining features of the European Union that give the integration process a systematic impetus toward expanding the scope of market competition, as well as dynamics of liberalization that emerge from these features. The defining features include the Community's comparative advantage in regulatory governance, or pursuit of integration through reliance on impartial rules rather than distributive or redistributive policy measures, and a bias toward economic liberalization embedded in the institutional structure and law of the EU. Two crucial dynamics are unleashed by the functioning of these defining characteristics of the EU. The first is a process of state hardening, achieved as governments bring binding European-level commitments into the domestic arena. This process typically redistributes power both within and across institutions in the domestic political economy—modernizers in center-left parties have been empowered, as have central bankers and finance ministry technocrats relative to other economic policy making elites. The second dynamic consists of the mobilization of private sector actors in response to implementation of the EC competition regime. The wedge of increased competition serves as a catalyst for new market entrants to employ Community competition rules to broaden liberalization and combat policies of their governments that disadvantage them in competition with public sector enterprises. Collectively, these characteristics and dynamics create a strong case for the initial expectation that competition is likely to spread to sectors previously protected from the reach of market liberalization.

The Single Market: Efficient Transmitter of Liberalization

The European Community's single market project is an efficient transmitter of the forces of economic liberalization. The single market project itself was a product of shifting domestic political coalitions that favored fiscal austerity and greater scope for competition at home. Along with center-right political elites, party modernizers on the center-left, economic policy makers in governments of the member states of the European Union (EU), the trans-European business community, and the institutions of the EU itself have since the mid-1980s sought to establish rules that foster sound fiscal and monetary management and greater economic competitiveness.

The implications of global economic shocks of the 1970s and 1980s for the political economies of West European countries have been widely analyzed. Vast increases in oil prices, the rise of newly industrialized economies and intensified international economic competition, and the increased speed and volume of international financial flows strained the institutional arrangements of industrialized democracies. Several important political developments followed. Social democratic governments found it increasingly difficult to sustain their commitments to full employment (Scharpf, 1991). Structural unemployment or fiscal deficits—in some cases, both—rose. The increase in capital mobility relative to labor mobility, along with constraints on fiscal resources, undermined institutional arrangements for labor inclusion in national-level bargaining over wages, prices and government spending (Kurzer, 1993).

While external economic constraints persisted into the 1980s and 1990s, what fundamentally changed in western Europe in the mid- to late-1980s is that many government, business, and financial elites in EU member states supported a strategy of making commitments that would lock in a particular path of economic adjustment. Agreement by EU member state governments to the objectives of a single market and a single currency made fiscal and monetary constraints an integral prerequisite of core economic and political objectives.[1] By pursuing a course of auto-binding, these groups increased the credibility of their commitments to austerity and undermined domestic political opposition.[2] Because of the perception of government failure shared by these ascendant groups (Majone, 1994; 1996), they sought to use their growing influence within policy making institutions to render the state less susceptible to particularistic demands for side payments by institutionalizing constraints on policy discretion—that is, by "hardening" the state.

Some political elites on the center-left sought to gain the upper hand in internal party struggles for modernization and enhanced electability. In France, for example, François Mitterrand saw the commitment to EMU as a means of improving the PS's image on the issue of fiscal management, and thereby improving the party's electoral fortunes (Dyson, 1999: 42). Southern European economic policy makers viewed the financial liberalization demanded by the Single European Act and membership in EMU as a means of reining in stubborn public deficits sustained by particularistic demands (Pagoulatos, 1999). The transfer of monetary policy sovereignty to a European central bank made monetary policy constraints much more tangible—and marketable to domestic constituencies—than the vague notion of a loss of monetary sovereignty to the force of international financial markets.

In short, the international economic constraints that had developed in the 1970s and persisted into the 1980s were by the 1990s nationalized, or domesticated; political actors seized on international economic pressures as an opportunity to restructure domestic political power. This process reinforced four factors that drive the liberalization of markets in European Union countries—two of them core features of the EU institutional apparatus, and two of them ongoing dynamics of national political economies:

1. *Regulatory governance.* The single market project, culminating in the process of economic and monetary union (EMU), strengthened a bias toward regulatory governance, in which the focus of policy making is on setting rules to secure and sustain free and fair competition rather than on the distribution or redistribution of resources.
2. *Institutional bias toward economic liberalization.* Closely connected to this development, effective regulation has placed considerable power and autonomy in the hands of a European Commission that is organizationally and ideologically biased toward market liberalization. National governments have ceded regulatory authority to the Commission precisely because of its technical expertise and political neutrality, attributes that render the enforcement of member state government commitments credible.[3] Moreover, the Commission's enforcement authority is supported by a European Court of Justice that is institutionally oriented toward advancing the cause of European integration by breaking down national-level protectionist barriers.

3. *State hardening.* Bringing binding constraints into the domestic arena amplified a restructuring of the distribution of power both within and across domestic political institutions. Central bankers and finance ministry technocrats have been empowered relative to other economic policy making elites, as have modernizers in center-left political parties.
4. *Private sector mobilization.* The process of market liberalization has had an impact on the mobilization and articulation of interests by private sector actors. Market liberalization has served as a catalyst for new market entrants to employ single market rules to broaden liberalization and combat policies of their governments that disadvantage them in competition with public sector enterprises.

European integration has not promoted these developments single-handedly; forces exogenous to policy making by national and EU political institutions fostered economic liberalization prior to the relaunch of Europe in the mid-1980s. However, agreement by member state executives to embark on monetary union endogenized and reinforced these processes, representing an effort to lock in and make credible their commitments to fiscal prudence, monetary discipline and price stability, and liberalization of markets, particularly those dominated by public enterprises (Moravcsik, 1994; 1998; Sandholtz, 1993a). The initial commitment of governments to these objectives empowered European Union institutions that are both ideologically and organizationally wedded to market liberalization. Furthermore, the liberalization process overseen by the European Commission has mobilized private sector actors, including individual firms and business associations, who increasingly use the regulations of an integrated European market to push for further liberalization of product and services markets. This development has broadened and hastened processes of privatization of public services (Smith, 2001a).

Knitting together these "market-making" mechanisms is the position of the European Commission at the hub of the European integration process. The Commission is the hub in two senses: (1) as the central point for information flows; and (2) as a privileged policy interlocutor, making it an attractive resource for domestic political elites pursuing strategies of state hardening. The Commission's strategic position at the center of the EU policy-making web gives it significant leverage to contribute to the preference-formation process of other actors (Nugent, 1995; Sbragia, 1998b). Adding further to the Commission's agenda-setting weight is the ability of the Commission to use the rule of law to its advantage, drawing on different aspects of its EC Treaty-based authority to justify policy initiatives, undergirded by decisions of the European Court of Justice.

Outcomes favoring the expansion of competition are fostered by the degree to which national government preferences have become endogenous to the integration process. National preferences are rendered endogenous through several mechanisms. These include changes in ideas, policy borrowing, or regulatory competition, which alter preferences by operating directly at the level of national executives making policy decisions. In addition, charged with setting the agenda for European integration, an entrepreneurial European Commission can have a powerful impact on the parameters of policy debate, whether through its choice of legal basis for a Community policy initiative or through the way it structures a proposal for legislation passed on to the Council of Ministers and European Parliament. Furthermore, the Commission can influence domestic policy making through processes of consultation that catalyze interest aggregation and articulation by domestic political interests (Mahoney, 2004). Consultation and the formation of policy networks have been critical to the Commission's efforts to promote sectoral liberalization.[4] And finally, Commission decisions in cases of government aid to industry can shift national positions on broader issues of sectoral liberalization.

The supranational competition policy administered by the European Commission represents the apogee of its regulatory powers. The Commission can exercise its competition policy authority through its capacity to investigate individual cases in which there are alleged breaches of competition rules and via its ability to reach decisions that may involve the termination of restrictive practices and even the payment of fines. In addition, Treaty powers enable the Commission to open entire sectors to competition by directive. Moreover, as analyzed in chapter 4, the reach of competition policy authority spread steadily to the public sector during the 1980s and 1990s.

Collectively, the institutional dominance of domestic political coalitions inclined toward neoliberal policies; the ability of policy makers to use European-level commitments to insulate themselves from the claims of domestic interest groups; the regulatory focus of European integration; the European Commission's agenda-setting abilities, competition policy powers, and commitment to apply these rigorously embedded in the Commission's most powerful administrative units; and the endogeneity of national government preferences to the European integration process powerfully promote a competition-enlarging process that generates a self-reinforcing liberal bias.

Regulatory Governance

The institutions of the EC have a comparative advantage in regulation, meaning that the Community has strong capacities for generating rules governing the operation of markets, and few of the financial or political resources required to create common spending programs involving political control of markets. As James Caporaso suggests, "The extractive capacity of EU institutions is nearly zero" (Caporaso, 1996: 39). The European Union therefore may be described as a "regulatory state"—a rule-making system grounded in the rule of law (McGowan and Wallace, 1996: 563). The defining characteristics of EU institutions are the exercise of judicial authority, possession of significant technocratic expertise, and extremely limited financial resources—attributes that give it substantial capacities to set the policy agenda, make rules, and "steer" policy development rather than fully controlling policy making (Sbragia, 1998b: 8).

The European Commission, charged by the Treaty of Rome with keeping the integration process moving forward, is far more capable of framing debate, articulating rules, and organizing support for legislation that removes barriers to the freedom of establishment and free movement of goods and services, than it is at generating policies involving large-scale investment or redistribution of resources. As a regulatory agent characterized by political neutrality, technical expertise, and unrivaled access to information, the job of the European Commission is to manage externalities at the European level (Caporaso, 1996: 39). Thus, the Commission seeks to prevent distortions to free and fair trade within the internal market (Majone, 1994: 90; Sbragia, 1998b: 16–17). Accordingly, the progress of European economic integration restricts the use of government aid to public enterprises when such aid distorts competition with the private sector, and encourages private sector competition in markets previously restricted to the public sector, as in telecommunications and postal services. Similarly, Community competition rules limit the use of social criteria in the awarding of contracts for goods and services by public authorities. Since national authorities face disincentives to regulate such activity on their own, there is need for a European-level regulatory authority to step in if the single market is to be meaningful (Caporaso, 1996: 41).

As Giandomenico Majone argues, the growth of regulation at the European level emerged from the experience of "government failure" at the national level—recognition of the ineffectiveness of the policies based on public ownership and expenditure that prevailed in western Europe from the 1960s to the 1980s (Majone, 1996: 1–2). The experiences of the 1970s and 1980s induced ideological changes across the continent in dominant conceptions about the role of government and its limits (McGowan and Wallace, 1996: 564). The demand for European regulation, moreover, has grown both as companies doing business in the single market have sought the cost advantages of uniform standards for the European market, and as interests disadvantaged in domestic politics, such as environmental protection and consumer rights groups, have seized upon EU institutions as an alternative site for interest articulation (Richardson, 1998; Sandholtz, 1996).

The regulatory focus of economic integration means that redistributive policies at the European level are extremely limited. Yet the regulatory environment may affect the use of redistributive mechanisms nonetheless. For example, single market legislation governing the procurement of goods and services by public authorities specifies that contracts must be awarded in open competition, based on price and quality rather than social criteria. Hence, the European Court of Justice has struck down an Italian law reserving 30 percent of public contracts for undertakings located in the Mezzogiorno. Despite its domestic social policy intentions, the Italian law discriminates against suppliers located in other EU states, and is therefore inconsistent with the principles of the single market.[5]

Ultimately, by vesting authority to regulate competition in the European Commission, the governments of EU countries have in effect separated the *means of distribution,* which remain at the national level, from the *means of regulation.* The result is that national- and regional-level distributional and redistributional policies are constrained by European-level competition rules. And there is evidence that European Community competition policy has promoted substantial convergence of national competition laws. Although the picture is not unilinear, Michaela Drahos, for example, finds substantial elements of convergence in the development of competition law in Germany, Austria, and the Netherlands (Drahos, 1999). Drahos points out that national competition policy governing restraints of trade and abuses of dominant market position may vary along three dimensions: (1) the scope of competition law; (2) the extent to which policy is guided by the principle of outright prohibition of restraints of trade versus a system with a higher threshold for ruling restraints abusive; and (3) the structure of the institutions implementing competition law, which range from government ministries, to independent agencies, to courts whose members represent societal interest associations. National competition law in Germany, Austria, and the Netherlands has faced modest direct pressures for convergence from European Community law. However, forces of convergence also have emerged from several indirect mechanisms. National industry associations have argued that distinctive national merger controls may discriminate against national companies, and that making competition rules consistent with European rules lowers transactions costs (Drahos, 1999: 21 and 29). National courts do not want to be overruled by European-level institutions. Given the supremacy of Community law over national law, these courts may seek to anticipate European-level decisions (Drahos, 1999: 15). Finally, national competition authorities (Germany's Bundeskartellamt, and national courts, e.g.) may wish to maximize their influence over the evolution of European competition law, which they can best do by adopting a competition policy regime similar to that prevailing at the European level (Drahos, 1999: 23).

The European Commission: Policy Initiator with a Liberal Agenda

Organizing common policies of investment or redistribution on a large scale requires fiscal resources beyond the means of the EU.[6] However, the European Commission's ability to act as a policy entrepreneur has taken market regulation further than the expectations of member state governments.[7] Determined to establish their credibility as regulators and to instill trust in the single market, officials of the Commission charged with overseeing the single market have an institutional interest in pursuing gaps in implementation, even when this involves conflict with member state authorities. Moreover, as discussed later, Commission officials generally have a deep philosophical commitment to the objectives of an efficiently functioning internal market, resulting in a zeal to remove barriers to free competition.

As scholars have analyzed extensively, the Commission pursues its commitment to an efficient internal market through a variety of mechanisms of "policy entrepreneurship," including broad consultation and the circulation of exploratory green papers as an agenda-setting device that can help to define policy problems, identify Community-level solutions, and foster the aggregation of interests supporting such solutions.

The relevance of the European Commission as a policy entrepreneur—and as a causal factor in European economic integration—is not unquestioned. First, this chapter began with an account of the single market that relies on shifting domestic political coalitions and national preferences to explain the support of national governments for the project, an essentially intergovernmentalist approach. Indeed, Andrew Moravcsik, the leading theorist of liberal intergovernmentalism, suggests that, on the whole, the Commission's entrepreneurial efforts are "redundant, futile, and sometimes even counterproductive" (Moravcsik, 1999: 270). Moravcsik arrives at this assessment of supranational leadership by examining decision-making processes in the major treaty-amending episodes in the history of European integration.

The defense of the significance of Commission entrepreneurship in the promotion of market liberalization is threefold. First, the liberal intergovernmentalist perspective focuses on the dominant role of intergovernmental bargaining in the determination of outcomes. As Wayne Sandholtz points out, it is not surprising that EU decisions look like interstate bargains. The critical question concerns the context in which the preferences brought to that process are formed (Sandholtz, 1996: 404). Liberal intergovernmentalism depicts bargaining as a sequential process, in which national preferences emerge from domestic political debate, and are then brought to the negotiating table. The EU is simply that—the negotiating table, a forum for bargaining with clearly defined rules. A multilevel governance perspective departs from liberal intergovernmentalism in viewing the European integration process as an independent factor in the determination of national preferences.[8] The preference-formation process, in other words, is interactive rather than sequential; preferences are endogenous.

As an example, Commission decisions on individual cases of state aid to industry can have decisive consequences for a government's position on whether or not liberalization is desirable in a given sector. As Scharpf (1999: 68–69) points out, Commission directives, with their sweeping impact, may encounter resistance within the College of Commissioners itself.

Where several national governments oppose sectoral liberalization, individual Commissioners may be inclined to adopt their national positions within the Commission, especially on questions outside their immediate policy area. When a decision on an individual case of competition-distorting government aid in a single member state is at stake, the Commissioner from the member state concerned may come under heavy pressure from national ministers to oppose the Commission's effort to apply competition rules rigorously. However, other Commissioners are more likely to support the case presented by the competition or internal market DG. No longer able to sustain a subsidy regime or other practices that advantage domestic enterprises and insulate the domestic market, the government that is denied the ability to subsidize a particular sector is likely to become an advocate of liberalization at the Community level (Schmidt, 1998: 174). Moreover, this shift in the preference of a single government can have dramatic consequences for the fate of a sector. In theory, by pursuing a single critical case in a member state, or replicating this in a small number of member states, the Commission may be able to tip the entire balance of the Council of Ministers in favor of support for sectoral liberalization.

Second, Moravcsik allows that the Single European Act is an exception among the five "grand bargains" he studies—the sole case in which the Commission played a vital independent role by solving coordination problems *within* states. The Commission accomplished this by fostering interest organization among businesses favoring the single market and correcting for "aggregation failure" by bringing together in a single initiative the many components of liberalization comprising the single market project, something that no single domestic ministry would have been able to accomplish, or even would have attempted (Moravcsik, 1999: 297).

Finally, rather than instances of major treaty amendment, decisions involving liberalization of public sector activities are "not-so-grand" bargains, whose dynamics are facilitated by the outcomes of the major bargains themselves, including the content of the 1957 Rome Treaty. Given independent powers to enforce treaty rules, the institutions of the EU have a significant impact on interpretations of the rules, the scope of activities to which they may be applied, and the discourse associated with those rules, all of which may produce consequences unanticipated by the national governments that were parties to the initial bargain (Sandholtz, 1996: 409–410).

In concert with national political elites favoring liberalization, senior Commission officials have fostered a discourse based on the idea that barriers to open competition within the European market were the very factors responsible for the weak economic performance of European countries in the 1970s and early 1980s—especially with respect to job creation—relative to their American and Japanese competitors. The European Commission's 1994 White Paper, "Growth, Competitiveness, Employment: The Challenges and Ways Forward into the 21st Century," was the original comprehensive statement of this perspective on Europe's economic difficulties. The White Paper was the product of Jacques Delors's effort to convince EU heads of state and government gathered at the June 1993 Copenhagen European Council to grant the Commission authority to investigate issues of employment and competitiveness. The central message of the White Paper is that EU member states must undertake reforms to augment the employment-intensity of growth, since even robust economic growth in the context of existing economic structures and policies is unlikely to have a substantial impact on persistently high unemployment (Commission, 1994b: 63, 79).[9] The analysis suggests that industrial and labor market policies across Europe have produced rigidities and lags in structural adjustment that account for the inability of European industry to respond efficiently to intensified international economic competition. Required are a reduction in state subsidies that sustain inefficient economic activity, a change in emphasis in public expenditure from social policy to productive investment, a shift in the locus of taxation from employment and investment to consumption, labor-market deregulation that reduces the risks of hiring faced by employers, austere fiscal policies, and wage restraint.

In the years following publication of the White Paper, national executives repeatedly endorsed this analysis following meetings of the European Council; even social affairs ministers of the EU member states came to embrace these policy objectives, accepting the argument that high social charges on labor discourage hiring and that generous unemployment benefits create a disincentive to job-seeking. The mid- to late-1990s witnessed a debate not over the substance of this policy course, but over the most effective way to implement such a program.

During this period, the liberalizing thrust embedded in the Treaty became more institutionally embodied in a European Commission with both an organizational and ideological commitment to liberalization. The Commission under Jacques Delors (President of the Commission, 1985–1995) seized on its Treaty-based authority to regulate the internal market as a vehicle for the aggrandizement of the Commission's role in the integration process. Since the Commission's most substantial powers are in the area of regulation and, especially, competition policy, those administrative units charged with breaking down restrictive practices blocking deeper economic integration—including subsidies to national enterprises and closed processes of bidding for public contracts—became dominant within the Commission, both ideologically and politically. Moreover, as the agent of multiple national governments with a range of policy preferences that decide on single market issues through majority voting rather than unanimity, the Commission's competition DG often has crafted measures that advance economic competition beyond the preferences of even modestly protectionist—or, for that matter, even cautiously liberalizing—governments.

"Hardening" the State

The advance of European regulation has been associated with efforts of national governments to "harden" their states, securing greater autonomy from societal demands. The purpose of hardening is to render the executive less penetrable by particularistic interests; in other words, "system effectiveness is given priority over representation" (Della Sala, 1997: 14). In most national settings, hardening has been deployed as a means of implementing fiscal austerity. This is especially true in cases of otherwise "weak" states, such as Italy, which for years prior to the Maastricht convergence process remained mired in uncontrolled spending on social policy, regional transfers, and government assistance to industry.[10] But efforts to augment fiscal autonomy have hardly been limited to the most extreme cases of penetrated states.[11] For example, economic integration has been fostered by and contributed to the hardening of the Spanish and French states as well.

Hardening is a self-reinforcing process: "as the space for the articulation of claims diminishes, it becomes easier to make decisions to continue to displace authority" (Della Sala, 1997: 30–31). Hardening has been accomplished through a realignment of the dominant policy-making coalition. The Italian case exemplifies this development, as hardening has been accompanied by the virtual domination of Italy's leadership posts by neoliberals and technocrats from the Treasury, the Bank of Italy, and the economics profession (Della Sala, 1997: 29). As Alberta Sbragia has found, "constraints negotiated at the European level" (Sbragia, 1998a: 19) became pivotal in the efforts of senior officials in the economics ministries—

including the Treasury Department and the Bank of Italy—to advance the cause of fiscal austerity and the institutional reforms required to lock in that objective (Sbragia, 1998a: 17).

The dynamics of economic integration redistribute power between domestic political actors in two ways. First, the regulatory functions of the European Commission bring it into intensive interaction with key domestic political actors. Because national governments have vested authority to define and enforce rules on economic competition in the Commission, members of national executives as well as private business associations and firms may experience enhanced opportunities to realize their interests by allying with the Commission. As the Italian case illustrates, economic integration has also served to redistribute power between domestic political actors by creating opportunities for actors favoring fiscal and monetary restraint to augment their status and political influence. This is true for finance ministry and central bank officials as well as modernizers in center-left political parties.

Located at the hub of the integration process, the Commission often serves as an ally for policy makers who in the face of domestic political opposition need additional leverage to promote privatization or a reduction in state subsidies to industry. In this way the Commission often operates in concert with, rather than in opposition to, the preferences of member state governments. As several scholars have argued, there are important ways in which the integration process "strengthens" the state (Milward, 1992; Milward and Sørensen, 1993; Moravcsik, 1994). This may take place in the form of "blame-shifting," which lowers the political costs of policy choices to which there are otherwise no legislative barriers. Alternatively, the demands of economic integration may furnish a faction within a ruling party or coalition with leverage in a struggle over economic policy.[12]

Blame-shifting featured prominently, for example, in Conservative government efforts to close down the shipbuilding industry in Britain during the Thatcher years. The Thatcher government invoked the European Commission's efforts to reduce shipbuilding capacity in Europe as a means of lowering the costs of pursuing the government's preferred policy of industrial diversification in England's decaying North (Smith, 1997). The advantages of colluding with the Commission that may accrue to policy makers in internal party or coalition government policy struggles is illustrated by the 1995 case of government aid to the state-owned Spanish airline, Iberia. In this instance, the ruling Socialist Party was divided between industrial modernizers who wished to transform the culture of state subsidization that had absorbed huge losses accumulated by Iberia between 1990 and 1994, and traditionalists who wished to preserve the status quo. The struggle between the modernizers, led by Spain's industry minister, and traditionalists, led by the minister for transport, reflected a larger contest within the Socialist Party over macroeconomic policy, pitting those favoring state shrinkage against those committed to sustained public investment and ownership.[13] The European Commission assisted modernizers by rejecting the claim from the Transport Ministry that Iberia's problems reflected special factors, such as Spain's recession, the devaluation of the peseta, and poor performance of the company's Latin American subsidiaries. Accordingly, the Commission allowed only part of the capital infusion into Iberia requested by the Spanish government, making this conditional on the sell-off of loss-making Latin American assets. This outcome ultimately strengthened the hand of those promoting fiscal discipline (Smith, 1997: 180–182).

Portraying economic integration more broadly as a means of constraining domestic political choice, Kenneth Dyson writes in his analysis of French motives for pursuing EMU that technocrats in the finance ministry and Banque de France viewed EMU as "an external anchor for domestic economic policy" marked by fiscal and monetary discipline.[14] Ultimately, "EMU was . . . called into service as part of a French domestic game to restructure power over economic policy" (Dyson, 1999: 38). Moreover, the preferences of finance ministry and Banque de France officials ironically were supported by leaders of the French Socialist Party. While President Mitterrand and others did not embrace such policies on ideological grounds, the electoral fortunes of the PS promised to improve to the extent that modernizers could overcome the party's association with fiscal profligacy (Dyson, 1999: 42). Like Italy's ascendant fiscal conservatives, Britain's ruling Conservatives, and Socialist modernizers in Spain, leaders of France's PS found Europe a convenient route to objectives that were elusive through exclusively domestic political means.

Mobilizing Private Sector Interests

In response to the broadening impact of the European Commission and Court of Justice, private sector actors increasingly look to the EU's supranational institutions to satisfy their preferences for freer and fairer competition.

As Karen Alter writes, the ECJ "has a policy bias in favor of dismantling national barriers to trade," which operates to the detriment of those who prefer national rules (Alter, 2001: 53, 229). This bias reinforces the institutionalized domination of monetary and fiscal austerity and market liberalization wrought by other institutional and policy dimensions of economic integration.

Mobilization by private actors at the European level has come about in a number of ways. Judgments of the European Court of Justice have empowered private actors and increased their awareness of their rights to utilize EU competition rules to their advantage. In the early years of the Community's legal system, there were very few cases of infringement of competition law heard; few legal precedents were established and private litigants essentially were discouraged (Alter, 2001: 213–215). However, over time, private firms and business associations have come to view EU competition rules—as defined and enforced by the European Commission, and interpreted by the Court of Justice—as a tool that could enhance their ability to pursue their economic interests. Moreover, as analyzed in chapter 3, partial liberalization represents the thin end of a wedge. Where liberalization has begun in a given sector, market entrants seek to use the competition rules to combat distortions of competition, and increasingly resort to legal remedies—the European Court of Justice—to seek redress.

These arguments extend to private enterprises that compete with providers of public services. Most public enterprises, as in the banking and postal services sectors, not only provide public services, but also engage in business that competes with the private sector. Where government aid to public enterprises exceeds that which compensates for public service functions, it yields an advantage in competitive activities and thereby violates EU competition rules. As these rules have become more fully articulated and more broadly enforced in concert with the single market project, private sector actors have come to view the European Commission, with its exclusive competence to enforce competition regulations, as an ally in rooting out government aid that distorts competition. As posited by Alter, "Domestic actors use European law . . . to achieve outcomes that they are institutionally and politically unable to achieve through the domestic legal or political process alone" (Alter, 2001: 52). Furthermore, the growing authority of EU law creates a "virtuous circle" in which private actors become "less sensitive to the political concerns of governments, more willing to question the limit of state authority, and more willing to challenge the status quo" (Alter, 2001: 218).

As understanding of EC competition rules has spread throughout the European business community, larger numbers of private firms have sought to use these rules to improve their ability to compete. Recent developments in the case of German banking reflect this broader mobilization. As argued in chapter 7, economic integration has made it possible for private banks to challenge the competitive advantages of the public sector Landesbanken in a manner that would not have been possible in Germany's federal system. Following the introduction of the euro, other European banks have taken a growing interest in the German market. Reflecting this emergent "Europeanization" of the banking sector, the European Banking Federation in 1999 submitted a formal complaint alleging violations of EC competition rules that was designed to provide the European Commission with additional leverage to probe the guarantees extended to the Landesbanken (*Financial Times,* December 2, 1999: 16). Indeed, German state and federal governments found themselves with fewer and fewer allies as they sought to defend the status of their public banks.[15]

Community rules limiting the use of state aid to industry have created a powerful symbiosis between the private sector and the European Commission. Studies of the development of the single market have explained how business sector mobilization preceded and catalyzed the single market process (Cowles, 1995). In the aftermath of that process, there was a steady increase in the activities of European-level interest associations, including business associations as well as environmental and consumer groups (Greenwood, 1997; Greenwood and Ronit, 1994; Mazey and Richardson, 1993, 1996). Similarly, market liberalization intensifies private sector engagement with the European Commission. As the Commission has fostered liberalization of postal services, for example, private sector competitors have sought to use rules constraining state aid to public enterprises to improve their competitive position. The Europeanization of the banking sector fostered by EMU follows this pattern. By taking advantage of the opportunity to shift the conflict from the national to the European level, Germany's private banks gained the Commission as a powerful ally. By strengthening Germany's private banks relative to the public credit institutions, the Commission advanced its own broader interest in more sharply defining the role of public services and limiting the impact of government aid on competition within the single market. Furthermore, the introduction of the single European currency amplified this effect by multiplying the number of actors with an interest in the institutional structures inside other EU countries.

Conclusion: Liberalization Without Limit?

Acceptance by EU member state governments of Community competition rules and collective constraints such as the Maastricht convergence criteria and the Stability Pact governing EMU was a product of national preferences emerging from coalitions of finance ministers, central bankers, center-right political elites, social democratic party reformers, and portions of the business sector. Consequently, the ability of national institutional structures to resist changes driven by these rules is severely compromised. While political resistance certainly remains possible, it is not a simple matter for national governments to back away from obligations implied by EU membership. As Wayne Sandholtz points out, the EU system is a complex of intertwined policies; this inhibits the singling out and reversal of individual policies that have become inconvenient or costly for some member states. In other words, as Sandholtz succinctly has summarized this, "membership matters" (Sandholtz, 1996). Provided the system as a whole generates benefits that exceed the costs of the undesirable policy, the member state will not abandon the entire project (Sandholtz, 1996: 411).

Recognizing the limits of national political resistance to the powerful forces of economic liberalization unleashed by economic integration, Philippe Schmitter asserts that "only those countries that elected not to join the EC/EU could confidently expect to preserve their quaint practices of informal collusion, associational concertation, and private interest governance" (Schmitter, 1997: 423–424). Making a related point from a practical perspective, Hans-Olaf Henkel, President of Germany's industry federation, the BDI, has concluded that Europe's single monetary policy and the EC's competition policy, "are stronger than any national populist" that seeks to abandon these commitments (*Financial Times*, December 8, 1999: 2).

In short, regulatory governance, state hardening, and mobilization of private interests generate a strong prima facie case for expectations of sweeping liberalization. Once an economic sector becomes the focus of competition policy, these mechanisms simultaneously erode protectionist elements and foster sectoral liberalization. As chapter 4 explains, the progressive extension of European Community competition policy to the public sector from the 1980s to the present has had dramatic consequences for protected public services. Indeed, the limits to this process are not at all obvious. Working toward an understanding of such limits, the following chapter begins to consider how the forces of liberalization interact with the inclination of public sector monopolists to adapt or resist.

3

EXPLAINING EUROPEANIZATION

Chapter 2 set out the case that the institutions and processes of European integration have the potential to impose a sweeping expansion of competition across markets in EU member states. This chapter looks more closely at the literature on Europeanization, which focuses on the impact of European integration on domestic politics. The examination of the Europeanization literature is designed to help identify the mechanisms by which European-level developments affect domestic politics. Challenging the picture portrayed in chapter 2, the literature calls into question expectations of unilinear change, revealing differences in the introduction of competition across sectors and countries. Outcomes, in other words, defy attempts to establish simple national or sectoral patterns.

The chapter also generates hypotheses regarding the conditions under which pressures for sectoral liberalization from the European level actually lead to augmented competition. The hypotheses focus on two crucial features of the nexus between European-level developments and domestic politics: the extent to which private sector competitors of public service providers mobilize in ways that amplify pressures from the European level for domestic adaptation, and whether protected public service providers respond to mounting liberalization pressures with adaptation or resistance.

Patterns of Continuity and Change in Public Services

Lodge (2000: 89) suggests that the very term "Europeanization" used to describe the effect of integration on domestic politics implies convergence. He posits that convergence of national systems is fostered by policy implementation and the strength of the European Court of Justice in enforcing law related to the single market; policy borrowing; institutional modelling;

and efforts to promote diffusion of best practice in the Community. Concurring with several other studies of the nature of Europeanization, Lodge argues that the policy preferences of national governments have become endogenous to the European integration process. This follows from the fact that national policy makers interact with their counterparts from other member states on a regular basis in Community institutions, such as meetings of the Council of Ministers and working groups (Cram, 1997; Lodge, 2000: 90; Sandholtz, 1996). In fact, while studies of the integration process suggest some dimensions of tentative convergence, the scholarship on Europeanization is hardly conclusive on this point. To date, evidence of the impact of economic integration is mixed, identifying elements of potential convergence and others of diversity that persists in the face of economic, political, and legal pressures.

Consistent with these findings, the market-making forces embedded in the single market process have not produced a uniform pattern of liberalization. Responses to pressures to introduce competition into many areas of public service provision vary not only cross-nationally, but across sectors as well. Competition has expanded unevenly within the European Union's public sector. Competition remains highly circumscribed in markets for the purchases of goods and services by public authorities at both regional and national levels across Europe. In contrast, Europe's telecommunications sector has been completely liberalized. Until the mid-1990s, most governments resisted the introduction of greater competition in the supply and distribution of electricity and gas, but liberalization has since advanced in these markets. At the European level, the postal services sector at the start of the twenty-first century mirrored energy markets in the mid-1990s, with only modest progress in Community-level liberalization. However, the pattern is very uneven across countries, with some having introduced extensive competition unilaterally, others on the verge of doing so, and others adhering to a more restrictive environment.

The United Kingdom was the first liberalizer of telecommunications services and equipment in the late 1980s; Germany resisted the former. This may have a simple explanation: Britain is, of course, a leading neoliberal political economy, while Germany, as numerous observers have found, is suffused with rigidities stemming from its highly structured systems of industrial relations and corporate governance.[1] Yet a decade later, Germany was prepared for liberalization of postal services, while the UK remained a laggard. Similarly, the UK has fully liberalized its electricity and gas markets, but was the target of European Commission action for failing to implement a Community Directive governing open public procurement in the water, energy, transport, and communications sectors (RAPID, March 9, 2000; press release IP 00/238). The Italian government has taken bold steps to reduce distortions to competition resulting from government aid to public enterprises, and has exceeded minimum competition requirements for the first two stages of electricity liberalization, but has made little progress in creating a competitive public procurement market. The government of France was a leader in introducing competition in telecommunications networks and services, yet slowed the introduction of competition in electricity production and supply to the point where it faced legal action by the European Commission in June 2000.

An analytical perspective focused solely on European-level legislation and the legal powers of EU institutions would encounter difficulties explaining this pattern of outcomes. In attempting to explain states of liberalization, this project therefore considers how domestic political structures mediate European-level forces for liberalization. Especially critical from this perspective is the behavior of actors in dominant political and market positions: are changes in their preferences, interests, or strategies necessary for the introduction of greater competition in public service sectors? If so, how and when do these changes come about? What is the role of private sector competitors who advocate enhanced competition? Support for Community liberalization measures from prospective market entrants or private sector competitors who attempt to use Community competition rules to dislodge a public enterprise from its dominant position may be catalysts for more aggressive efforts by the European Commission to gain support for sectoral liberalization. But under what conditions is support for sectoral liberalization among these actors sufficient to induce national governments to back Community-level liberalization initiatives?

Theoretical Approaches to Europeanization

Two concerns are central to the emerging literature on Europeanization—the impact of European integration on national political economies. First, what are the mechanisms by which European integration creates forces of change? And, second, what are the mediating factors that determine the contours of the outcome—that is, the depth and timing of domestic political change? Intergovernmental bargaining may very well explain the decision to create Europe's single market; the subsequently enlarged autonomy of Community institutions is central to explaining the application of single market competition law to public services long governed by politics rather than market rules. But the critical question that follows is this: what are the consequences when the force of Community regulation meets domestic political structures?

Attempts to advance economic liberalization within the single market may emerge from any of three sources. And causal arrows may flow from the national to the European level, or vice versa. First, efforts to introduce competition in sectors monopolized or dominated by public undertakings may derive directly from the demands of national governments, which themselves may be the product of either autonomous preferences of powerful government ministries or the demands of influential domestic constituencies. Here, following any internal struggles that take place during the process of policy formulation, we would expect the implementation of liberalization to proceed fairly smoothly, with most conflict confined to negotiations over the scope and timing of sectoral liberalization. As described in Table 3.1, governments may seek sectoral liberalization as a means of reducing the flow of subsidies to protected public service providers and thereby improving the fiscal implications of public service provision—in short, as a means of hardening the state.

Second, identification of liberalization as a policy objective may emerge from the demands of private sector competitors of public sector undertakings. One of the most significant emergent mechanisms favoring the broadening of competition is the ability of private sector actors who compete with public sector activities to utilize European-level institutional channels—the investigatory and enforcement powers of the European Commission and the European Court of Justice—to demand tighter application of European Community competition rules. In essence, the existence of multiple institutional levels composing the European polity, along with the rigor of European Community competition policy, create a political counterpart to the economic aspect of capital mobility. This *political mobility* of capital derives from the ability of private sector actors to move outside regional or national political arenas in order to combat government practices that privilege public enterprises or reserve entire sectors for public services and thereby exclude private competitors. Hix and Goetz refer to this as a new opportunity for capital to pursue an "exit strategy" (Hix and Goetz, 2000: 12). This is a

TABLE 3.1: **Sources of Liberalization in Europe's Single Market**

Source of Liberalization Initiative	Objective	Domestic Response to Liberalization Proposal
National governments	State "hardening"	Resistence likely to be muted; conflict confined to scope and timing of liberalization
Private sector competitors of public service providers	Larger market share for private sector competitors	Resistance from public service providers who dominate sector depend on the degree to which they've undertaken organizational reforms to prepare for competition; competition complaints at European level likely to spur reforms of public sector monopolists
Initiative of European Commission	Desire of powerful single market and competition DGs to broaden scope of competition as a means of promoting economic dynamism and success of the single market; advancing the cause of European integration	Same as response to pressure arising from private sector competitors, though Commission entrepreneurship and the threat of ECJ action can alter attitudes of public service providers toward the costs and benefits of reform and liberalization

crucial development because, however privileged the position of business in national political economies, that privilege is constrained by the autonomous preferences of the state. However, political mobility gives business added leverage to challenge government practices that protect public sector economic activities at the expense of private sector competitors.

Chapter 4 examines some of the many cases in which private sector actors have invoked European Community competition rules in an effort to rein in the discretion of public authorities and thereby broaden competition in market segments served by the public sector. When private sector competitors seek to promote sectoral liberalization through the EC, resistance from public undertakings that dominate the sector will depend upon the extent to which they have embarked on or plan reforms that prepare them to compete. The threat of market opening created by a private sector competition policy complaint also can serve as a catalyst for public sector reforms.

And, finally, the supranational European Commission may define gaps in the single market that it seeks to close. The Commission's effort to advance sectoral liberalization on the European agenda may be driven by a broader interest in promoting integration, or by the political ascendance within the Commission of directorates general (DGs) responsible for the single market and for competition policy. These DGs have a powerful ideological commitment to economic liberalism as a means to promote economic dynamism, and an institutional interest in the success of the single market. As chapter 2 established, the Community's comparative advantage in regulation and its bias in favor of negative integration, or the removal of barriers to free competition, over positive integration, or common policies, foster the expansion of markets. In addition, the European Commission is skilled at directing the attention of governments to incomplete elements of the single market project and finding support for its cause among sympathetic policy makers. This has important consequences for policy initiatives and the substance of policy proposals, which, according to the EC Treaty, are guided by the Commission. Also, the strong liberal bias of the Commission's most powerful administrative units, the DGs for competition and the single market, tends to amplify the weight of liberal sentiment among member state governments and shapes proposals for Community legislation, and influences the nature of policy networks cultivated by the Commission to help draw national government preferences closer to Commission proposals. Finally, the EC Treaty grants extensive independent powers to the European Commission in the area of competition policy, giving the Commission substantial leverage to root out distortions of competition within the single market.

As Table 3.1 suggests, the fate of liberalization initiatives that have origins in Commission agenda-setting may depend in part on the effectiveness of Commission entrepreneurship, but also will be especially sensitive to the strength of domestic resistance to liberalization within member countries, which may in turn be affected by such pressures as the threat of action by the European Court of Justice.

Cases of the second and third types—which are by no means mutually exclusive given the likelihood that the Commission will encourage complaints about restrictive practices from private sector competitors of public sector undertakings where it wishes to advance competition—are theoretically the most interesting. In these cases, the drive for liberalization comes from the European level; though certainly there is no neat separation between the European and national levels, a liberalization initiative originating with the Commission is more likely to conflict with domestic preferences. What happens, then, when domestic interests in sustained protectionism encounter the force of EC treaty rules backed by Community law?

Explaining Liberalization: Hypotheses

Table 3.2 portrays the universe of possible interactions between national- and European-level "projects" of public sector reform. As the table shows, EU institutions may have designated a sector for liberalization in the name of the single market, or the sector may remain off the liberalization agenda. National governments may wish to open a sector to private competitors, or they may wish to sustain political regulation. Where there is support for liberalization among public authorities, and the prospect of Community-level legislation to liberalize the sector, those governments taking unilateral action have the opportunity to capture first-mover advantages. Once national monopolists have absorbed the costs of adjustment to a competitive environment, they may be well positioned to defend their national market share and expand into the markets of partner single market countries.

When a national government favors increased competition, the government will face an incentive to try to place or advance sectoral liberalization

TABLE 3.2: **Interactions Between the Single Market Project and National Government Policy Preferences**

EC Project: National Project:	Liberalization	No Liberalization
Liberalize	First-mover advantages	Attempt by national government to enlarge market gains by reaching agreement at Community level
Sustained Political Regulation	Legal confrontation or political negotiation over the timing and extent of the introduction of competition	Elite cartel between Commission and member state governments threatened by private sector actors

on the single market agenda. As Fritz Scharpf points out, the ensuing bargaining process between liberalizing and protectionist governments within the Council may be asymmetrical; some countries, particularly those with small domestic markets, will have a greater stake in liberalization than others (Scharpf, 1999: 105). Vanguard liberalizers are in a strong position to compete, and also have an interest in Community-wide liberalization. But asymmetries do not necessarily favor outcomes involving liberalization. Countries with plans for national liberalization measures—those in the second stage of liberalizers—may withhold support for Community measures, fearing that laggard countries will use state resources and monopoly profits to expand into their national markets, gaining competitive advantage through delayed implementation.[2] And even vanguard liberalizers may withdraw support from a liberalization initiative when the concessions required to forge a qualified majority go too far in indulging protectionist impulses, choosing to wait for a more rigorous future measure.[3]

The section on the lower right of the table, in which neither the European nor the national project favors sectoral liberalization, reflects collusion between national and European elites. As chapter 4 details, such collusive arrangements have come under increasing threat as actual and potential private sector competitors of protected public service providers have challenged the ability of national governments acting in concert with the European Commission to decide when to expand the reach of Community competition policy. The public broadcasting sector is a good example of this phenomenon. For the effort to understand Europeanization, the lower left area—representing the instance when a national government seeks to sustain political regulation in the face of a liberalizing project at the European level—depicts an especially interesting interaction. Can sectoral liberalization be imposed on reluctant governments by force of European institutional and legal authority?

The Force of Europeanization and the Political Mobility of Capital

The previous section highlighted two defining questions for the study of domestic political change in response to pressures from the European level: How does European integration create forces of change? What factors mediate domestic political adaptation? The first question concerns the nature and intensity of forces of change. Theoretical accounts of pressures for change tend to focus on the distance between European policies and their structural requirements, on the one hand, and domestic policies and structures, on the other. As Börzel and Risse contend, "*The lower the compatibility between European and domestic processes, policies, and institutions, the higher the adaptational pressure*" (Börzel and Risse, 2000: 6, italics in original). When European norms and rules are consistent with those at the domestic level, they neither create compliance problems nor generate important changes in political opportunity structures in domestic politics (Börzel and Risse, 2000: 6).

In the case of the Community competition regime, the tension emerges as sectors long dominated by public sector monopolists fall under competition rules. As explained in chapter 4, this is a process that gathered momentum with the implementation of the single market program during the latter 1980s and 1990s. Accordingly, a first potential explanatory hypothesis for the parameters of liberalization could be located at the European level:

Hypothesis I

The scope and timing of liberalization are a product of the intensity of European-level pressures for sectoral change.

In particular, the political mobility of capital—the ability of competitors of protected public sector enterprises to move outside the national political arena to pursue liberalization through European level institutional and legal channels—may be a prime catalyst for European-level liberalization pressures. Capital's political mobility can operate as a powerful weapon in the cause of economic liberalization. For example, complaints concerning violations of Community competition rules initiated by private sector actors have undermined elements of regional policy in Italy, overturning a public statute predating the single market that required that authorities purchase a fixed percentage of goods and services from firms headquartered in the Mezzogiorno. The ability of private capital to appeal to the Community regulator, the European Commission, and the European Court of Justice for firm application of competition rules enlists private sector interests in the process of opening public sector activities to competition. An opening to competition in a market segment previously monopolized by the public sector may invite in competitors who then become advocates for further competition. This occurred, for example, in postal services, when United Parcel Service used its participation in the liberalized segment of the German postal services market to bring to the European Commission and, eventually, the European Court of Justice, complaints against the German public sector operator, Deutsche Post (DPAG).[4] UPS argued that DPAG was abusing its dominant market position in letter services to engage in predatory pricing in package delivery services. UPS also alleged that DPAG was using monopoly profits for a vast range of acquisitions designed to boost its global market share.

The impact of capital's political mobility may begin at a national level and then spread outside the national setting to a European level. First, a complaint by a competitor can turn the application of EC competition policy rules toward a particular public undertaking in a member state. This may lead to changes in the financial relationship between that undertaking and the state, or even in the institutional structure of the public service in question. But the effects may go beyond the single country in which the public undertaking operates. As Susanne Schmidt has shown, when practices protecting a country's public sector monopoly must be relinquished because they are declared incompatible with Community law, the government will change its position from defense of restrictive public sector practices to support for sectoral liberalization at the Community level. This shift in national preference increases the likelihood that the Council of Ministers representing national governments will approve Community-level measures to expand competition.[5] Schmidt demonstrates this with reference to airport ground-handling services. With sectoral liberalization initially opposed by a group of seven states large enough to block Council approval of a directive, the European Commission in 1995 won support for a liberalization proposal after stimulating reforms in three of these countries by threatening to use its treaty powers to declare restrictive public sector practices incompatible with the treaties (Schmidt, 2000: 47).

Private sector advocates of fuller competition may become critical strategic allies of a European Commission attempting to build a coalition of governments supportive of liberalization. For example, as Wayne Sandholtz has demonstrated, this was an important element in the process of liberalization of Europe's telecommunications sector (Sandholtz, 1993b). Successful efforts by private sector actors to pursue interests at the European level therefore may reinforce the liberalization agenda of the European Commission. In some cases, these actors may even force the hand of a Commission that acknowledges political constraints and therefore wishes to exercise restraint in promoting competition. The consequence, as Fritz Scharpf writes, is that "no area of service public is now beyond the challenge of European competition law" (Scharpf, 1999: 61).

An emphasis on capital's political mobility and the tension it can generate between European-level objectives and national-level policies and institutions yields a corollary of the first hypothesis regarding the parameters of economic liberalization:

Hypothesis I(a)

The scope and timing of liberalization are a function of European-level pressures for adaptation—in particular, the extent to which private sector competitors of protected public enterprises employ EU channels to combat restrictive practices of governments.

According to this hypothesis, outcomes will depend on the strength of capital's incentives to act at the European level and the degree to which the complaints of potential market entrants and competitors of public sector monopolists induce action by European level institutions—the European Commission and Court of Justice. Once competitors call attention to restrictive public sector practices, the regulatory authority of the European Commission and legal authority of the European Court of Justice substantially determine the scope of liberalization. The primary source of variation of outcomes is therefore the difference—across countries and sectors—of incentives for capital to act at the European level. In evaluating the empirical evidence relative to each of the explanatory hypotheses, chapter 8 spells out in detail the factors that determine the strength of these incentives.

Domestic Political Costs

The second question at the core of the study of Europeanization is this: what factors mediate between European-level forces for adaptation and domestic political outcomes? As most studies of Europeanization acknowledge, any theory of domestic political change demands clear specification of mediating variables. Thomas Risse, Maria Green Cowles, and James Caporaso identify several factors that mediate between the adaptational pressures of Europeanization and domestic political structures, including the number of domestic veto points, the ability of formal institutional structures to facilitate change, and domestic organizational and policy cultures (Risse, Cowles, and Caporaso, 2001: 9–12). Markus Haverland highlights the importance of institutional veto points, asserting that national systems with centralized structures (Britain, the Netherlands) adapt much more readily to European-level pressures than fragmented or decentralized polities that permit broad access to the policy making process (Germany)

(Haverland, 2000: 84–85). Christoph Knill and Dirk Lehmkuhl cite changes in opportunity structures as the primary mechanism of change in areas of market-making or negative integration; the scope of change depends on the extent to which European policies redistribute resources between domestic political actors (Knill and Lehmkuhl, 1999: 3, Table 1; 6). One of the contributions made by Risse, Cowles, and Caporaso is that they shift the literature's lingering focus on the impact of European integration on the relative power of national executives to consideration of the redistribution of power among a wider range of domestic actors. Underscoring the conception of Europeanization as a shift in opportunity structures, these authors work from the assumption that domestic actors generally will seek to take advantage of the availability of additional resources provided by the Europeanization process or the opening of new avenues to pursuing their objectives (Risse, Cowles, and Caporaso, 2001: 11).

Beyond these perspectives, might we glean additional insights into the process of Europeanization from the broader literature on the international system and domestic political change? In developing an approach to domestic change in response to external pressures in the EU context, we can benefit from the understanding provided by investigations of political change outside the European integration literature: in particular, studies of international trade regimes and of institutional transfer. For example, Dennis Patterson and Dick Beason have examined the impact of pressures on the Japanese government to stimulate their economy stemming from the response of the United States to a large and growing bilateral trade deficit with Japan. Studying a period from the mid-1970s to late-1990s, these authors find that pressures from the government of the United States are an important explanatory factor for the adoption of economic stimulus packages by Japanese governments. In fact, their findings suggest that such foreign pressure, or *gaiatsu,* is the single most powerful explanatory factor for the adoption of economic stimulus packages.[6] But Patterson and Beason also note that pressure from the United States on the Japanese government to stimulate domestic demand was constant for nearly two decades. While Japanese governments sometimes were responsive to these pressures, there also were prolonged periods in which the Japanese did not cooperate. External pressure alone therefore does not explain policy outcomes. In their study, Patterson and Beason find that Japanese economic policy responded to U.S. pressures when those pressures coincided with the need of governing parties to expand their electoral support (Patterson and Beason, 2001:

508–509). External pressures do not automatically translate into domestic policy outcomes; such pressures are mediated by a critical domestic political factor: the need for the incumbent government to mobilize additional political support.

Studying similar terrain, Leonard Schoppa has examined how the United States pursued the bilateral Structural Impediments Initiative as a means of reducing its ballooning trade deficit with Japan by pressing for structural reforms in the Japanese economy that would make it more receptive to imports from the United States (Schoppa, 1993). The United States urged several types of structural reform. However, results varied significantly across policy areas. Schoppa finds a systemic explanation for this pattern of outcomes inadequate, since U. S. priorities for Japanese reform and the level of external pressure from the United States did not correlate with the pattern of change in Japan's economic structures. Schoppa's explanation instead focuses on transformation of the domestic policy process. Consistent with the later findings of Patterson and Beason, one of the primary mechanisms of transformation was "participation expansion," consisting of the mobilization and inclusion of additional actors in policy making. Conditions for participation expansion include politicization of the policy issue and the existence "at the elite or mass level or both" of "latent support" for reforms promoted by external pressures (Schoppa, 1993: 373). As Schoppa summarizes these conditions, in order to induce domestic policy change, external pressures must "resonate with domestic politics in certain ways" (Schoppa, 1993: 383). Again, it is not simply the nature and intensity of external forces for change that determine outcomes, but also their differential impact on domestic political actors and configurations of interest articulation.

Similarly, in his examination of institutional transfer in *Imitation and Politics,* Wade Jacoby finds that domestic political receptors facilitate change even in situations of highly asymmetrical power relations. Criticizing existing approaches to the relative success of institutional transfer for portraying transfer either as inevitable (the literature on neoliberal convergence) or impossible (due to path dependence or the embeddedness of institutions), Jacoby finds that successful institutional transfer requires domestic political agency, or the "pulling in" of institutional change by indigenous reformers. This holds even in the case of the allied occupation authorities in post-World War II Germany, in which one would expect the occupiers to all but dictate the terms of reform (Jacoby, 2000: 3). There are two crucial strengths of the Jacoby argument that potentially may be extended to the present study. First is the insight that even actors with substantial authority or resources with which to impose change cannot do so without the participation and consent of those who are the objects of change. Second, since domestic political change is neither inevitable nor impossible, outcomes are contingent rather than predetermined.

Application of these insights to the study of European competition policy and its impact on the public sector would require investigation of two questions: (1) To what extent do the consequences of pressures from the European level to broaden competition depend on the ability of sectoral change to service domestic political needs; and (2) to what degree does the impact of European-level pressures depend on their ability to activate latent interests favoring a reduction of protectionist practices? Recent work by Paulette Kurzer examining the impact of European integration on domestic political culture offers a preliminary indication of the usefulness of these mechanisms for understanding the Europeanization process. Kurzer finds that domestic political interests are at the center of a movement toward partial convergence within the EU (Kurzer, 2001). While the free movement of people across borders has altered attitudes toward "moral regulation"—involving such issues as alcohol and drug control and abortion rights—Europe's single market has created possibilities for the participation expansion identified by Schoppa. In the case of alcohol control in Finland and Sweden, single market policies have mobilized interests including "liquor producers, the food retail sector, conservatives (and) urban young professionals" in opposition to state controls (Kurzer, 2001: 178).

European Community policy initiatives requiring national-level policy and institutional reforms hardly carry the force of the plans for reform of allied authorities administering occupation zones in post-World War II western Germany. Nonetheless, Jacoby's analysis promotes the general point that changes in policies and institutions cannot be imposed against the objections of indigenous interests, especially those with some institutional purchase, however fertile the larger reform environment. Accordingly, the literature on international forces and domestic political change yields a second set of hypotheses based on the notion that the scope and timing of liberalization depend on a supportive domestic environment. Whereas the first set of hypotheses emphasizes the strength of external forces for broader competition, this second set focuses on the domestic political costs of sectoral change.

But how might the Europeanization process foster a supportive domestic environment where initially there is firm opposition to liberalization from public sector monopolists and their political supporters? To begin with, let us assume that those initially in dominant market and institutional positions are pivotal actors in any process of change of domestic institutions. Those who manage public sector institutions and deliver public services, such as national or regional electricity, telecommunications, and postal service operators, maintain a substantial degree of control over the policy process through several means:

1. *Control over discourse.* Actors in dominant market and institutional positions have an advantage in shaping the discourse surrounding sectoral change. Based on their knowledge, experience, and familiarity to the public, their claims about the potential costs and benefits of sectoral change are likely to dominate domestic policy debates.
2. *Risk aversion.* Compounding the potential bias against rapid and thorough sectoral liberalization fostered by point (1), the debate over liberalization of public services is inherently asymmetrical. This is because of the risks to public service provision posed by liberalization and the fact that liberalization represents a move from a known to an unknown set of conditions. Competition arguably threatens the delivery of some services, or raises the prospect of significant price increases for some consumers (for example, rural residents in the case of postal services). Only in the case where existing public services are widely recognized as intolerably inefficient do protected public service providers lose the advantage of being able to make a credible case against sectoral reform based on the risk to public services.
3. *Institutional support.* Public service providers are likely to have well-developed networks of political support in governing institutions. While some ministries—finance ministries in particular—may favor sectoral liberalization because of the beneficial fiscal consequences, government ministries responsible for regulating public service providers are likely to be sympathetic to the problems and costs of rapid sectoral adjustment.

Those in dominant market positions do not necessarily act as veto points. As discussed earlier, such actors may perceive an opportunity to derive first-mover advantages from early liberalization. But where public sector monopolists initially view sectoral liberalization as a threat to their interests, EU efforts to expand competition are likely to be frustrated unless Europeanization somehow alters the role of protected public service providers in national policy formulation. As reflected in hypothesis IIa, one possibility is that public sector monopolists alter their calculations of the costs and benefits of sectoral liberalization:

Hypothesis IIa

Where public service monopolists oppose European-level liberalization initiatives, liberalization's prospects depend on the extent to which the Europeanization process induces those in dominant market and institutional positions to revise their assessments of the relative costs and benefits of competition.

A second prospect is that dominant market occupants experience a reduction in their weight in national policy formulation. Hypothesis IIb articulates the causal relationships implied by these developments:

Hypothesis II, corollary b

Where public service monopolists oppose European-level liberalization initiatives, liberalization's prospects depend on the extent to which Europeanization fosters a shift in domestic interest aggregation that reduces the weight of dominant market occupants in national policy formulation.

The empirical materials examined in chapters 5 through 7 reveal how the types of change expressed in hypotheses IIa and IIb may or may not occur. Chapter 5 shows that an insufficient number of public authorities have revised their assessments of liberalization to bring about an open, competitive regime for the purchase of goods and services by local, regional, and national governments. And, relative to the continued widespread use of protectionist practices by procuring authorities, few private sector actors have submitted complaints about violations of the Community public procurement regime. In contrast, private sector complaints about violations of competition rules have been numerous in the postal services sector, as discussed in chapter 6. Yet postal services providers have in some EU member states been reluctant to revise their assessments of the costs and benefits of liberalization, slowing the sectoral liberalization process. Chapter 7 shows a similar pattern, with sectoral change coming only after a protracted period of standoff and then negotiation between public service operators, their political supporters, and the European Commission, though the outcome—far-reaching sectoral reform—has differed from that in the postal services sector. As explained in chapter 7, a complaint by a private sector competitor of Germany's public sector banks was the driving force behind European-level pressures for reform of practices that distorted competition in the German banking sector. However, staunch resistance to change from the public sector banks meant that commensurate reforms came with a substantial time lag, and only after the support of national political elites shifted away from the large state banks.

Before reviewing the evidence provided by these cases, chapter 4 turns to the progressive extension of European Union competition policy to the public sector, which has brought European-level pressures for broader competition into more direct contact with the objectives of public service providers in EU member states.

4

EUROPEAN COMMUNITY COMPETITION POLICY AND THE PUBLIC SECTOR

Chapter 3 identified the dynamics of the Europeanization process according to which European integration may restructure interest articulation in the domestic political arena. The chapter raised questions about the mechanisms that foster such change and the factors that determine its timing and extent. Chapter 3 also discussed some of the factors that motivate private sector actors and governments to pursue liberalization of markets, including markets served by the public sector. But how has the set of rules and treaty obligations encompassed by European integration and originally focused on bringing freer and fairer competition to private markets come to impinge upon the public sector in the first place? Why have treaty rules ostensibly designed to break down market barriers established by private sector actors come to reach into the public sector?

Overview

The European Union's commitment to a liberal economic order is rooted in the founding treaty of the Community, the Treaty of Rome (Majone, 1993: 156; Sbragia, 1998b: 10). The objectives of eliminating barriers to free and fair trade and distortions of competition within the common market are central to the Treaty. However, until the 1980s, much of the potential for liberalization enshrined in the Treaty of Rome remained dormant. The European Commission had developed few autonomous capacities to define the policy agenda, and in most member states elite cartels between government ministries and public sector managers favoring public ownership and subsidization of public enterprises remained firmly entrenched. A combination of a shift in dominant conceptions of the role of government, manifested in both policy making and business communities, and a European Commission empowered by the 1986 Single European Act and by decisions by the European Court of Justice, began to mobilize the bias inherent in the EC Treaty.

This process consisted of two critical changes in the application of Community competition law to the public sector during the 1980s and 1990s. First, as the European Commission oversaw implementation of the single market program, it began actively to apply restrictions on state aid to industry to relations between governments and public enterprises.[1] Over time, the Commission challenged government aid to public enterprises in a growing range of sectors and forms. This required governments to make their financial relationships with public enterprises more transparent, demanded in many cases that they restructure those relationships as a condition of the Commission's approval of aid packages, and strengthened the position of governing officials who wished to put public enterprises on a more market-based footing. Second, the Commission grew more active in its application to the public sector of Treaty articles restricting abuses of dominant market position.[2] Successive decisions of the European Court of Justice narrowed the scope of exclusions from Treaty rules for undertakings charged with providing public services. This gave the European Commission a powerful instrument with which to attack restrictive practices in the public sector, and raised the prospect of sweeping sectoral liberalization in public services. This potential was fully realized in the telecommunications sector, and Court decisions in the early 1990s in cases involving restrictions on energy imports and on private supply of some postal services suggested that the measures applied to end public sector telecommunications monopolies possibly could be applied to broaden competition in the energy and postal services sectors as well.

The extended application of state aid and competition rules to the public sector generated an additional development that further strengthened the hand of the European Commission as guardian of free and fair competition in the single market. The Treaty allows private actors to bring to the attention of the Commission alleged violations of competition law by competitors. The burgeoning application of state aid and competition rules to state relations with public enterprises during the late 1980s and early

1990s opened new opportunities for private sector actors. Private sector firms and business associations in most member states previously had little domestic scope to combat privileges granted by the state to public sector competitors. Community rules designed to reduce distortions of competition resulting from restrictive public sector practices made it possible for private firms to challenge these practices at the European level. The relationship with the European Commission was a symbiotic one, as the Commission itself came to rely on private complaints as an important source of legitimation for its expanding state aid agenda. However, the Commission also proceeded cautiously, refraining from the application of the state aid regime in politically sensitive areas and thereby sustaining a cartelistic relationship with elites in the national governments. But beginning in the mid-1990s, European Court decisions threatened even this limit to the reach of state aid policy by conferring enhanced rights on "third parties"—those who are not direct parties to a transaction or relationship between the government and an enterprise, but who have a material stake in the consequences—who lodged complaints with the Commission. Henceforth it would be more difficult for the Commission to avoid fully investigating economically meritorious but politically inopportune cases.

As legal scholar David J. Gerber has described these developments, "For almost three decades the predominant, almost exclusive, focus of enforcement and intellectual development within Community competition law was private conduct. . . . During the last few years, however, concern about governmental activities has shaped the development of Community competition law" (Gerber, 1994: 140). Following an account of this politically important extension of competition rules to the public sector, the chapter presents some of the most significant cases in which private sector actors competing with public sector activities appealed to Community competition law in order to combat restrictive public sector practices. In all the cases covered, involving sectors from government procurement to postal services, assaults on the protection afforded public sector competitors scored legal victories. At the same time, favorable legal outcomes in these cases did not translate directly into the broadening of competition in markets served by the public sector.

This chapter begins with an analysis of competition law and the public sector in the context of Europe's single market project. The chapter then articulates how competition between the public and private sectors increases pressures for sectoral liberalization. The relevance of Community competition policy has grown both through the European integration process itself and through autonomous reforms of the public sector undertaken by various governments. When the economic integration process fosters sectoral liberalization, it enlarges the arena in which public sector services compete with the private sector. This competitive realm represents an arena of contention that is heightened by the existence of European Community competition rules that permit private sector actors to challenge practices of governments that may restrict competition. Independently of developments at the Community level, domestic policy reforms may create a competitive sphere or increase the portion of a market that is open to competition. Alternatively, public sector enterprises may adopt business practices that bring them more directly into competition with private firms. For example, beginning in the late 1980s, the progressive involvement of Germany's large public sector banks in such activities as international investment banking intensified competition with commercial banks. Similarly, the French post office has expanded its activities into the insurance sector. In these enlarged realms, private sector competitors of public enterprises have with increasing frequency appealed to Community competition rules to enhance their market opportunities. Based on these dynamics, the chapter analyzes how the extension of competition policy draws in additional market entrants, calls forth more rigorous application of Community competition laws, and intensifies pressures for reforms of public sector practices. Once this occurs, however, the consequences of the application of competition policy must be negotiated between the European Commission and actors in dominant institutional and market positions within the member states. Ultimately, the implications of the enlarged realm of European Community competition policy flow from political rather than legal processes.[3]

Processes of public sector change therefore are a product of the "supply" of liberalization resulting from the progressive development of a European competition policy and the "demand" for liberalization emerging from political mobilization of critical actors. Liberalization is most likely to occur when private sector actors mobilize to invoke EC competition rules, and the European integration process generates incentives for critical domestic interests to push for liberalization. On the other hand, liberalization may meet resistance at the level of domestic interest articulation. In other words, the institutions of the EU, especially the European Commission, are sometimes effective at nurturing shifts in government policies that promote the single market. However, the integration process also may strengthen forces of resistance to economic liberalization. The chapter establishes that, however great the pressures emerging from decisions on competition cases, the competition policy tools of the European Commission and Court of Justice do not by themselves explain the scope, timing, and extent of extensions of competition into public sector activities.

European Community Competition Rules and the Public Sector

Why did national governments agree to competition rules with such vast potential to constrain the use of public sector resources in the first place? A functional approach to regimes suggests two reasons. First, in order to capture the benefits of cooperation established in the EC Treaty, national governments required a neutral arbiter to enforce the rules. In the case of competition policy, the absence of an enforcement authority would undermine the benefits of cooperation, leaving a prisoners' dilemma in which each member state would face an incentive to subsidize domestic industry more heavily than its partners, and all would be worse off as a result. Second, a neutral authority also would be necessary to resolve situations unforeseen by the Treaty—cases of "incomplete contracting" (Pollack, 1997). Still, the competition rules represent a clear case in which "autonomous enforcement powers enable IOs" (international organizations) "to push practice and policy in directions not foreseen nor mandated by the Member States" (Sandholtz, 1996: 408).

In the early decades of the common market, the Commission operated within parameters established by the national governments. The functions of the Commission in administering rules governing industrial aid were to coordinate the application of regional financial aid in accordance with the wishes of the Council to minimize the risk of competitive regional subsidization. The Commission clarified the definition of regions that should be targeted for aid, assessed degrees of regional imbalance within the Community to determine permissible aid intensities, and managed the process of extending the applicability of regional aid guidelines in the wake of Community enlargement. The Commission also played a supportive role to the Council of national government representatives in developing guidelines for the control of aid in declining sectors, such as textiles, and helped foster the orderly reduction of overcapacity.

The EEC Treaty explicitly recognizes the potential for distortions of trade within the common market caused by the granting of industrial aid. While EEC Article 92(1) (Article 87 (1) in the Amsterdam Treaty effective 5/1/99) establishes that state aid is in principle incompatible with the common market, Article 93 EEC (Amsterdam Article 88) gives the European Commission the task of controlling state aid. The state aid rules apply to transfers of resources from any public authority—national, regional, or local—or any enterprise serving as an intermediary of the state. The rules cover transfers in almost any form, from outright grants, loans on terms more favorable than commercial arrangements, tax exemptions, or loan guarantees, to accelerated depreciation allowances. Article 92 (paragraphs 2 and 3) enumerates exemptions from the state aid rules for regional aid to assist the development of regions with relatively low living standards or high levels of unemployment. The exemption clauses identify these economically troubled areas both in relation to the EU as a whole and within national contexts. In other words, the exemptions are designed to permit assistance to both the Community's poorest regions and, reflecting the political bargaining that shaped the Treaty, less advantaged regions in every member state. Article 93(3) requires member states to inform the Commission of plans to grant aid and stipulates that proposed aid measures may not be put into effect until the Commission has certified the compatibility of the aid with the common market. While EEC 93(1) charges the Commission with reviewing aid schemes and authorizes the Commission to propose appropriate measures "required by the progressive development . . . of the common market," Article 93(2) gives the Commission authority to require that states "abolish or alter" aid that it deems incompatible with the common market. The procedure embodied in 93(2) allows the Commission to impose conditions on approved aid, including "restrictions on the type, amounts, intensities, beneficiaries, purposes and duration of aid."

The extension of these rules to public undertakings, though possible from the outset of the EEC, did not begin in earnest until the 1980s. This process developed only slowly, since the European Commission started with very little information about the extent of government aid to public enterprises. Public sector transparency became a Commission priority when a series of large state aid cases in the mid-1980s in sectors with increasingly serious overcapacity—such as motor vehicles—made clear both the vast extent of the gaps in the Commission's information and the impossibly opaque relations between governments and public sector enterprises in some member states.[4]

Overall, the competition rules established in the EEC Treaty were clearer with regard to private sector enterprises than relative to treatment of state activities (Scharpf, 1999: 51). Treaty Article 86 (Amsterdam 82) protects against abuses of dominant market position by firms. Article 90 (Amsterdam 86) raises a series of ambiguities concerning the application of this clause to public enterprises. In this sense, "Article 90 operates in the borderland between economics and politics" (Dommering, 1993: 72). On the one hand, paragraph (1) of Article 90 requires that member states adhere to the competition laws when granting special or exclusive rights to public undertakings.[5] On the other hand, Article 90(2) exempts "undertakings entrusted with the operation of services of general economic interest." A third paragraph makes the Commission responsible for the application of Article 90, and empowers it to address decisions or directives to member states.[6] Decisions represent Commission rulings on individual instances; directives are Commission judgments regarding entire sectors across member states. In either case, Article 90(3) gives the Commission power to act unilaterally, without the consent of either the Council of Ministers or the European Parliament. This contrasts with the way that single market legislation normally is made, with the Commission possessing the sole right to initiate legislation, but its proposals subject to the approval of national government representatives in the Council of Ministers and of the European Parliament.

The potential significance of the Article 90(3) provision is clear: were the Commission to develop a narrow conception of services "of general economic interest," the Commission could open entire sectors to competition by fiat if supported by the European Court of Justice (ECJ). However, the dominant expectation during the early years of the common market was that Article 90 would never lead to the subjection of the public sector to the competition regime. From this perspective, "Article 90 seemed to have fallen into a deep sleep" (Pappalardo, 1991: 30). The tension between restrictive practices that protected public services and free competition was to be resolved only in the context of the single market project, when repeated challenges to the Commission's use of Article 90(3) powers by national governments were rebuffed by the ECJ, and the balance shifted decisively toward a highly circumscribed interpretation of exemptions for "services of general economic interest" under Article 90(2).

There are contending accounts of the origins of the ambiguity embedded in Article 90. One view suggests the article resulted from a unitary rational decision. The framers of the Treaty sought to sustain a neutral position in the contest between free competition and state planning; the components of the Article therefore reflect balance rather than tension (Gardner, 1995: 78). Another interpretation is that the provisions represent a tradeoff between the concerns of different member states. With relatively small public sectors, the Benelux countries insisted on writing Article 90(1) into the founding Treaty to guard against unfair competition between their private firms and enterprises in the large public sectors in France and Italy. The French and Italian governments, in turn, demanded Article 90(2) to prevent European economic integration from impeding their uses of the public sector (Page, 1982). In either case, the implications could only be clarified by the case law of the ECJ. Indeed, as early as 1974, the ECJ provided an interpretation of this tension that placed the burden on national governments to demonstrate that the application of competition rules would unduly restrict the delivery of services of general interest (Conant, 2002: 97).

The European Commission first used Article 90(3) in 1980. The product was a binding Commission directive on public sector transparency requiring member state governments to provide information on their financial relations with public undertakings. In justifying this measure, the Commission argued that it could not carry out its treaty obligation to ensure that governments not grant undertakings aid incompatible with the common market without a clearer view of these relations.[7] Little detail was known, at least at the European level, about the extent of government subsidies; comprehensive, reliable data on levels of government aid to industry simply did not exist. In some countries, as in the French and Italian cases, relationships between government ministries and aided national enterprises, or between local political parties and aided firms, were privileged and deliberately opaque. Indeed, the French and Italian governments, joined by the UK, petitioned the ECJ to annul the Commission's public sector transparency directive. Foreshadowing a theme that was to feature prominently in several efforts to constrain the Commission's use of Articles 90, 92, and 93, these governments argued that the effect of the directive was to discriminate against public undertakings, in violation of Treaty Article 222, which pledges the Community to neutrality with respect to ownership (Ottervanger, 1993: 75). But the Court rejected this argument, asserting that, since public and private undertakings operate in different situations, the directive is not discriminatory.

In the 1980 transparency directive, the Commission stressed the need to distinguish the state's role as owner from its role as regulator. The reporting requirements established by the directive called on public authorities at all levels to provide information on assistance given directly to undertakings as well as that channeled through intermediary entities; the directive required public authorities to give financial data on all forms of aid, from outright grants of capital to returns on public funds falling below normal market levels and "compensation for financial burdens imposed by the public authorities" (Article 3). Until 1985, public undertakings in the water, energy, transport, public credit, and posts and telecommunications sectors were excluded from the directive (Article 4).

The 1980 directive ultimately had dramatic consequences for the application of state aid policy in the context of the single market project. As the information available to the Commission increased, so too did its application of the state aid rules to new sectors and a broader range of aid types. The European Commission's first systematic survey of aid to industry in EC countries, completed in 1989, revealed stunningly high levels of aid across the Community, with aid to industry totaling approximately 3 percent of GDP, and much of this going to public enterprises. Putting this level of aid in perspective, a *Financial Times* article from the period pointed out that "Governments give more to companies in state aid than they get back in direct taxes, and in some countries, the volume of state aid is bigger than the entire budget deficit" (*Financial Times,* November 20, 1989: 6). Armed with data on the vast sums with which public sector enterprises and services were underwritten, the Commission in the early 1990s fostered a discourse that coupled the theme of fair competition within the single market with competitiveness vis-à-vis external competitors, particularly Japan and the United States. The 1994 "White Paper on Growth, Competitiveness and Employment" discussed in chapter 2 was a centerpiece of this effort. The economic convergence process that followed the 1992 Maastricht Treaty bolstered the scrutiny of public sector funding by amplifying fiscal pressures. Along with this process, the discourse of competitiveness strengthened the hand of modernizers within national governments seeking to rein in public sector subsidies. These reformers found an ally in the European Commission.

The case of aid to Spain's national airline, Iberia, illustrates the point well. In 1994, a state holding company planned the second large transfer of resources to the Spanish air carrier in less than four years, potentially violating Commission guidelines on aid to state airlines. The governing Spanish Socialist Party (PSOE) harbored competing views about the treatment of Iberia. A traditionalist faction was determined to sustain generous public investment. A modernizing group was committed to shrinking the state sector and reforming management of public enterprises so that decisions would be made based on business practices rather than political calculations. Modernizers in the PSOE found allies in EC Competition Commissioner Karel van Miert and in Transport Commissioner Neil Kinnock, who was determined to tighten implementation of state aid rules in the aviation sector. A new Iberia management team put in place by Socialist Party modernizers relied on assistance from the European Commission as it sought to implement a cost-cutting program, which included redundancies and wage cuts. Since the Commission would not approve state aid unless it financed restructuring that enhanced the financial viability of the enterprise, Iberia management could credibly warn that the Commission would not approve the desperately needed capital infusion from the state holding company without agreement on the cost-cutting package. Ultimately the Commission approved a portion of the planned capital transfer, with conditions attached to the approval that endorsed the position of PSOE modernizers.[8]

As the Iberia case indicates, even with the authority bestowed on the Commission in the Treaty, the Commission depended on domestic political partners to enact its state aid policies. Any potential application of EC Treaty Article 90 was far more contentious, because it carried the threat of the Commission unilaterally banning restrictive practices. Nonetheless, ECJ jurisprudence during the second half of the 1980s and the early 1990s significantly strengthened the ability of the European Commission to use Article 90 to break down restrictive practices in the public sector. During this period there was a marked shift in the balance of interpretation of the exemption clause of Article 90 (i.e., paragraph 2). Whereas the ECJ's early interpretations of the clause asked how far exclusive rights of privileged undertakings could be extended before they ran afoul of competition rules, by the early 1990s the ECJ had stood this approach on its head. Instead, the Court now attempted to define the minimum extent of exclusive rights necessary to ensure the financial viability of the services of general economic interest provided by these undertakings (Gardner, 1995: 79, 82). As legal scholar D. G. Goyder asserted in the late 1990s, "The Court is clearly not disposed to interpret Article 90(2) broadly, even where the functions performed by the undertaking are central to the proper functioning of the economy of a Member State" (Goyder, 1998: 537). Moreover, the Commission signaled its willingness to take advantage of its growing authority. In its 1990 report on competition policy, the Commission's competition policy DG asserted that although private firms were responsible for many barriers to trade within the Community, "at the present stage of integration . . . the barriers are greatest in the markets currently subject to State regulation" (Commission, 1991a: 50).

A number of cases demonstrated that Article 90 could be a potent constraint on restrictive practices in sectors where private firms also could offer the service provided by a public enterprise. For example, in 1991 the ECJ ruled that the German Civil Code violated Article 90(1) because it prevented private sector recruitment agencies from offering job placement services in competition with the German Federal Employment Office. The Federal Employment Office had been granted the exclusive right to offer such services by Germany's Law on the Promotion of Employment (Gardner, 1995: 81). But the most publicized and far-reaching use of Article 90 came in the telecommunications sector. The first telecommunications decision took place in 1985, when the ECJ ruled in the British Telecom case that "the provision of telecommunications services was subject to the competition rules of the EC Treaty and had to be regarded as a normal economic sector with no exceptional status" (S. Schmidt, 1998: 172–173). As Susanne Schmidt explains, this opened a policy window which the Commission immediately exploited by following up on private complaints against existing telecommunications equipment monopolies in Germany, the Netherlands, Belgium, Italy, and Denmark (S. Schmidt, 1998: 173). Thereafter the Commission issued a series of directives covering distinct parts of the telecommunications sector based on Article 90(1). In June 1988 came a directive requiring liberalization of terminal equipment; this was followed in 1990 by a Commission Directive on liberalization of telecommunications services. Both directives were challenged in court by national governments, but in decisions of 1991 and 1992, respectively, the Court backed the Commission's use of Article 90, confirming the Commission's authority to deal with entire sectors rather than simply individual infringements (Hancher, 1993: 18). Further directives introduced competition in satellite services and equipment (1994), cable television (1995), and alternative networks (1996); full liberalization of services and networks applied from 1998 on.[9]

While much scholarly attention has focused on telecommunications, the Commission's role and ECJ decisions in cases in electricity and postal services appeared to foreshadow a similar pattern of Commission-driven liberalization in those sectors. In the second half of the 1980s, the Commission used Article 90 to ensure competition in the international express segment of the postal services market. The Commission invoked Article 90 to overrule restrictions placed by some governments on private international express carriers that favored public sector express services.[10] The most significant case involved postal services reform in the Netherlands, a case that both affirmed the Commission's authority to overrule restrictive practices imposed by national laws affecting public services and underscored the need for the Commission to consult extensively with national governments before using this authority.

In October 1988, the Dutch government adopted a new law that replaced the state post office with a private law company, PTT-Post, wholly owned by the government. The law assigned PTT-Post the public service duty of transporting letters and packages throughout the country at a uniform rate, granting PTT-Post in exchange an exclusive franchise on the transport of letters weighing up to 500 grams. The law excepted from this provision guaranteed express delivery services, but only if they were offered at a higher price than the normal express delivery provided by the state-owned company. This segment of the market previously had been open to competition. In November 1988, the European Commission informed the Dutch government that the restriction on private express courier services established by the Dutch postal law amounted to a price agreement and was therefore an illegal restraint on competition. The restriction could not be justified by the need to provide a service of general economic interest because the revenues earned from express delivery services were not necessary for the funding of those public service functions (ECJ, 1992). The government of the Netherlands contested this claim, and asserted that the price restriction was necessary to ensure both letter delivery services and the normal express transport service. In March 1990, the government of the Netherlands brought an action calling for the European Court of Justice to invalidate the Commission's decision. Several private express associations, including two Dutch express courier associations, the European Express Organisation, and the Association of European Express Carriers, intervened on the side of the Commission. The ECJ upheld the Commission's use of its Article 90(3) powers to take direct action against a measure having an anticompetitive effect enacted by a member state government. However, the Court found that the Commission had failed to give the Dutch government a further hearing following Commission consultations with the private industry associations in the sector. The complaint of the Dutch government was thereby upheld on procedural grounds and the Commission's decision regarding the Dutch law was nullified, though the Court endorsed in principle the Commission's right to reach decisions based on Article 90.

Finally, in 1991 the Belgian government brought criminal charges against Paul Corbeau, an individual operating a private express delivery service in Liege. Corbeau was accused of violating the 1956 Belgian postal monopoly law, which gave the state postal monopoly the exclusive right to collect, transport, and deliver all mail throughout the national territory. The Liege criminal court referred the case to the ECJ for a preliminary ruling on the interpretation of Articles 86 and 90 of the EEC Treaty. Intervening on behalf of the Belgian government, the Spanish, British, and Irish governments argued that the postal service monopoly meets the criteria for exemption under Treaty Article 90(2), that the mere existence of a dominant market position does not imply an abuse of that position, and that the financial viability of the public service obligation requires prohibitions against activities that might undermine the viability of the service.[11] However, the Court found that it is a violation of Treaty Article 90 for a government monopoly to prohibit an economic operator from offering value-added services distinct from the service of general economic interest.[12]

In the energy sector, the Commission followed the European Court's 1991 telecommunications decision by informing those member states maintaining exclusive import and export rights for electricity and gas that they would have to abolish these restrictions (Hancher, 1993: 19). In addition, the 1992 Almelo case established that electricity supply is not exempt from the competition provisions of the Treaty restricting vertical agreements or abuses of dominant market position. The case was referred to the ECJ by a Dutch court for a preliminary ruling when the municipality of Almelo challenged the exclusive purchasing clause imposed by the regional electricity distributor on local electricity distributors, which prevented imports of electricity from other sources. The ECJ reasoned that because the electricity distribution system in the Netherlands was comprised of a series of contractual relationships reaching downward from electricity generators to regional and then local distributors and ultimately to end users, it was possible that energy generators and regional distributors collectively occupied a dominant market position (ECJ, 1994). The exclusive purchase agreement represented an abuse of this position, contravening Article 86. Moreover, the prohibition on electricity imports affected trade between member states, and therefore violated EEC Treaty Article 85.

Overall, the legal authority accruing to the European Commission between the early 1980s and late 1990s facilitated a process of momentous political consequence that began with the promotion of transparency in relations between government and public enterprises and led to close scrutiny of decades-old public sector monopolies. Ironically, while the case law of the European Court of Justice during the second half of the 1980s and first half of the 1990s clarified the legal authority of Community institutions with regard to Article 90, it also more deeply politicized the application of Community competition law to the public sector. Or, as David J. Gerber puts this, "a political institution . . . replaced a judicial institution as the driving force within the competition law system" (Gerber, 1994: 137).

Developments at the political level during the second half of the 1990s underscored the politically sensitive nature of the application of competition law to public services. First, despite the prospects created by the PTT-Post, Corbeau, and Almelo cases, the Commission did not attempt to extend the reach of Article 90 beyond telecommunciations liberalization. Lisa Conant writes that, rather than a signal that the Commission could employ Article 90 at will, the use of the Article 90 "crowbar" in the telecommunications sector was politically permissible only because most national governments embraced the sectoral liberalization objectives pursued by the Commission (Conant, 2002: 102). Similarly, Roland Sturm and Stephen Wilks asserted in the midst of Commission efforts to advance electricity liberalization that in contrast with the telecommunications sector, "political sensitivities have been such that the Commission has not dared to use Article 90" (Sturm and Wilks, 1997: 17). In electricity and postal services, the very objective of sectoral liberalization was highly contentious. While the experience of the mid-1980s to mid-1990s suggests that the Commission might have garnered legal support for an Article 90 approach to these sectors, it would have faced political outrage from several member state governments. As chapter 6 shows, the Commission in fact moved cautiously in the electricity and postal services sectors. If Article 90 had any impact at all, it was through the implied threat that the Commission could resort to harsher measures. Indeed, Sturm and Wilks suggest that in the electricity sector, the Article 90 threat created a bargaining incentive for the French and German governments, which ultimately were responsible for concluding the outlines of a deal on sectoral liberalization in 1995 (Sturm and Wilks, 1997: 17).

By the second half of the 1990s, the Commission's conception of services of general economic interest, building on the series of Article 90 cases that had preceded, established that this category would give little protection to remaining public sector monopolies engaging in commercial activities. The Commission gave systematic expression to this standpoint in a 1996 communication to the Council on "Services of General Interest in Europe."[13] The communication reflected an effort by the European Commission to codify the scope of application of Community competition policies to public services, largely in response to conflicting political pressures. Speaking to those governments concerned about the ever-expanding application of Community competition rules to public sector activities, the Commission defined services of general interest according to the principles of equality, universality, and continuity, and asserted that the objective of the treaty was to strike a balance between safeguarding public service functions and promoting European integration. This balance is reflected in the limitation of the remit of Article 90 to economic activities of the public sector; the Article does not extend to non-economic activities such as compulsory education and social security or the provision of external and internal security and the administration of justice (Commission, 1996c: para. 18). However, also addressing the demands of some governments for firmer application of competition regulations to protected public sector activities, the communication emphasized that not all general interests must be met by public services; in many cases, these interests can be served by the market.

On balance, the interpretation of Community rules on services of general economic interest presented in the Commission's 1996 communication tilted heavily in favor of broadening competition. First, the communication equates the public interest with the interest of consumers—best served by augmenting competition and thereby increasing efficiency in order to improve the quality of public services and lower prices.[14] Central to the regulation of services of general interest is the principle of proportionality, which, outlined in Article 90(2), states that any restrictions on competition designed to protect services of general interest can not exceed what is necessary to guarantee fulfillment of the public service mission. In other words, the fact that a public undertaking performs a service of general interest does not entitle the undertaking to extensive subsidies; the extent of public support must be proportional to the cost of the public service function. Finally, the communication underscores the need for oversight of universal service providers by independent regulatory bodies. A central requirement of effective oversight is the application of firm rules for the separation of the commercial and public service accounts of public entities that both provide services of general interest and engage in commercial activities that compete with the private sector.

The EU's 1996–1997 intergovernmental conference on treaty revisions that led to the Amsterdam Treaty provided evidence of the persistence of conflicting political pressures on the European Commission. On the one hand, some national governments wished to see fuller application of the competition rules to the public sector, while others were concerned that the reach of competition rules threatened their conception of public services. Ultimately the Amsterdam Treaty (signed October 1997; entered into force, May 1, 1999) included as a concession to the French government and others concerned about the tendency of competition rules to undermine public services a new Article 16, which stipulated that, without prejudice to existing articles governing undertakings providing services of general interest and state aid,

> given the place occupied by services of general economic interest in the shared values of the Union as well as their role in promoting social and territorial cohesion, the Community and the Member States, each with their respective powers . . . shall take care that such services operate on the basis of principles and conditions, which enable them to fulfil their missions.[15]

A similar rhetorical acknowledgment of the special role of public services in EU member countries ensued when national governments at the March 2000 Lisbon European Council requested that the Commission update its communication on services of general interest. This new communication recognized the legitimacy of different models of universal service provision. The two primary models discussed are compulsory public service and the single provider model. According to the first, all operators are charged with the duty of providing services of general interest, thereby promoting competition and permitting users of the service to choose their providers. The second model designates a single universal service provider while requiring all operators in the sector to contribute to the financing of the service (Commission, 2000b: Sec 3, para. 15). The Lisbon Council also reiterated its support for Article 16 and its recognition of the value of services of general economic interest. Yet, demonstrating the continued march of liberalization in practice, the Council simultaneously called for the accelerated liberalization of the gas, electricity, transport, and postal services sectors. Moreover, the European Commission in 2000 reiterated the core themes of its 1996 communication, including the central role of the interests of citizens as consumers of public services, the need to separate regulatory functions from the operation of public services, and the Commission's authority to assess the proportionality of any restrictions on competition designed to ensure provision of services of general economic interest. The Commission cited the experience with liberalization in telecommunications and air transport as evidence of the success of sectoral liberalization in improving service availability and lowering prices, as well as enhancing the global economic competitiveness of European industry.

The Political Mobility of Capital

The gradual but substantial extension of EU competition rules has contributed to a second development that reinforces the infusion of competition into public sector activities. This consists of the response of private sector actors to opportunities opened for firms and business associations by Community competition law. Analyses of the globalization process cite the rapidity and volume of transnational capital flows as a primary force for political change. Capital's high degree of mobility relative to labor redistributes power between the two, with significant political consequences. Paulette Kurzer, for example, has attributed the demise of corporatism in small open economies to capital mobility, which left capital with little incentive to remain committed to social concertation with organized labor (Kurzer, 1993).[16] Capital's political mobility may have somewhat similar consequences for the relationship between elements of the business sector and the state. The political power of business in capitalist society is limited by autonomous state interests, which have long shielded public services and state enterprises from competition. Prior to the development of Europe's multilayered polity, individual firms and business associations had fewer opportunities to penetrate these protected sectors. The evolution of the European Community's single market rules empowered private sector actors to move outside the national arena in order to pursue their interests in broader competition at the European level.

Indeed, in some cases the political opportunity opened up for firms and business associations that compete with public sector activities has been especially dramatic. First, there are cases in which financial arrangements for public services are codified in public or budgetary law that cannot be challenged in national courts. This is true, for example, of the institutional guarantees extended by municipal and state owners of German public law financial institutions, an arrangement that accompanies their public law status. Spain's public broadcasting companies receive grants from regional government authorities pursuant to budgetary laws. In these instances, private sector competitors are powerless to pursue claims in national courts that these provisions distort competition.

Second, the ability of firms to challenge restraints on competition in areas where public sector activities compete with the private sector has challenged privileged relations between national government ministries and public enterprises where those relations are especially close and impenetrable, as in the French public sector. For private sector firms in this setting, using European-level institutional channels may represent their most promising chance to counterbalance the political potence of their public sector counterparts.

And finally, the growing authority of the European Commission as a locus of enforcement of Community state aid policy also has represented a sharp change in the political opportunity structures of large multinational corporations with an economic but limited political foothold in individual European political economies. This explains, for example, the European-level legal strategy pursued by United Parcel Service in its effort to penetrate the Deutsche Post-dominated German parcels market. Rather than lobbying the European Parliament to support greater liberalization of the postal services sector, UPS has focused on submitting to the Commission allegations of illegal subsidization and other forms of distortion of competition practiced by Deutsche Post. Chapter 7 analyzes this development more fully.

The political mobility of capital has progressed in stages, in response to the development of the European Community's competition regime. Restrictions on government aid to industry are not a novel product of the single market process; they were, in fact, set out in the Treaty of Rome establishing the European Economic Community. As discussed earlier, through the 1970s, the primary role of the European Commission in enforcing a Community-level state aid policy was to manage the orderly reduction of overcapacity in declining sectors and to prevent costly subsidy competition. The European Commission's directorate for state aid sought to achieve this objective by translating the preferences of member state governments into frameworks governing such areas as regional aid and sectors with overcapacity such as textiles, autos, and shipbuilding.

As the European Commission sought to implement the provisions of the single market program beginning in the second half of the 1980s, it relied on complaints from third parties as a crucial enforcement mechanism in several policy areas, including the public procurement and state aid regimes, especially concerning government aid to the public sector. These complaints either spawned or supplemented ECJ actions initiated by the European Commission against governments for violating single market rules. These included pathbreaking actions in the public procurement sector, such as the Dundalk case originating in Ireland that set a precedent for restricting national content or standards clauses for public works projects, and the Italian DuPont de Nemours case which established constraints on the use of local preferences as an instrument of regional or industrial policy.

As implementation of single market legislation began, the European Commission was in a position to foster as well as limit the development of the single market. Government ministers frequently lobbied the Commission's internal market or competition directorates on behalf of specific decisions or sectors. Though the Commission relied heavily on the private sector to support the single market project, it was relatively autonomous from private sector interests in setting the operational agenda for single market implementation, allowing the Commission to judge which complaints it would pursue and which it would neglect. These decisions were as much political or administrative as meritocratic. That is, they were guided by political judgments about the level of political support for the application of competition policy and by the Commission's resource constraints. The Commission's internal market and competition policy directorates at times even cultivated complaints as useful fodder for battles with individual governments in sectors or cases in which the internal market or competition policy directorates were prepared to move forward. Those whose complaints about the treatment of public sector competitors were not pursued by the Commission perceived little recourse.

As the single market became progressively more institutionalized, awareness of the rules and of the Commission's investigative and enforcement powers, and of its activism, spread. Additional sectors were affected by the liberalization process, and initial steps toward liberalization drew in market participants who became advocates of greater competition. These developments multiplied the number of complaints from the private sector, particularly from firms competing with public sector activities. Third party complaints, in fact, began to overwhelm the institutional capacity of the Commission's competition policy directorate. Reflecting the way in which "policy creates politics" (Pierson, 1993), the growing involvement of trans-European and subnational actors in the monitoring of state aid has been fostered by the expanded application of state aid policy accompanying implementation of the single market program. Recognizing this increased significance of nonstate actors in defining the terms of the state aid regime, Claus-Dieter Ehlermann, former Director-General of the Competition DG, has written that state aid is "no longer controlled exclusively or principally in the interest of other Member States, but also, and perhaps even more so, in the interest of the competitors of the intended beneficiaries of the aid" (Ehlermann, 1995: 1219).

Table 4.1 documents the large and growing number of complaints and their increasing share of overall detected cases of suspected infringement of Community law.[17]

As the volume of complaints from private sector competitors mounted during the 1990s, the Commission's limited staffing and the labor-intensive nature of investigating alleged violations of single market rules induced the

TABLE 4.1: European Community Law: Infringement Cases By Origin

Year	Complaints	Total Cases	Complaints as a Percentage of Total
1996	819	2155	38.0
1997	957	1978	48.4
1998	1128	2134	52.9
1999	1305	2270	57.5
2000	1225	2434	50.3
2001	1300	2180	59.6

Sources: Various European Commission Annual Reports on Monitoring the Application of Community Law, including Eighteenth Annual Report, Brussels, July 16, 2001, COM (2001) 309 final; and Nineteenth Annual Report, Brussels, June 28, 2002, COM (2002) 324 final.

Commission to become more selective about the complaints it was willing to investigate (Maselis and Gilliams, 1997: 103). In response, firms and industry associations lodging complaints with the European Commission became more assertive about the treatment of their complaints by the Commission. Beginning in the mid-1990s, a series of cases before the European Courts marked a shift in the nature of legal proceedings in the single market area. There were a larger number of actions against the Commission by third parties dissatisfied with the Commission's dismissal of their complaints against public sector competitors. These included cases in the French postal services sector, the Italian chemicals industry, Spanish broadcasting, and German postal services, all decided in favor of private firms and against the Commission.

The irony of this development is that the very nonstate actors whose reliance on Community competition rules had been a source of growing Commission enforcement authority became an emerging constraint on the autonomy of the Commission in the application of state aid policy. Initially, newly mobilized constituencies enhanced the ability of the European Commission to determine outcomes. However, these constituencies also made demands that, in turn, required the Commission to undertake new tasks and expend additional scarce resources. As these demands have mounted, they have encroached on the Commission's independent agenda-setting abilities. Furthermore, they have strained the elite cartel between the Commission and national government ministers that facilitated the stricter application of state aid rules in some areas along with restraint in others. As this development implies, to the extent that private firms and business associations successfully have used Community state aid regulations and legal mechanisms to extend the application of competition rules to public sector activities, they may also constrain governments that wish to preserve the privileges of some public undertakings.

The following section discusses some cases in the early phase of single market construction, in which the Commission relied on private complaints to legitimate its efforts to combat distortions of competition by governments through the use of state aid or public procurement practices. The discussion then moves into more recent cases in which the Commission has resisted investigating complaints forwarded by private sector actors, and in which challenges to the Commission in the European Court have threatened the Commission's autonomy to define the agenda for further infusions of competition into areas served by the public sector.

Private Complaints and the Expansion of Commission Agenda-Setting Authority

In the early years of single market construction, from the mid- to late-1980s, the European Commission sought to build authority and establish precedents for the use of European Community law to extend the reach of the single market. Complaints from private sector actors about alleged violations of Treaty provisions stemming from political regulation, though not a sufficient condition for action by the Commission, helped legitimate the Commission's actions. This was a critical function as the Commission drew on Treaty provisions in order to challenge institutionalized public sector practices. While this legitimation function was especially important in the first few years of the single market process, it remains important even after the establishment of a wide range of precedents for Commission action in the fields of state aid and public procurement. For example, a complaint lodged with the Commission by the European Banking Federation in December 1999 added to the legitimacy of the Commission's effort to alter the system of public sector guarantees extended to Germany's public law banks by their state and municipal government owners. As discussed in chapter 7, the European federation's complaint about the advantage given to Germany's public sector banks within the euro-zone underscored the case long made by Germany's private sector banks and contributed to an erosion of support for the public sector Landesbanken from Germany's political parties at the federal level.

Private sector complaints were instrumental in elevating the single market in public procurement—the vast market composed of purchases of goods and services by local, regional, and national governments—to the top of the Commission's agenda. Cases that preceded completion of the secondary legislation for the single market regime in 1993 drew on EC Treaty Article 30, which prohibits quantitative restrictions on the flow of goods between member states or measures having this effect. Article 30 was instrumental in the Commission's responses to complaints concerning restraints on competition generated by restrictive national standards requirements as well as public procurement practices establishing regional preferences. Moreover, these cases provided an early indication that the Commission could rely on private sector contractors to help the Community achieve an enforceable and effective single procurement market.

The protectionist effect of national standards was central to the 1987 Dundalk pipeline case (ECJ, 1988). In this case, the Commission brought an action against the Irish government when the Dundalk Urban District Council in a public tender for construction of a water main specified that asbetos cement pipes supplied by the contract awardee would have to meet a standard certified only by the Irish Standard Mark Licensing Scheme, effectively ruling out products from other countries. The Commission's action followed complaints from two companies, an Irish contractor and a Spanish supplier of water pipes. The unsuccessful Irish contractor complained that it was excluded from competition even though the pipes manufactured by its Spanish supplier were certified by the International Organization for Standardization, a worldwide federation of national standards institutes. Only a single firm—located in Ireland—produced pipes meeting the standard specified by the Dundalk Urban Council in its contract. The complaint lodged by competing firms was not the sole cause of the Commission's decision to pursue the case. But the complaint provided the Commission with greater legitimacy and authority to act on a mid-1980s review of public procurement directives that highlighted their inadequacy and to follow through on the high priority given to public procurement legislation in the 1986 Single European Act.[18]

A complaint lodged by a competing firm was also instrumental in the assault on the use of public procurement as a form of regional aid policy in the DuPont de Nemours case. In this case, ultimately decided by the European Court of Justice in 1990, the Court ruled that Italian public authorities could not reserve 30 percent of their purchases of goods and services for undertakings permanently established in the Mezzogiorno, as required by Italian law (Millett,1992: 76; Commission, 1994a: paragraph 264). According to the Court, the 30 percent quota violated Community public procurement rules because it discriminated not only between regions within the country, but also against suppliers from other EC countries (ECJ, 1990).

Several additional cases involving preferences granted by the Italian government as instruments of regional redistribution reinforced the general thrust of the Dupont de Nemours judgment against national or regional preference schemes. Among these is the 1992 Lottomatica case, in which the Italian government limited competition for a contract to set up and operate a computerized lottery system to firms having a majority of their shares in Italian public ownership (Arrowsmith and Fernandez Martin, 1993: 334). In 1992, the Court also ruled that contracts awarded under the terms of Italian Law Number 80/87 violated the provision of freedom to provide services contained in Article 59. The Italian law required that a proportion of public works contracts be awarded to subcontractors located in the region in which the contract was to be fulfilled, and also gave preference to local firms in choosing which contractors should be invited to submit bids (Arrowsmith and Fernandez Martin, 1993: 339).

Private Complaints Threaten the Elite Cartel

Complaints from competing firms about protectionist public procurement practices and state subsidies to the public sector that distorted competition were critical to the European Commission's efforts to establish authoritative policy regimes in these areas. They also facilitated substantial Commission control over the single market agenda and enhanced Commission autonomy relative to national governments. However, as the single market became institutionalized, third parties perceiving violations of competition rules were no longer content simply to lodge their complaints and hope that the Commission would devote resources to a full investigation. Increasingly, these parties have challenged the Commission when they have perceived that it has too readily dismissed their allegations.

Where private actors have not been able to rely on the Commission because of political constraints on that institution, they have turned to the European Court of Justice as an additional instrument for pursuing their interest in freer competition. Judgments of the ECJ have expanded the opportunities for private sector actors to utilize European-level institutions as a locus of interest articulation and a means of preference satisfaction. This route of political action has become an effective means for private sector competitors of public enterprises to attack the distortions to competition resulting from the granting of industrial aid by national governments. Firms increasingly have resorted to the European Court of Justice to broaden their rights to have their complaints against public sector subsidies thoroughly investigated by the European Commission, which has exclusive authority to regulate government aid to enterprises. As a result of Court judgments, private enterprises have acquired enhanced rights to challenge governments that grant subsidies to public enterprises on grounds that they violate EU competition rules. To the extent private firms and business associations acquire such rights, this makes it more difficult for a cautious European Commission to sustain privileged relationships with members of national executives seeking to shield public enterprises from the full brunt of competition law. The landmark case in this regard emerged from the French postal sector, when private firms providing security services used the European Court to challenge the legality of a subsidized security enterprise set up by the French Ministry of Posts and Telecommunications.[19]

The enterprise set up by the French postal service, Sécuripost, received numerous forms of favorable treatment from France's Ministry of Posts and Telecommunications. In 1989, several French business associations and individual undertakings providing services competing with those offered by Sécuripost, including Sytraval[20] and Brink's France, submitted a complaint in which they requested that the Commission initiate an investigation of illegal state aid pursuant to Articles 92 and 93 of the EC Treaty. After several exchanges with the French government, the Commission ultimately announced on December 31, 1993, that no state aid existed according to the available evidence. In March 1994, Sytraval and Brink's France brought an action for annulment of the Commission's decision before the Court of First Instance.[21] The action filed with the Court asserted that the Commission had failed to provide Sytraval and Brink's with adequate reasons for dismissing their complaint, as required by Article 190 of the EC Treaty.[22] The Court of First Instance ruled that the Commission had not made its reasons for rejecting the complaint sufficiently clear to enable the complainants to defend their rights and for the Court to exercise its power of review (Court of First Instance, 1995).

In its appeal of the lower court's decision, the Commission argued that the EC Treaty obligates it to do no more than provide the complainant with a copy of its decision addressed to a member state. In April 1998, the European Court of Justice, while taking a more limited view of the Commission's obligations than the Court of First Instance, nonetheless confirmed that the Commission must provide "clear and unequivocal" reasoning for reaching the conclusion that arguments put forward by complainants fail to demonstrate the existence of state aid.[23]

The Court of First Instance (CFI) in particular has sought through its decisions to enhance the rights of third parties lodging complaints with the Commission.[24] In September 1998, the CFI ruled in the case of BP Chemicals as well as that of Gestevisión Telecinco. In the first, the Commission had permitted a third consecutive capital injection into EniChem, a subsidiary of the Italian public undertaking ENI.[25] BP Chemicals, a UK competitor of EniChem, argued that the Commission was obligated to open a formal investigation into the third capital injection, since ENI was continuing to incur losses despite the two prior injections of funds designed to facilitate restructuring. The Court ruled that the Commission was not in a position after a preliminary examination to overcome doubts about the compatibility of the capital injection with Community state aid rules. The Commission therefore had infringed BP's rights as an interested third party, and the CFI supported BP's request to have the Commission's decision annulled. The second case, Telecinco, emerged from complaints lodged with the Commission by one of Spain's three private television companies, which competed for advertising revenues with public sector broadcasters. The Telecinco complaint alleged that grants to public sector regional television companies by regional governments and subsidies granted to the public television authority by Spain's central government were incompatible with the single market. This complaint languished with the Commission for four years.

The delay in the Commission's assessment of the Telecinco complaint was not simply a case of bureaucratic omission, and identifies a sector shielded by the elite cartel between the Commission and national governments. The delay demonstrated the Commission's reluctance to make judgments about how to enforce state aid rules in the area of public broadcasting in the absence of political support for intervention in the sector. When Telecinco submitted its complaint, the European Commission was in the early stages of an internal debate over how to value public service obligations and the level of compensation for public service functions that could be permitted without distorting internal market competition. Ruling in favor of Telecinco, the Court judged that the Commission had failed in its obligation to come to a timely decision on a state aid complaint (Court of First Instance, 1998).

The UPS case, emerging from a 1994 complaint that ultimately led to a September 1999 CFI decision, was similar to Telecinco in two senses. First, the delay also reflected the unwillingness of the Commission to move into a sector in which political preparations for further liberalization had not been completed. Second, the CFI found that the Commission had failed to fulfill its obligation to act on a complaint. In 1994, United Parcel Service approached the European Commission with evidence that the German postal service was using profits generated by its monopolized letter handling services to subsidize its parcel delivery services, in which UPS and other firms competed with Deutsche Post. While there was potential merit in the complaint and the Commission favored the introduction of greater competition in the sector, it was in the midst of negotiations over liberalization in the energy sector, and postal services were not yet atop the liberalization agenda. Moreover, most national governments, including those in France, Germany, and the UK, were not yet prepared for more competition in the sector. The Commission would not take decisive action until it had prepared the ground politically and generated support in the Council of Ministers. In response to the resulting delay, UPS ultimately sued the Commission in the European Court of Justice for its failure to act. In September 1999, the Court of First Instance ruled that the European Commission had failed to fulfill its obligation to act on the UPS complaint in a timely fashion.[26] Once again private sector legal action threatened the Commission's ability to set the agenda for expanding competition in Europe's single market.

A growing range of actors seeks to utilize the Commission's role in regulating state aid to check undesired policies of governments. In a case brought before the Italian courts in 1997 and referred to the Court of Justice for a preliminary ruling, employees of the Italian post office argued that the exemption of the post office from laws limiting fixed-term employment contracts constitued an illegal state aid that advantaged the Italian post office in relation to its competitors.[27] Arguably, societal mobilization in response to the application of state aid policy has generated a new form of checks and balances in the domestic politics of European Union countries.[28] This explains why, when the Commission filed its appeal of the Sytraval decision before the Court of Justice, the Commission was joined before the Court not only by the French government, but also by the governments of Germany, Spain, and the Netherlands. What was at stake for each of these governments was the susceptibility of their industrial policies to challenge by private sector actors—including not only actors from other member states, but from their own societies as well.

Actors in Protected Sectors: Adaptation and Resistance

Two developments have subjected public sector monopolies to tougher regulatory scrutiny in the countries participating in Europe's single market.

The first concerns the nature of public service providers themselves; the second involves their intensified competition with private sector firms. Governments' intensified fiscal prudence has induced fundamental changes in the provision of public services. Public service providers have been charged with greater self-sufficiency in the financing of their public service obligations; this has been done in part through diversification into commercial activities. Some governments have been willing to open to competition segments of markets previously monopolized by state enterprises. The extent of this opening varies across countries, with some opening broadly and others liberalizing only modestly to ease the adjustment costs faced by public service providers.

Both the introduction of competition in portions of public service markets and the growing commercialization of public sector activities have enlarged the sphere in which private firms and public entities compete. As established in the current chapter and in chapter 2, factors operating at both national and European levels have created a strong tendency toward the infusion of greater competition into public service sectors. Chapter 2 discussed the liberalism of the European Commission's powerful single market and competition DGs and their agenda-setting abilities. This chapter has analyzed how a Commission committed to competition sought to constrict the ability of governments to shield public service providers from Community competition rules by virtue of their public service obligations. Additionally, in the course of implementing the Single European Act, the Commission extended the application of rules governing state aid to industry to public sector activities.

Moreover, the political opportunity for private sector actors to pursue their interest in broader competition through European channels disrupts the Commission's exercise of single market agenda-setting authority. This especially threatens the implicit balance that permits the Commission substantial autonomy vis-à-vis national governments in exchange for its respect for political sensitivities in the application of competition regulations to the public sector. Beyond this, decisions of the ECJ have facilitated the European Commission's effort to narrow the field of exemptions from Community competition rules on grounds of public service provision, and have strengthened the implied threat of unilateral sectoral liberalization by the Commission.

As analyzed in this chapter, the expanded reach of EU authority into the public services sectors has altered the regulatory environment in which public and private competitors operate. How, when, and to what extent should we expect this regulatory environment to constrain protection of state-owned public service providers?

The empirical evidence presented in chapters 5 through 7 explores instances in which the liberalization objectives of national actors coincide as well as those in which the "national project" is at odds with the "European project." The latter obtains when a government prefers to sustain protection of a sector, despite the general environment of state hardening, fiscal prudence, and ever-widening competition. In such cases, pressures to alter the system of political regulation initially may be minimal because the European Commission has not attempted or been able to organize sufficient political support to advance sectoral liberalization on the single market agenda (reflecting the restraint marking the elite cartel between the Commission and national executives). But, as this chapter has shown, such instances increasingly may be undermined by complaints—backed by the threat or reality of legal action—from third parties, including other national governments with more open markets in the sector in question and, especially, private sector firms or business associations competing with public service providers.

How might we conceptualize the process that emerges from the tension between forces pushing for the opening of a sector to greater competition and those for sustained protection? The progressive extension of Community competition rules to public services suggests the potential for a comprehensive transformation of the public sector. What role do national governments, institutions, and public sector actors play in defining the terms of this transformation? To what extent do pressures on governments to remove barriers to competition increase as third party complaints bring the legal mechanisms of the Community directly to bear on restrictive practices? Under what conditions are private complaints likely to be forthcoming in the first place? And what impact have these complaints had in practice?

The role of law in the application of Community competition rules is intimately related to the issues posed by the political mobility of capital. What happens when Commission or ECJ decisions determine that political regulations distort competition within the single market and that protectionist practices must be abandoned? Does sectoral transformation automatically follow? In short, what is the relationship between legal decisions and political change? The application of law in the EU often is constrained by politics. This is reflected, for example, in the Commission's hesitation, as discussed above, to apply the full force of Article 90 to the liberalization of the electricity and postal sectors.[29] The application of law to national government practices that are inconsistent with the single market typically is accompanied by negotiations to resolve conflicts short of all-out legal confrontation. Moreover, legal proceedings decide principles; they do not resolve precisely how to observe such principles in practice. Consequently, even after legal proceedings have been concluded, implementation of a legal decision is a negotiated process.

The questions following from the application of law indicate that a receptive domestic political environment may be decisive for the ultimate outcome. But the domestic environment is neither static nor independent of European-level processes. National responses to pressures for greater competition in public service sectors are the product of complex interactions between adaptational pressures from the European level and domestic political institutions and actors. Relaxation of barriers to entry in public services sectors may therefore depend upon the support (or at least the absence of opposition) of critical domestic political actors who come to perceive liberalization as desirable or at least acceptable.

Who are these actors, and how might they alter their estimates of the costs and benefits of sectoral liberalization? As indicated in the case studies examined in chapters 5 through 7, pivotal domestic actors are those in dominant institutional or market positions, such as national or regional public service providers, or political party leaders at national or regional levels. In a protected environment, supporters of the introduction of greater competition who are market or institutional "outsiders" seeking greater scope to compete with public undertakings, such as domestic private firms seeking a larger market share or transnational corporations pursuing greater access to domestic markets, initially may not have as formative a role as market and institutional "insiders" in the policymaking process. However, entrenched public sector monopolists and their supporters become more likely to alter their positions toward liberalization following a revision of their estimates of the benefits of competition relative to the costs, a reduction in the costs of liberalization resulting from compromises on the scope and extent of liberalization, or an increase in costs due to the threat of legal action. The first change will depend on the relationship of the public sector monopolist to their own government and any unilateral changes in domestic regulation, as well as the decisions of other governments about opening their own markets to competition. The second change involves bargaining within the Council of Ministers and between the Council and the European Commission. Revised estimates due to the threat of legal action follow from actions of the Commission and the European Court of Justice.

Given the significance of domestic receptiveness to European-level pressures, one of the burdens on the empirical material in the next three chapters is to reveal when and how domestic political actors occupying pivotal positions in the national policy formulation process may (or may not) revise their assessments of the consequences of liberalization.

5

GOVERNMENT PURCHASING: THE PERSISTENCE OF PROTECTIONISM

This chapter presents the first of three empirical cases that address the question raised in chapter 3: what happens when European-level legal mechanisms mandating the opening of a sector to competition confront domestic political environments that resist liberalization? Collectively, the cases encompass a full range of outcomes, both in terms of the scope of competition actually introduced and the timing of liberalization. Our first case, concerning the market for contracts in goods, services, and public works awarded by governments at all levels—local, regional, and national—is an instance of resistance to competition sustained both over time and across a vast market expanse. Public sector purchases totaled some 1.5 trillion euros in 2002. This explains the seriousness with which European Community institutions approached the task of injecting competition into public procurement as part of the single market project. The chapter establishes that this sense of purpose, and the extended reach of Community law that accompanied implementation of the single market program, have not by themselves been sufficient to undermine the abilities of public authorities to use public resources to pursue political objectives, even where those objectives conflict with the overarching commitment to economic efficiency inherent in the EC.

Overview

By 1993, the institutions of the European Community had enacted the legislation required for completion of a single European public procurement market, potentially introducing competition into the huge market for purchases of goods and services by governments at all levels in member states.

Drawing on EC Treaty articles prohibiting restrictions on the free movement of goods, the rights of establishment, and the right to perform services within the single market, the Commission had proposed "positive" legislative measures supplementing these prohibitions, including procedures for purchasing of supplies, commissioning of works, and contracting for services by public authorities at all levels—local, regional, and national.[1] As national governments transposed these measures into law,[2] the European Community formally moved toward a single market in public procurement.

However, as this chapter demonstrates, in practice little interpenetration of national markets ensued; legislation was a necessary but not sufficient condition for the genuine introduction of competition. Political leaders of the EU member states had supported the single market in public procurement, the appropriate legislation had been crafted by the European Commission and approved by the Council of Ministers, and single market public procurement rules had significantly altered domestic administrative practices. Yet more than a decade after the formal completion of the single market in public procurement, there is only limited cross-border competition for public works and supplies contracts within the EU, and closed local, regional, or national public contracting practices constrain the emergence of a single European market.

National governments support competition in the 1.5 trillion euro public procurement market because of the gains in efficiency and competitiveness it promises. Moreover, the fiscal benefits to be captured by competitive procurement coincided with objectives of budget consolidation central to the process of economic and monetary union accompanying the single market. As an additional ingredient in the recipe for sectoral reform, the European Commission has supplied supranational leadership by promoting awareness of the potential benefits to governments and mobilizing support for a legislative package. Yet in successive Commission reviews of the progress of the internal market, public procurement persistently ranks among the "missed targets" of efforts to complete the project.[3]

Why, despite national support and supranational leadership, as well as the existence of a formal public procurement competition regime at the European level, does the sector remain characterized by substantially closed markets? To what extent have private sector firms relied on the Community competition rules to take action against protectionist practices? Has protectionism been abetted by the failure of private firms to mobilize on behalf of more open procurement markets? To what extent is the limited nature of sectoral liberalization the product of resistance to competition by public authorities themselves? What might be the source of such resistance?

This chapter first examines the rationale for and development of the single market in public procurement. The chapter reviews several early legal tests of the regulatory regime in which Community-level directives, along with the ability of capital to pursue interests at the European level as an alternative to the national political arena, appeared to have advanced the cause of liberalization. The chapter then turns to the protectionist practices that remained widespread a decade after attainment of the formal legislative framework for competition in government purchasing markets. The chapter concludes by addressing why neither greater regulatory rigor nor the ability of private competitors to challenge violations that restrict competition have decisively opened public procurement markets.

Public Procurement: The Stakes for Public Authorities

Public procurement, the contracting by government for public works and goods and services, is a routine function performed by all public authorities. However, it is also an instrument of industrial and social policy. In addition to satisfying the operating needs of public entities, the process of awarding contracts for goods or services by public authorities may be guided by regional development objectives—such as support for firms headquartered in the Italian Mezzogiorno, or for contracts that create jobs in Northern Ireland[4]—social objectives such as providing jobs for the long-term unemployed, or a desire to sustain or develop particular technologies or skills as a means of promoting national industrial competitiveness (Arrowsmith, 1995; Bovis, 1997: 6; Crauser, 1993; Winter, 1991). Public contracts also may be used to sustain locally or strategically important companies, for which a public authority may be the chief or sole customer. Consequently, the European Commission in seeking to open vast national public procurement markets to intra-Community competition (and, with the inclusion of 1994 GATT Agreements on government procurement, international competition more broadly)[5] confronts a range of entrenched national political traditions and local or regional policy preferences, as well as a host of technical challenges. Moreover, "1992," with its connotations of an operational internal market, hardly marked the completion of the single market in public procurement; rather, it marked the end of the Community's initial assault on protected markets.

That assault began in 1985, with the crafting of the single market initiative. Public procurement was given a central place in the single market project. This was so for three reasons: the low level of cross-border penetration of public procurement markets; the tremendous size of the market for public sector contracting; and the potential multiplicative effects of public procurement liberalization. Although public procurement received little attention during the decade and a half preceding the Single European Act, the 1985 White Paper on completing the internal market referred to the protection of individual national public procurement markets as "one of the most evident barriers to the achievement of a real internal market" (Commission, 1985: 23).

In the decade following the Single European Act, the relevant administrative units of the European Commission, with approval from the Council of Ministers of the member states, established a comprehensive regulatory framework for public procurement. Supranational regulation has induced the progressive harmonization of previously diverse national approaches to public contracting. Indeed, the explanation for the growth of regulatory governance based on both the supply of regulation from EC institutions and the demand for regulation from governments (Dehousse, 1992; Majone, 1994) offers an insightful account of the emergence of Community public procurement policy. Recognizing that the use of public contracts for purposes of social, regional, and industrial policy has bred serious inefficiencies that damage the competitiveness of European suppliers in global markets and waste public resources, officials at both EU and national levels considered it essential to introduce more competition into public sector contracting. The Commission was able to win support for regulation at the European level, which would define common procurement rules for all member states. Placing market integration first, these rules were designed to eliminate preferential treatment of national industry in government purchasing, whether for purposes of industrial restructuring, regional development, technological promotion, or employment policy objectives (Arrowsmith, 1995: 254).

Public procurement accounts for 16 percent of EU GDP,[6] roughly the equivalent of the Belgian, Dutch, and Spanish economies combined. The figure is proportionally higher for Denmark, Germany, the Netherlands, Sweden, and the UK.[7] There are nearly half a million public authorities within the member states that award contracts for supplies or works; at least 110,000 of these are directly affected by Community public procurement rules (Commission, 1996a: 21).[8] According to the study of the costs of non-Europe that accompanied the drive to establish the single market, protected procurement markets represented perhaps the single most significant non-tariff barrier in the European Community; they also amplified the problems of completing a single European market by promoting different national design standards that create barriers to interoperable infrastructure in such areas as rail transport and power supply (Commission, 1988: 4). Across EC member states, purchases of goods and services from foreign suppliers were much lower than import penetration for the economy as a whole.[9]

Unlike member state aid to industry, public procurement is not explicitly mentioned in the EEC Treaty. However, the process of public contracting within the single market is captured by several Treaty Articles. Article 7a establishes that the internal market shall allow for the free movement of goods, persons, services, and capital. Article 30 prohibits quantitative restrictions on imports between member states, or any measures having the equivalent effect. The right of establishment of nationals of one member state on the territory of another, and freedom to provide services are enshrined in Articles 52 and 59, respectively. Treaty language sets the foundation for internal market development by prohibiting forms of discriminatory activity between member states. But, as in other policy areas, this "negative" integration has had to be supplemented by measures that define the terms by which the spirit of the Treaty should be honored. This is the function of EC legislation, consisting in the area of public procurement of a set of Council directives that establish a legal framework for open public procurement markets.

In contrast to policy regulating government aid to industry, the Commission does not have the exclusive authority to set the rules for compliance with the terms of the Treaties and must instead rely on the Council to pass legislation that it proposes. In other words, in public procurement policy, the Commission's dependence on the Council is both political and procedural. Since the EC Treaty does not contain explicit provisions for public procurement, the Community's role in regulating public contracting derives from general Treaty principles on the free movement of goods, the freedom to provide services, and freedom of establishment. Consequently regulation of public procurement markets requires secondary legislation—

directives or regulations—that must be approved by a qualified majority of the Council of Ministers of member state governments.

In order to promote public procurement liberalization at a Community level, the European Commission has emphasized several potential benefits of more transparent and open public procurement: improved government efficiency and accountability (Commission, 1996a), global competitiveness of European suppliers, and technological innovation. In the campaign for a competitive European market for government purchasing, the Commission's internal market directorate and other proponents of open procurement asserted that competition and transparency will save governments and taxpayers money and reduce the incidence of fraud and corruption (Commission, 1996a). Unless the requirements of public tenders and the terms of contracts awarded are published, procurement decisions are an inherently non-transparent, low-cost form of subsidy (Weiss, 1993: 16). The study of the costs of non-Europe contracted out to private consultants by the Commission in order to bolster the case for the single market estimated that price competition in sectors with little prior competition, cross-border competition, and economies of scale due to restructuring of industry in previously protected sectors would generate between 8 and 19 billion ecus (the accounting unit predecessor of the euro) of savings annually in public expenditure (Commission, 1988: 6–7).

Additional arguments on behalf of competitive procurement include the claim that competition would render European suppliers of goods, services, and public works more competitive globally, enabling them to compete more successfully around the world in increasingly open procurement markets. Implementation of EU procurement directives, by enhancing competition, also would induce price reductions, and, therefore, efficiency gains. Finally, because procurement markets tend to be concentrated,[10] the relevant sectors typically are controlled by oligopolies that stifle product innovation. Intensified competition would boost innovation in products and processes, further enhancing the competitiveness of European suppliers (Commission, 1991b: 16).

Clearly, the completion of the single market and realization of the economic benefits foreseen by the European Commission depend on success in liberalizing public procurement markets. The Commission's effort to give renewed impetus to completion of the project, embodied in its June 1997 Action Plan for the Single Market, highlights the central importance of public procurement and the concern that the wide-ranging supranational legislative framework completed in the early 1990s proved insufficient to secure the objective of a single European market for purchases of goods and services by local, regional, and national public authorities.

The Regulatory Framework

From the launching of the single market program in 1985, the European Commission set out to integrate public procurement markets according to the principles of openness, nondiscrimination and efficiency. These principles were to be operationalized by requiring Community-wide publication of public tenders, prohibiting award criteria that discriminate against foreign contractors, and establishing commercial criteria as the sole basis for the awarding of contracts (Arrowsmith and Fernandez Martin, 1993: 324).

Shortly after the launching of the single market project, an evaluation of policy in these areas suggested that the environment of recession in the 1970s and the lack of harmonization of standards left national procurement markets largely closed. Noncompliance with EC directives dating to the early 1970s, moreover, often was deliberate, consisting of frequent use of restricted tendering procedures and splitting up of contracts to keep contract values below the threshold captured by EC regulations (Commission, 1986: 4). Furthermore, critical sectors—transport, telecommunications, and energy—were omitted from the scope of existing directives.

The mid-1980s evaluation indicated that even where there was compliance with the public procurement directives, it was limited to publicity at the beginning of tender procedures. The process of awarding contracts remained opaque and little information was available to competing suppliers both about the terms of winning bids and any further negotiations that might take place after the awarding of the contract. It was typical for public authorities to limit the time allowed for submission of bids to an extent that effectively ruled out participation by contractors from outside the local or national market.

The European Commission's effort to infuse public procurement markets with more competition in the context of the single market program operated from the implicit assumption that crafting appropriate legislation, garnering member state support, and ensuring enactment of the legislation at the national level would have the desired effect. Accordingly, this was the focus of the Commission's 1986 Action Progam. The Action Program was divided into three parts—more fully applying the directives, improving the directives, and extending the directives to excluded sectors. Better application included efforts to achieve correct transposition of the directives into national law, to establish even application across public authorities—through the use, where appropriate, of the infringement procedures set forth in the EC Treaty (Article 169)—and to eliminate the use of national technical standards as a barrier to open procurement (Commission, 1986: 5).

In order to improve on the directive for supplies contracts, the Commission first proposed that the use of restricted tendering procedures be limited. With the launching of the single market project in 1985, only 24.7 percent of public supply contracts advertised in the *Official Journal of the European Communities* were awarded by open competition.[11] In addition to advocating that open procedures become the norm, the Commission proposed that public authorities be obligated to use European rather than national technical standards, and that more time be allowed for the preparation of tenders. The Commission advocated similar reforms for public works contracts; in 1985, only 30.1 percent of contract notices published in the *Official Journal* followed an open procedure.[12] In addition, the Commission called for prepublication of annual works programs in order to give contractors general information about upcoming market opportunities; it also extended the directive to public enterprises controlled directly or indirectly by public authorities (Commission, 1986: 7). The Commission also planned the establishment of a public procurement unit both to improve implementation by providing information to public authorities and enterprises and to identify infringements of Community law by surveying published tenders.

Citing the critical value in terms of both market size and contribution to economic development of those sectors excluded from the directives, including transport services, water and energy production and distribution, and telecommunications, the Commission called for the introduction of competition and pursuit of market integration in these excluded sectors. Finally, to create conditions for the enforcement of the regulatory regime that would not rely exclusively on the (wholly inadequate) oversight capacities of the European Commission, the updated directives required that governments ensure the availability of remedies in national courts for aggrieved contractors. This also undergirded the single market principle of giving interested parties enforceable rights to nondiscriminatory treatment.

Measured by the objectives of the 1986 Action Program, subsequent developments in regulation of public procurement markets reflected a substantial impact of Community policy. First, by 1993, all the objectives set out in the Commission's work program had been incorporated into legislation, including a 1988 amended Supplies Directive, an amended Works Directive in 1989, and a Utilities Directive for the excluded sectors in 1990. In addition, in 1992, the member state governments approved a directive on procurement of services by public authorities, including such activities as maintenance and repair contracts, auditing and bookkeeping, market research, financial services, and computer services. This was particularly significant given that services account for one quarter of all public sector procurement (Arrowsmith and Fernandez Martin, 1993: 326–328).

The June 1993 directive on the award of public works contracts is illustrative of how the European Community—through the collaboration of the Commission and national governments operating in the Council of Ministers—operationalized the Action Plan. The directive broadened the definition of covered contracting authorities. It also more precisely specified restrictions on the use of negotiated (as opposed to open) tendering procedures, and tightened restrictions on the practice by which public authorities circumvented earlier directives by breaking up contracts into small lots that, taken individually, fell below the financial threshold captured by the directive. The 1993 directive required that tenderers eliminated in preliminary stages of competition or ultimately rejected have access to written information explaining the award decision. The legislation also established guidelines designed to prevent the use of national standards or requirement of specific products or processes that can serve as a barrier to open competition. Finally, the directive codified common pre- and post-award publicity rules, and set out precise time periods to allow tenderers sufficient time to prepare and submit bids.

With the support of national governments in the Council of Ministers, the European Commission had by 1993 established "an exhaustive supranational regulatory framework in the public procurement area" (Fernandez Martin, 1996: 287). As the following section discusses, the measures comprising this framework—including the directives themselves and European Court of Justice rulings on directives produced between 1988 and 1993—have had a substantial impact on the administration of public procurement within the member states.

National Law and the Public Procurement Directives

The first phase in the implementation of the revised public procurement regime required the transposition of Community directives into national law; this would be followed by application and monitoring. While differences in national administrative systems created some problems for transposition of Community legislation to the national level, the instruments available to the European Commission proved sufficient to overcome these difficulties. In particular, varying approaches to transposition gave the directives different bases in national law. In some cases, this left individual contractors with no foundation on which to pursue alleged violations of the directives. However, Community infringement procedures enabled the Commission eventually to ensure proper transposition of Community legislation. In instances where lags in transposition lingered, as in the case of transposition of the Services Directive by Greece, the Commission by virtue of the 1992 Maastricht Treaty acquired an additional enforcement tool—the provision in Article 171 of the TEU permitting the Commission to ask the Court to levy a fine against a member state government for failing to comply with a judgment of the Court.

The effort to overcome problems in the national transposition phase is illustrated by the 1995 judgment in the *Commission v. Federal Republic of Germany*, in which the Commission took the German government to the Court for failing to properly comply with the 1988 supplies directive and the 1989 public works directive (ECJ 1995). The case emerged after the German government followed its traditional administrative procedure of altering public contracting rules informally, through the use of an internal administrative circular drafted by committees consisting of representatives of local authorities, business, and trade union representatives. The Commission argued that this did not amount to proper transposition of the directives because it did not create a right for citizens and suppliers to rely on the rules as a basis in law for bringing alleged violations before national courts. Indeed, Germany was not alone in this method of transposing the directives—Denmark, Luxembourg, and the UK all transposed the 1988 supplies directive by administrative circular, as did Denmark for the 1989 public works directive (Commission, 1994a). Directives, unlike regulations, leave the choice of means of transposition to national governments. However, in its ruling, the Court agreed with the Commission that transposing a directive by administrative practice is not sufficient to provide citizens with an awareness of the full extent of their rights and does not protect tenderers against actions by contract-awarding authorities that violate Community directives (ECJ 1995: I-2317–2318).

The implications for German public procurement practices were significant. As Peter Huber points out, prior to the Europeanization of Germany's public procurement process, parties competing for public contracts had no legal standing with which to challenge public contracting processes (Huber, 2001). Government purchasing in Germany, as stipulated in the budget statutes of both the federal government and the Länder, traditionally was a matter of civil contract, governed by internal administrative regulations impenetrable to private sector competitors. As Huber suggests, "Judicial intervention in the award procedure was unknown." In short, "public procurement existed in the hidden depths of administration and was therefore especially inclined to abusive practice" (Huber, 2001: 36). The transformative effect of European Community regulations on German public procurement law are demonstrated by the gap that has emerged between the legal regime governing procurement that falls within the scope of the EC directives, and those contracts that fall below the specified thresholds and continue to be governed by Germany's traditional administrative procedures (Huber, 2001).

Implementation and Infringements of the Regulatory Regime

More intractable problems have emerged in the day-to-day application and enforcement of public procurement regulations. As the theory of regulatory governance suggests, the costs of implementing public procurement regulations produced at European level are to be borne by national and local public authorities. Yet it is precisely in the area of implementation that the liberalization of public procurement markets has run aground.[13] While the European Community and the Commission in particular possesses a comparative advantage in regulation because regulatory governance depends on expertise, neutrality, and credibility rather than financial resources, the same is not true for monitoring and enforcement, for which the Commission lacks adequate manpower. Ultimately, despite the fairly rigorous set of directives governing public procurement, the European Community has achieved relatively little of the desired impact in terms of market opening, efficiency gains, and attendant structural adjustment of European suppliers. Public authorities have found means to evade the spirit of the procurement directives and to continue exercising the autonomy to which—as in the cases of Swedish municipalities or German Länder—they are accustomed.

The European Commission learns of possible infringements either through its own monitoring, which typically consists of comparing information gleaned from local press with information reported—or not reported—by governments to the EU for Europe-wide publication in the *Official Journal of the European Communities,* or through third-party complaints.[14] The Commission's internal market unit ultimately pursues infringements through the instrument of EC Treaty Article 169, which is the appropriate response to the failure of a member state to fulfill its Treaty obligations. The process is lengthy and cumbersome. Where the Commission believes a public contracting process violates a Community directive, it first sends a communication to the relevant public authority requesting information. If the internal market directorate deems the response unsatisfactory, the Commission can deliver a "reasoned opinion" calling on the authority to comply with the directive in question within thirty days. Only if the authority does not meet these terms can the Commission bring the case before the Court. However, this process must allow time for the suspected offender to submit its observations, for assessing the submission and drafting a reasoned opinion, and finally for giving the party an opportunity to comply. Between 1976 and 1992, the European Commission invoked the Article 169 procedure before the ECJ fifteen times in public procurement cases.[15]

The central question surrounding the infringement process is its relevance. If infringement proceedings are fully exhausted only after the contract in question has been carried out, the infringement process may be rendered impotent. The point is highly apt given that the average duration for ECJ proceedings is approximately two years (Arrowsmith and Fernandez Martin, 1993: 336). Two possibilities can make the infringement process effective: if the Commission or courts have the power to suspend a contract pending the outcome of an infringement proceeding, or if courts award damages to injured parties after the fact. The European Commission has sought authority to suspend a contract award, but the member state governments have been unwilling to grant the Commission this power (Arrowsmith, 1993: 14; Arrowsmith and Fernandez Martin, 1993: 338; Winter, 1991: 750–751). However, the ECJ has been willing to suspend contract awards where they are not yet fulfilled, as in cases involving, respectively, the renovation of a waste disposal plant and the establishment of an automated lottery system, both in Italy (Arrowsmith and Fernandez Martin, 1993: 336–337; Bovis, 1997: 86–87).

National courts also exercise this authority; the EC public procurement directives require that national governments provide for the availability of effective remedies. However, though subject to minimum requirements imposed by Community law, the precise procedures governing public contracting and the remedies available where breaches occur are a matter of national law.[16] This reveals why there may be substantial incentives for third parties to bring complaints before the European Commission rather than national courts, since national courts may be more reluctant than the ECJ to suspend contract awards as a means of interim relief (Arrowsmith, 1993: 8, 25), and also may be hesitant to award damages to an aggrieved party beyond the costs of preparing and submitting a bid for a contract from a public authority.[17]

In some instances, Community enforcement actions—whether from the Commission or, at a later stage in the process, from the Court—have challenged fundamental tenets of national industrial or regional policy. The Dupont de Nemours case, guided by a preliminary ruling by the European Court of Justice, provides an illustrative example. A 1986 Italian law required that all public authorities or entities owned (even partly) by the state purchase at least 30 percent of their supplies from undertakings established in the Mezzogiorno. When a local health authority excluded Du Pont de Nemours Italiana, an Italian subsidiary of a German company, from competing for a public supply contract in accordance with the law, the company brought a complaint before an Italian regional administrative court. That court referred questions regarding the compatibility of the national law with EC law to the ECJ. The European Court ruled that reserving a portion of public contracts for goods produced in particular national regions discriminated against goods produced in other member states and thereby violated EC Treaty Article 30, which prohibits quantitative restrictions on the flow of goods between member states or measures having this effect (Commission, 1994a: paragraph 264; Fernandez Martin and Stehmann, 1991: 216; Millett, 1992: 76).

Establishing a similar prohibition against national or regional preference schemes, the Court also ruled in 1992 that contracts awarded under the terms of Italian Law Number 80/87 violated the provision of freedom to provide services contained in EC Treaty Article 59. This Italian law focused on public works contracts, reserving a portion of subcontracting for regional firms and giving preference to local firms in choosing which contractors should be invited to submit bids (Arrowsmith and Fernandez Martin, 1993: 339).

Still, the enforcement process by itself has not been a powerful tool in the Community's push for open public procurement markets. In contrast with the regulatory regime governing government aid to industry, Court decisions on public procurement policy typically are driven by Article 169, which establishes procedures for instances of infringement of Community law, rather than from expansive interpretations of principles sketched out in the Treaties. Because the Commission's authority to regulate state aid derives directly from Treaty articles, Court jurisprudence has focused on interpretations of these articles as much as individual infringement cases. The Court's interpretations often have augmented the Commission's authority to regulate state aid to industry. In Article 169 infringement proceedings, even where the Court decides in favor of a complaint, the authority created for the Commission is quite circumscribed. Indeed, as one official from the Internal Market DG suggests regarding public procurement regulation, the Court "could create a revolution" were it to use Treaty principles as a basis for jurisprudence.[18] The Court, however, has chosen not to do so.[19]

Given these limitations on the legal mechanisms at the service of public procurement liberalization, how might we measure the relative success of efforts to create a competitive market for public sector purchasing at the European level? The following section evaluates several possible measures.

Measuring Public Procurement Liberalization

One measure of the relative success of European-level efforts to infuse competition into markets for public purchasing is the level at which the regulatory framework operates. As established by the discussion to this point, a rigorous and relatively comprehensive regulatory regime has resided at the European level for at least a decade; the original, albeit less effective, EC-level regulations go back three decades. Moreover, as alluded to in the previous discussion concerning public procurement in Germany, the Community regulatory regime has altered significantly national administrative practices.

Still, the mere existence of a regulatory framework says nothing about its effectiveness—the extent to which competition prevails in practice and the degree to which contractors are pursuing and winning contracts across national borders. Assessing the degree to which local, regional, and national markets remain protected therefore requires supplementary measures.

The European Commission itself has emphasized transparency as a yardstick of progress toward competitive public procurement markets. Transparency may be measured by the number of public contracts actually advertised at Community level, as required by EC law. As Table 5.1 indicates, this number exploded following the introduction of new directives governing public procurement beginning in the late 1980s:

However, while public notices are a starting point for a more competitive environment, they are a more useful measure of the *potential* for open competition than of the degree to which competition exists in reality. The number of notices published still provides no information about the frequency of cross-border tenders and the number of contracts awarded to suppliers from member states other than that in which the public authority is located. Moreover, as estimated by the European Commission, the number of tenders published represents only a fraction of the total public procurement market—tenders published in 1998 equaled 1.87 percent of EU GDP, compared with a total market of at least 11–12 percent of GDP; calls for tender published in the Official Journal in 2002 represented only 16 percent of the total value of public procurement in the EU.[20] In addition, many notices published do not comply fully with publication requirements, such as fully specifying the criteria for awarding the contract (Commission, 1997: section 2.2).

A more telling measure therefore is the share of public purchasing contracts awarded to firms competing across borders. Cross-border awards, in fact, continue to account for only a small fraction of public contracts.[21] According to the European Commission's 1998 review of the public procurement sector, import penetration in the public sector increased only

TABLE 5.1: Public Tender Notices in EU Official Journal and the Single Market in Public Procurement

Year	Number
1987	12,000
1995	54,731
2002	106,346

Sources: Commission (1996a:5); "The Impact and Effectiveness of the Single Market," Communication from the Commission to the European Parliament and Council, October 30, 1996, section 3.6; and Commission (2005: 9).

marginally, from 6 percent in 1987 to approximately 10 percent a decade later (Commission, 1998a: section 1). A 2003 study based on a survey of 1,500 firms in eight EU member states indicates that cross-border procurement is considerably more frequent when taking account of the use of local subsidiaries by foreign firms (that is, firms from EU member states other than the home country of the public authority offering the procurement contract). While only 3 percent of all bids submitted represent direct efforts by firms to win contracts across borders, 30 percent of all bids are made by foreign firms using local subsidiaries. Direct cross-border tenders have a below-average success rate, but firms using foreign subsidiaries win contracts at a rate roughly equal to that of domestic firms (Commission, 2004a).

Additionally, an open, competitive market would be characterized by substantial price convergence of public procurement goods across borders. A decade after completion of the regulatory regime for competitive public procurement, there was scant evidence of such convergence. More recent studies indicate some price convergence, though the results are uneven across sectors and there remain substantial savings to be captured from additional convergence of import and export prices of procurement goods (Commission, 2004a: 19).

A revealing indicator of the impact of the legislative framework in place at the European level concerns the infringements uncovered by the Community's enforcement mechanisms. Recent infringements include cases in which public authorities do not recognize the certifications of foreign contractors; those in which contracts are broken up into smaller parcels that individually fall below the threshold at which EC directives take hold;[22] and instances in which competition is restricted, whether to public law bodies or locally established firms. The pattern shares many features with the sorts of infringements common prior to the establishment of a comprehensive regulatory framework at the Community level, thereby suggesting that protectionism continues to pervade the public procurement process.

As Arrowsmith notes, of the more than 1,000 complaints and investigations scrutinized by the European Commission in a nine-month period during 1990–1991, the overwhelming majority consisted of requirements for qualification of foreign contractors that served as barriers to market entry.[23] A substantial body of anecdotal evidence from recent infringements suggests that these practices persist across EU member states more than a decade later. In an infringement proceeding pursued in spring 2001, the European Commission asserted that the Municipality of Rome in awarding a contract for the printing of city publications violated a 1992 Community public procurement directive and the legal principles of mutual recognition and freedom to provide services. The city authority required that any foreign-issued documents submitted as part of a contract tender be legalized by the Italian authorities.[24] In a similar infringement also identified early in 2001, the Commission found that the Belgian government discriminated against foreign contractors in the competition for public works contracts by requiring that contractors, even if certified in other member states, petition for and gain recognition from the appropriate government ministry.

In several cases in Italy, local authorities have sought to circumvent Community regulations by splitting public services contracts into parts that fall below the euro 200,000 threshold at which they must be advertised at Community level. This was the approach employed by the city of Genoa in a contract for planning of construction to be carried out on local school buildings, as well as that used for a contract to set up and manage a computerized accounting system for the local health authority in Frosinone.[25]

In France, local development agreements concluded under the Town Planning Code exempt local development projects from publicity and competition requirements. And studies designed to prepare local development agreements can only be carried out by public or semipublic bodies under French law, eliminating competition in the provision of these services. The Italian government has placed a similar restriction on the contract for design, construction, and management of the planned Messina straits bridge, which can be awarded only to a concessionaire wholly owned by public authorities or Italian firms.[26]

While a substantial share of infringement cases involve France and Italy, violations of the competition rules governing the single market for public purchasing—and the pattern evident in France, Italy, and Belgium of persistent preferences for national suppliers of goods and services and continued stipulation of national standards without reference to international equivalents—are by no means limited to these countries. The UK has been referred to the ECJ for failing to extend competitive procurement procedures to entities operating in the public utilities sectors (water, energy, transport, telecommunications); Austrian Länder have been slow to implement Community directives giving suppliers the opportunity for rapid and effective redress in instances of violations of public procurement rules; and, in Germany, contracts for engineering services often are awarded through negotiations with preferred contractors rather than open competition, a procedure permitted under EC regulations only in exceptional circumstances and with justification that has not always been provided by the relevant public authorities.

Protectionism's Persistence: Inadequate Enforcement or Perverse Incentives?

Ultimately, the puzzle of the public procurement sector is that a comprehensive legislative framework at the European level notwithstanding, genuine competition has been slow to penetrate markets for public purchases of goods and services across EU member states. Thus, the European Commission's conclusion in its review of the sector that public procurement "is one of the internal market areas where there are the most problems both in terms of communication of the implementing measures and in terms of the quality of implementation" (Commission, 1996a: 7).

We may endeavor to understand the ongoing protection of public procurement markets at either of two levels: the inadequacy of the enforcement mechanisms undergirding the EC regime, or the response of the actors affected by regulation of the sector. It is certainly the case that the European Commission lacks the resources to unilaterally ensure effective enforcement of Community public procurement directives. Aside from a substantial staffing increase for the relevant enforcement unit in the Internal Market DG of the Commission, a virtual impossibility given sensitivity on the part of the Parliament and the Commission itself to criticisms of EU bureaucracy, as well as the reluctance of national governments to fund an administrative expansion of the Commission, there are two possible mechanisms of more effective enforcement. The first is the development of independent regulatory bodies at national level that would monitor the compliance of public authorities with Community law, deter violations, and help achieve a much more effective public procurement regime. Sweden, for example, already has such an authority, and the Commission's Internal Market DG argues that national authorities would build up the credibility of the public contracting regime sufficienctly to deter violations (Commission, 1996a: 17). National governments, though, have resisted the call to take on the enforcement burden.

A second option would be for the Council to grant the Internal Market DG greater surveillance authority. The Commission has probed the prospect of requesting powers similar to the potent authority it wields in the investigation of restraints of competition involving market abuses and the exercise of dominant market position. However, in the political environment of suspicion of bureaucracy, and of fiscal austerity and national assertiveness that has prevailed since the late 1990s, there is no political support in the Council for such an extension of the Commission's powers. Industry, too, opposes the idea of more extensive investigative powers for the Commission.

We turn, then, to the actors whose behavior is affected by the attempt to infuse competition into the public procurement process. The analysis requires that we distinguish between those who are expected to apply the rules and those subject to them. Looking at the incentives facing those applying Community rules for competitive public purchasing, Fernandez Martin argues that the disjuncture between formal success (the regulatory framework at the Community level) and practical failure (persistence of protected local, regional, and national markets) results from the studied reluctance of public authorities to apply the rules. As for the motive behind this reluctance, he suggests that Community public procurement policy has upset the balance between efficiency criteria critical to the internal market and social criteria valued by public authorities (Fernandez Martin, 1996: 55–57).[27]

While national governments may endorse the efficiency objectives of open procurement markets, individual public authorities at subnational levels appear to be enmeshed in a prisoners' dilemma in which no single authority is willing to bear the costs of achieving that collective efficiency. According to internal market rules, public procurement contracts are to be awarded on the basis of cost effectiveness rather than to support social or political objectives. But individual public authorities face strong disincentives to open public tenders to competition unilaterally. From the perspective of public authorities, the competitiveness of the European supplier base in global markets is a public good for which they individually are unwilling to pay. The case for competitive government purchasing is that the long-term impact on the price and quality of goods and services and the price, quality, and process of public works will provide direct benefits to public authorities.[28] But, for each individual public authority, these benefits tend to be opaque, while the costs of abandoning regional preferences or support for local or national firms are highly visible and immediate.

Indeed, the high costs public authorities place on adhering to the rules reflects a tension at a broader level. This tension between the competition dimension of Europe's single market and the substance of the European social model has waxed and waned since the inception of the single market project—but remains unresolved. As discussed in chapter 8, developments since the 2000 EU summit in Nice demonstrate a growing desire on the part of powerful member states (France and Germany) to consider specific social objectives more fully in the application of competition policy—for example, by developing policies to bolster individual economic sectors rather than focusing narrowly on stricter competition policy. In effect, the French and German governments are challenging the position long defended by the Commission, that competition and social objectives are at least compatible, if not complementary. Evidence of this tension in the application of public procurement policy includes recent efforts by the European Commission to communicate to governments and to the European Parliament—long concerned with this issue[29]—means by which social objectives can be pursued by public authorities within the confines of Community public procurement rules (Commission, 2001b).

The persistent exercise of protectionism by public authorities in the public procurement sector also raises questions about the responses of firms competing for public sector contracts. If violations of the competition rules abound, why aren't complaints to the European Commission or national courts able to secure a competitive environment? Why has capital's political mobility—the ability of firms competing for public sector contracts to pursue their demands for fair competition at the European level—been insufficient to eliminate protection of public procurement markets? In fact, relative to the widespread failure of public authorities to follow the provisions of the Community regime for competitive public procurement, few private competitors have pursued complaints about violations of competition rules. How might we explain this, and under what conditions or set of incentives might capital be more likely to exercise its political mobility?

Public purchasing encompasses demand for a wide range of goods and services; there is potential for a large number of competitors in public procurement markets. Some firms have privileged relationships with public authorities and, therefore, a vested interest in the existing system of awarding public contracts. In addition, for some prospective market entrants, the incentives to pursue complaints against public tender procedures that appear to violate European competition rules may not clearly exceed the costs.

Since public contracting is essentially an iterative "game," suppliers may not be willing to "bite the hand that feeds them," believing that they will be excluded from future tender competitions if they bring an authority before national courts for violating competition law or file a complaint with the European Commission. In short, private firms that lose contracts because they are awarded on grounds other than value for money often are unwilling to pursue competition complaints because any benefits generated are public goods—at most, the reopening to competition of the tender in question—while the costs accrue privately.

Furthermore, the late 1980s study of the "costs of non-Europe" that proved so valuable in launching the single market process—a study that cited dramatic potential benefits of opening public procurement markets to competition—generated a policy based on the assumption that suppliers would compete for contracts across borders once the economic barriers to doing so were removed. However, as the slow respose to the Community legislative regime demonstrates, many suppliers anticipate high costs of entry into foreign markets (including, for example, the investment required to gather information about local market conditions) that would persist even with contract award procedures fully open to competition. In such cases, there is little incentive for firms to challenge perceived violations of rules for competitive public procurement.

Ultimately, then, incentives facing both sets of actors—public authorities responsible for applying public procurement rules and contractors subject to them—appear to be inadequate to move the Community toward fully competitive public procurement markets, regardless of the strength of the legal basis for such a regime. The issue of the incentives for private firms and business associations to challenge protectionist practices through European-level channels—that is, the extent of capital's political mobility—is a core concern of the book, addressed more extensively in the concluding analysis in chapter 8. That chapter also considers more general lessons from the European Community public procurement regime about limits to the advance of competition in markets served or controlled by the public sector.

The following chapter turns to a case in which efforts at the European level to foster liberalization of a particular public sector market—national postal services—have met resistance despite strong incentives for competitors and potential market entrants to challenge protected public service providers. Indeed, other factors, including a fertile domestic reform environment and strong supranational leadership from the European Commission, also favor liberalization of the sector. However, revealing the powerful constraints on Community liberalization processes, governments fearing the consequences of asymmetrical liberalization and unreciprocated market access have been hesitant to agree to expanded competition in the sector.

6

DELAYED DELIVERY: POSTAL SERVICES LIBERALIZATION IN COMPARATIVE CONTEXT

Chapters 4 and 5 demonstrated that EC legislation and legal mechanisms have been insufficient to create a single European market in some sectors served by public authorities. This chapter portrays another instance in which establishing a single market in a sector served by public service providers—postal services—remains an elusive goal despite efforts dating to the late 1980s and several other factors favoring the expansion of competition. These include the clear and sizeable collective economic gains attainable from a single European postal services market, fertile reform environments in EU member states, and supranational leadership from the European Commission, which proved so critical to the complete liberalization of Europe's telecommunications sector between 1989 and 1998. Moreover, in contrast to the case of public procurement, where firms seeking public contracts to provide goods or services to public authorities face significant disincentives to invoke EC legal mechanisms, numerous private sector competitors of national postal monopolies (including express carrier and package delivery firms) have lodged complaints with the European Commission about abuses of dominant market position by entrenched monopolists.

The study of efforts to liberalize Europe's postal services sector demonstrates that Europeanization is not only a one-way process transmitting forces of convergence around European norms to national political economies; interactions at the European level may also reinforce impulses to protect national practices. Whereas in other sectors—telecommunications, for example—Europeanization has implicated the institutions of the EU in transmitting forces of liberalization, in postal services Europeanization has had some perverse effects, including an increase in protectionism in some member states in response to the inability of governments to move beyond a minimalist Community-level competition regime and fears of the consequences of asymmetries in the opening of markets.

Overview

In 1989, the Council of Ministers of member state governments asked the European Commission to investigate the prospects for liberalization of postal services—a request initiated by a French government interested in establishing a Community-level regulatory framework. More than a decade later, during which there was very limited progress toward a competitive market, a proposed Community directive that would significantly broaden competition in the postal services sector at the Community level was killed in a December 2000 meeting of the Council of Telecommunications Ministers—with France leading the opposition. When a further sectoral liberalization measure finally was agreed by the Council and European Parliament in 2002, it was a circumscribed step that ensured that much of the postal services sector would be closed to competition until at least the end of the decade.

Why this glacial pace of liberalization in postal services? The outcome is all the more curious because objective conditions indicated that the time was ripe for a substantial liberalization of this sector. These included growing recognition among political elites of the potential economic impact of postal services liberalization; a mounting set of challenges to the restrictive practices of national providers from private sector competitors; and the development of a more favorable constellation of national positions in the Council of Ministers as governments independently modernized their national postal services and put them on a more competitive footing.

By the late 1990s, the desire of the European Commission as well as national governments to develop the efficient, low-cost mail services required to fuel a European e-commerce revolution to rival that of the United States lent fresh urgency to the objective of enhancing competition in the provision of postal services. Mail costs showed considerable cross-national variation. Moreover, in nine of fifteen EU countries, the rate for sending a letter within the EU exceeded the domestic letter rate, from 7 percent (Ireland) to as much as 100 percent (Spain) (Pricewaterhouse Coopers, 1998:

30, Table 2.11). Delivery times were considerably shorter for the transport of mail across long distances within countries than short distances from one country to the next, evidence of significant border effects that belied the concept of a single European market. The quality of service varied greatly for different cross-border deliveries: 95 percent of first-class letters arrived within three days following the date of posting from Germany to the Netherlands; from Italy to Spain the rate was 25 percent (Pricewaterhouse Coopers, 1998: 29, Table 2.9).

A succession of complaints to European-level institutions from competitors against abuses of dominant market position by national carriers added to the impetus behind liberalization. A 1994 complaint against Deutsche Post lodged with the European Commission by UPS, alleging that the German postal carrier was abusing its market dominance and subsidizing services in the competitive segment of the market with surpluses from its monopoly activities, was the first of these. In February 1998, the British Post claimed that Deutsche Post was assessing surcharges and slowing delivery of bulk mailings from the UK.[1] A complaint by a group of private sector express services organized into the European Express Organisation concerning national postal carriers' use of monopoly profits to finance acquisitions and enlarge market share followed.[2] In short, by enlarging the number of private sector competitors and enriching the stakes, even the minimal opening of the sector had increased pressures for further liberalization.[3]

In the face of these antitrust and state aid complaints, the European Commission's Industry Directorate General in early 1999 sought to pursue a comprehensive approach to the problem—further liberalization of postal services. Nonetheless, the nepotism and mismanagement scandal that forced the resignation of the College of Commissioners in March 1999 halted action on a draft directive prepared by the Commission. This left the problem of postal services liberalization in the hands of a new Commission, which took over in a political climate hostile to bold initiatives. Yet pressure on the new Commission to move ahead increased when the Court of First Instance ruled in September 1999 that the Commission had failed to fulfill its obligation to act on the 1994 UPS complaint in a timely fashion (ECJ, 1999).

Despite the minimal Community-level progress of postal services liberalization prior to 2000, individual member state governments had been promoting and preparing national postal service providers for greater competition. Sweden and Finland were the leaders, having eliminated their postal services monopolies and fully liberalized both incoming and outgoing cross-border mail. The Netherlands had fully opened direct mail—advertising and mass marketing—to competition and lowered the threshold for protection of a reserved sector (the monopolized sector considered necessary to secure the financial means to perform universal service functions, including letter delivery to all parts of the national territory at a uniform price) to 100 grams as of June 2000, going well below the 350-gram limit established in the Community postal services directive that went into force in early 1999 (Directive 97/67/EC). Spain had abolished the postal services monopoly for local and direct mail, though not for cross-border mail, and Italy had also placed direct mail outside the monopoly held by Posta Italiane.

The reserved monopoly in Germany had been lowered to 200 grams for ordinary mail, and 50 grams for direct mail. The altered status of Deutsche Post promised to give a critical boost to prospects for sectoral liberalization. In the early 1990s, Deutsche Post's financial standing relied heavily on its monopoly position. Responding to demands from Germany's business sector for better service and perceiving the implications of the Commission's investigation into the 1994 competition complaint by UPS, Deutsche Post in the second half of the 1990s moved aggressively to prepare for intensified competition. Between 1998 and 2000, Deutsche Post spent more than $6.5 billion acquiring U.S. and European companies in the freight transport, distribution, and express delivery sectors in order to build a global shipping and delivery network. With Deutsche Post prepared for competition, the German government was in a position to serve as an advocate for postal services liberalization.

Finally, the European Commission's proposed directive on postal services liberalization was, in characteristic fashion, the culmination of a lengthy process of consultation with a wide range of interested parties. These included PostEurop, the association of Europe's public sector postal operators, which had voiced concerns about the impact of liberalization on the ability of national postal services to fund their universal service obligations. These reservations coincided closely with concerns represented in the Council of Ministers by some national governments, including France. Moreover, the Commission's May 2000 proposal represented a step back from the much more aggressive liberalization concept advanced by the European Commission prior to the demise of the Santer Commission in spring 1999. The new proposal, for example, reflected the Commission's sensitivity to concerns, especially strongly held by the French government, about stipulating a date for the complete opening of the sector to competition.

Given this incorporation of interests of opponents of rapid liberalization; the desire shared by governments to bolster economic growth; pressures on the Commission from private sector competitors; the outcome of legal proceedings against national monopolists; and a shifting constellation of national government preferences in favor of liberalization, it appeared in fall 2000 that the ground was prepared for a significant step in the liberalization of postal services. Yet, surprisingly, the December 2000 Council of Telecommunications Ministers indicated that any progress in broadening competition in postal services through Community action was blocked, with those countries supporting rapid liberalization (Sweden, Finland, Netherlands, Germany, Denmark, Belgium, and Austria) unwilling to back a minimalist proposal endorsed by the European Parliament, and advocates of greater caution (France, UK, Spain, Portugal, Italy, Greece, Luxembourg, Ireland) blocking a more ambitious approach (*Bulletin Quotidien Europe*, No. 7871, 29 December 2000: 5).

Why, despite the alignment of factors favoring liberalization of the postal services sector, had the process come to this impasse? Almost a decade earlier, the European Commission had played a crucial role in forging transnational collective action to introduce competition in the telecommunications sector, achieved through a December 1989 decision of the Council of Ministers to liberalize telecommunications services as of April 1, 1990. As the analysis of telecommunications liberalization offered by Wayne Sandholtz suggests, Community-level action requires a permissive environment of adaptation at the national level, along with leadership from the Commission to galvanize a collective response (Sandholtz, 1993b). The service demands of the business sector and the legal pressures from competing private sector firms have fostered an environment of structural reform and liberalization in national postal services that constitute a permissive environment for European Commission leadership. During the 1990s, almost every national postal service in the European Union underwent major institutional reform. These ranged from privatization of the Dutch postal service (actually in 1989) to the restructuring of the Belgian, Danish, Finnish, German, Italian, Spanish, and Swedish postal operators as state-owned independent companies (Comandini, 2000: 148–152). On the side of EU institutions, the Commission has endeavored to advance the cause of postal services liberalization where possible through familiar channels of entrepreneurship, including studies of the sector that provided a basis for recommending measured steps toward liberalization; cultivation of networks of interests supportive of competition; and publicizing the essential role of postal services liberalization in the effective functioning of Europe's single market. In short, the conditions for transnational collective action seem to have been met. Why, then, was the Commission unable to forge a qualified majority coalition supportive of its liberalization initiative in this case? Why have postal services proved so resistant to liberalization?

This chapter provides a foundation for answering these questions by placing the Community effort to liberalize postal services in comparative context with liberalization of the telecommunications and electricity sectors. In telecommunications, liberalization efforts initiated in the 1980s culminated in full sectoral liberalization, ultimately completed in 1998. Telecommunications liberalization had progressed smoothly—despite the reaction of some governments against the methods employed by the European Commission—once actors in dominant market and political positions became convinced that liberalization could serve their interests. In the electricity sector, early Community-level liberalization efforts were unsuccessful. Europe's electricity sector in 1996 was in much the same position as the postal services sector in 2001: stalled despite repeated liberalization efforts and the strong support of several member state governments. But eventually a shift toward Council support for electricity liberalization emerged when institutionally entrenched actors in the French electricity sector—the electricity monopoly Électricité de France (EdF) and the French Industry Ministry—became convinced that they could preserve their interests in the context of a modest Community-level liberalization initiative.

In postal services, national providers that retained dominant positions in markets and political institutions, and in some member states—the UK and France in particular—were slow to be convinced of the benefits, or even of the prudence, of broad sectoral liberalization. This forestalled Community-level agreement on the introduction of greater competition into postal services by leaving governments divided into roughly equal groups of liberalizers and protectionists. The more or less bimodal distribution of national positions left only narrow prospects for the emergence of a winning coalition. Moreover, the experience of the electricity sector complicated the prospects for the success of any postal services legislation. Asymmetrical opening of electricity markets, especially the lag in French compliance with the Community electricity directive that came into force in 1999, was a source of tension between governments. As a consequence, in postal services, liberalizing countries not only withheld their support from minimal proposals, but also were prepared to retreat from their own commitments to market opening in order to prevent state-owned postal service monopolists from other EU countries from gaining unreciprocated access to their markets.

The chapter begins with accounts of telecommunications and electricity reform, the way each was facilitated by European-level forces that encouraged dominant market and political actors to embrace Community-level liberalization, and the reassessment of national positions that resulted. The chapter then turns to postal services. The account of the sector starts by establishing the place of postal services liberalization on the single market agenda from the late 1980s through implementation of the first halting step toward Community-wide postal services liberalization in 1997. The remainder of the chapter focuses on the momentum behind further injection of competition into the sector in the late 1990s and the nonetheless highly constrained scope and pace of liberalization well into the first decade of the twenty-first century.

Reflecting the dangers of using single case studies to draw conclusions about the explanatory power of different theoretical accounts of the European integration process,[4] it is possible to tell either of two stories about postal services liberalization: the best of times, or the worst of times. After the passage of fresh legislation governing the sector in March 2002, one can spin a tale of the success of postal services liberalization following the steady application of policy entrepreneurship by the European Commission and the consequent evolution of favorable national positions. However, in 2001, one could easily have told a story of relative failure, in which Community-level liberalization was stalled despite ardent efforts by the European Commission to foster greater competition in the sector. But the case ultimately is one involving a muffled introduction of competition, demanding that we explain the modest and retarded liberalization of postal services.

Placing developments in the postal services sector alongside those of telecommunications and electricity reveals the recursive nature of national policy formulation in a European context. Unsurprisingly, national government support for liberalization depends on an assessment of the relative costs and benefits of competition versus sectoral protection. But the assessment of those costs and benefits is revised throughout the European-level policy debate. With EU governments roughly evenly divided into pro- and anti-liberalization camps, two factors became critical to the outcome: changes in preferences of the countries near the center of the distribution; and leadership within either group that was willing to provide the collective goods required to secure the cohesion of its position. France clearly led the protectionists. While Germany was the potential leader of the liberalizers, its fears about asymmetrical liberalization resulting from delays in implementation of any Community directive—especially by the French—fostered a focus on reciprocity that left the German government unwilling to provide these collective goods. This was reflected in the decision of Germany's Economics Ministry in March 2001 to extend protection of the German postal services monopoly until 2007, a retreat from its plans for further unilateral postal services liberalization beginning in 2003. Whereas in other sectors—telecommunications, for example, Europeanization has implicated the institutions of the EU in transmitting forces of liberalization, in postal services Europeanization has had some perverse effects, including an increase in protectionism in Germany in response to the inability of governments to agree on a Community level regulatory regime.

Telecommunications Liberalization: Europe as Catalyst

The Community-wide introduction of competition in the telecommunications sector, as discussed in chapter 4, often is cited as an example of the market-making powers of the EC and of the European Commission in particular (Majone, 1994; Sandholtz, 1993b; S. Schmidt, 1998; Schneider, Dang-Nguyen, and Werle, 1994). Rather than waiting for the Council to reach agreement, the Commission drew directly on its Treaty powers—using Article 90—to restrict activities of state enterprises that diminish competition. In 1988, the Commission issued a directive introducing competition in terminal equipment, and, in 1990, a further directive liberalized telecommunications services, excluding basic telephony, as well as mobile and satellite communications.[5] By 1998, telecommunications networks and services were fully liberalized.

Three critical points emerge from the sizeable literature on liberalization in the telecommunications sector. First, telecommunications systems were protected national terrain until the mid-1980s; at this point, technological changes and the pressures of market competition from Japan and the

United States produced a fertile reform environment at the national level in most EC member countries. Accounts differ over the constituency for reform—some underscore the support for enhanced competition in the sector among telecommunications equipment producers, service providers, and users of advanced telecommunications services (Sandholtz, 1993b: 246). Others depict a much narrower constituency for sectoral liberalization, confined largely to consumers of telecommunications services, while both equipment producers and service providers were satisfied with the protected environment (Schneider, Dang-Nguyen, and Werle, 1994: 484).

This leads to the second point, concerning the crucial role of the European Commission. Even accounts that vary in their assessments of the initial forces for sectoral liberalization agree that the Commission was instrumental in forging a collective process of expanding competition throughout the Community, though they differ in their analysis of the mechanisms through which this occurred. For those who see a broad reform constituency at an early stage, the role of the Commission was to give shape to the thrust for reform, providing the leadership required for collective action to take place (Sandholtz, 1993b). In other words, while pressures for reform and preferences for some form of sectoral liberalization were widespread, the specific policy outcome was largely of the Commission's design.

An alternative viewpoint focuses on the role of the Commission in the preference formation process itself; the consultation process that followed the issuance of the Commission's 1987 green paper on telecommunications liberalization in essence mobilized the constituency for sectoral liberalization that ultimately prevailed in national politics. According to the policy network analysis carried out by Schneider et al., the Commission's effort to mobilize telecommunications users was highly successful. In Germany, for example, the Commission's interaction with representatives of German parties, firms, and interest associations molded domestic telecommunications reform (Schneider et al., 1994: 491–494). Germany's domestic reform, moreover, brought it into a closer fit with proposed Community-level measures. With larger global forces at work, the Commission also played an important intermediary role in French telecommunications reform (Schneider, 2001). In general, the telecommunications green paper critically shaped European telecommunications policy in large part because of effective "marketing" by the Commission (Schneider et al., 1994: 489). The Commission "se(t) the pace for a constant and convergent development of their legislation in the direction defined by the Commission itself" (Schneider et al., 1994: 494).

Finally, whether the European Commission was the leader that forged a collective reform outcome among willing but tentative governments, or the catalyst that fostered the emergence of coalitions that prevailed in the national political arena, the Commission by no means imposed its aspirations for broader competition on either national governments or dominant market participants such as national telecommunications administrators. Evaluating the relationship between the European Commission and national governments through a principal-agent model, Schmidt argues that the use of Commission directives to push telecommunications liberalization is best understood more "as a controlled delegation of rights than a significant example of agency loss" (S. Schmidt, 1998: 181). This is a crucial point, because, as discussed in chapter 4, the Commission's resort to direct action through Article 90 did not transfer readily to other sectors with less favorable reform environments at the national level. This is true in particular of the energy sector, where the infusion of competition has been gradual, and has demanded significant compromise and flexibility on the part of proponents of sectoral liberalization.

The Electricity Sector: Liberalization, Flexibility, and Reciprocity

Analyzing the process of energy sector liberalization from the perspective of the mid-1990s, Roland Sturm and Stephen Wilks assert that "attempts to create a single market in energy are one of the most spectacular failures of the Single Market Programme" (Sturm and Wilks, 1997: 17). Liberalization of Europe's electricity sector, which formally began with a December 1996 European Council directive that was to be implemented by February 1999, may be considered a Commission-initiated process, an effort to extend Community competition law to energy networks. Pressure from markets was less intense than in the case of telecommunications, in which technological innovation created its own logic of liberalization (Schmidt, 1996a: 45). Moreover, in contrast with the telecommunications sector, national structures in the electricity sector were highly varied, as reflected in the difference between France's centralized system and the much more diffuse and fragmented German electric utility system (Eberlein, 2000: 84; Eising and Jabko, 2000: 15).

At the outset of the process in the late 1980s and early 1990s, few EU member states embraced the idea of sectoral liberalization, with only the UK and Portugal, then Finland and Sweden, favoring this outcome. Rainer Eising and Nicolas Jabko argue that the initial array of member state preferences left "very little bargaining room for the emergence of a European directive" (Eising and Jabko, 2000: 4). As a consequence, gaining support for electricity liberalization demanded a high degree of flexibility in the Community approach to liberalization. This included a shift in the tactics of the European Commission from liberalization by administrative fiat (the Article 90 route) to liberalization by intergovernmental agreement.[6] This required a retreat from plans for a unified EU regulatory framework in favor of somewhat more diverse national frameworks that achieved liberalization in theory, but at the cost of a far less effective competition regime in practice.

Seeking to build on the momentum of telecommunications liberalization, the Commission followed its 1988 Green Paper on "The Internal Market for Energy"—its traditional means of articulating a rationale and mobilizing support for the expansion of the single market to a sector—by drafting an Article 90 directive to impose competition on the sector in accordance with Community law. The Commission coupled this approach with pressure on individual member states, which it created by initiating infringement proceedings against import and export monopolies in nine countries.[7] The European Commission's use of its treaty authority and threat of legal action placed substantial pressure on national governments to accede to sectoral liberalization. However, other sources of pressure—particularly complaints from competitors seeking greater market access—were muted. This was so for two reasons. First, suppliers wished to maintain their local or regional monopolies, and therefore tended to cooperate rather than to compete (Sturm and Wilks, 1997: 17). Second, as Susanne Schmidt explains, this desire to defend existing monopolies implied that electricity suppliers were willing to offer special pricing to large volume users (Schmidt, 1996a: 44). This undermined the incentives for large users to lodge complaints about violations of EC competition law against the electricity suppliers. As Schmidt points out, this represents a critical difference from the telecommunications sector, where complaints were motivated by an interest in competing with dominant suppliers (S. Schmidt, 1998: 180).

When the Commission met with strong political resistance both from national governments and the European Parliament, it quickly backed off its aggressive Article 90 approach, though insisting that in principle it retained the right to employ this tool. The first Commission proposal for a Council directive, which came in 1992, called for liberalization of networks by allowing third-party access to transmission lines and "unbundling" of transmission networks—encompassing electricity generation, transmission, and distribution—that would be necessary to prevent network operators from favoring their own companies in the transport and distribution of electricity. By 1993, this proposal was watered down in response to opposition, especially from France, to the third-party access provision. As a large surplus producer of electricity, France initially had been a strong proponent of liberalization; Electricité de France (EdF), the state-owned electric utility monopoly, wished for the removal of barriers to exporting electricity to the markets of other EC countries. However, EdF soon recognized that Community-level liberalization—especially third-party access rights and network unbundling—would threaten its monopoly control over the French market (Eising and Jabko, 2000: 10). The new proposal allowed for third-party access (TPA) to be negotiated rather than achieved through uniform regulation (Conant, 2002: chapter 5; S. Schmidt, 1998: 177). Rather than simply opposing sectoral liberalization outright at this point, the French government offered an alternative—a "single buyer" model. While there would continue to be a single network operator—leaving intact the EdF monopoly—liberalization would take the form of a market for electricity in which third parties could buy electricity from other sources at lower prices and sell it to the network operator (S. Schmidt, 1998: 177).

Ultimately an amended version of the proposal was put to the June 1996 Council of Energy Ministers. The proposal was accepted unanimously; the German, British, and Dutch delegations led the push for Council approval (Sturm and Wilks, 1997: 17). Support for the legislation was the result of a Franco-German deal involving "an uneasy compromise between the German preference for negotiated third-party access, and the French 'single buyer' model designed to protect Electricité de France" (Sturm and Wilks, 1997: 17). This compromise included, at German insistence, a reciprocity clause to allow member states to protect their markets against the consequences of uneven market opening across member states. The resulting December 1996 EC directive providing for liberalization of electricity generation and supply[8] required governments to open at least 27 percent of their markets to competition by February 1999, 30 percent by February 2000, and 35 percent by February 2003.[9]

Flexibility was incorporated into the liberalization process in three ways that made it simultaneously palatable to both the French government and more enthusiastic liberalizers. First, the quantitative levels of market opening stipulated in the directive were minimum figures. Governments were free to open larger shares of their markets—as almost all (France, Greece, Portugal excepted) chose to do. Second, while the directive called for all member states to establish open access to electricity networks, individual governments could choose any of three different means of enacting this requirement. The first of these was "negotiated third party access" (negotiated TPA), according to which eligible customers would negotiate the terms of network access with the network operator. A second option was regulated TPA. In this case, access to the network is based on a published set of tariffs applicable to all customers. The third alternative was the "single buyer" model, in which the transmission service operator (TSO) would buy all electricity consumed in the network from domestic as well as foreign producers on a competitive basis. With any of these approaches, the objective was for the TSO to guard the interests of the network rather than the narrower interests of a particular enterprise, and to "regar(d) all market players as its clients, and not as its competitors" (Commission 2001a: section 5).

Finally, the electricity liberalization directive requires that national or regional monopolies that generate electricity, own the transmission network, and sell electricity, be "unbundled." This does not require the breakup of vertically integrated electricity companies, merely the separation of management and accounting systems for electricity generation, transmission, and distribution. Beyond management unbundling, member states could choose "legal unbundling"—creation of a legally distinct transmission system company—or the full separation of a company owning all transmission assets and having no other interests in electricity generation or distribution ("ownership unbundling") (Commission, 2001a: section 5).

The situation in Community electricity markets at the end of 2000 revealed to the European Commission as well as member state governments that liberalization of the energy sector was at best a partial success. First, it was clear to all parties that a single European energy market by no means existed. Intra-Community trade in electricity amounted to only about 8 percent of total electricity production—far less than levels of trade in other networked sectors of the single market, such as telecommunications and financial services (Commission, 2001b: 9, section 2.4.1). In addition, transmission operators in some states—France foremost among them—were moving slowly and by some account deriving advantage from their status as laggards. By the end of 2000, France had opened the minimum 30 percent of its market. With the exception of Greece (which had a two-year extension on its deadline for implementing the directive), Ireland (which had a one-year extension), and Portugal, other states had gone beyond the minimum 30 percent required by the directive; the EU average share of the electricity market open to competition was 66 percent (Commission, 2001a: section 2.2). Moreover, France, along with only Greece and Portugal, planned no more than the mimimal required market opening of 35 percent by 2003 (at which point seven EU countries expected to have their electricity markets fully opened to competition). Although France was by far the largest net exporter of electricity in the EU, the French government and EdF remained cautious about exposing the domestic market to competition.[10]

This caution was reflected in both the pace and substance of the resulting French energy law. Although the 1996 EC energy directive required states to implement its provisions by February 1999, France's National Assembly approved a national law adhering to the minimal requirements of the directive only in February 2000. In the interim, the European Commission opened legal proceedings against the French government for failing to implement the EC electricity directive, and the Dutch government invoked the directive's reciprocity clause to restrict French electricity imports. The French law established RTE (Reseau de Transport d'Électricité) to serve as the transmission service operator; rather than being legally separated, RTE was set up as an independently managed entity within EdF. In June 2000, the European Commission initiated infringement proceedings against France because the national law imposed a three-year minimum period on contracts with electricity suppliers, contrary to the EC electricity directive, which places no such constraints on network access (European Report, 2000c).

Meanwhile, member states that had opened up their markets to a significant extent became stronger proponents of further liberalization. The share of the market in which consumers were free to choose their suppliers was not the only contentious dimension of sectoral liberalization. As reflected in the provisions of the 1996 Electricity Directive for network access and unbundling of management of the transmission system, national governments and transmission systems operators (TSOs) could protect their markets in two additional ways. According to the Commission's March 2001 assessment, network access was not a serious problem, since fourteen of fifteen member states (Germany being the exception) had chosen the regulated third-party access option. The status of unbundling, however, varied considerably across countries. In addition to France, most of Germany, Scotland, and Northern Ireland had opted for the minimalist approach of management unbundling. Italy, Belgium, the Netherlands, Portugal, Ireland, Denmark, and much of Austria chose legal unbundling. And the most thoroughgoing step of ownership unbundling was undertaken in Finland, Sweden, England and Wales, and Spain (Commission, 2001a: section 5). As with quantitative differences in the share of the market open to competition, the lack of uniformity in provisions for network access generated pressures from the more open member states for greater reciprocity of market opening.

The ability of companies like Électricité de France to use monopoly profits to boost their operations in competitive markets was a particular source of tension. The root of the problem was the heterogeneity of utility structures across countries, ranging from the highly centralized, state-owned monopoly in France to local, private utility companies in the UK—the later subject to acquisition; the former impenetrable.[11] Following passage of the December 1996 electricity directive, EdF launched a wave of aquisitions that would give it a foothold in the national markets of other EU countries. These included the acquisition of substantial assets in England and Wales,[12] and a controlling interest in Energie Baden Württemberg (EnBW), Germany's fourth largest energy utility (an acquisition the German government initially threatened to block in response to France's delay in implementing the 1996 EC electricity directive). Highly controversial was EdF's acquisition of a stake in Italy's second largest producer, Montedison. Revelations following the acquisition suggested that the purchase gave EdF a 20–25 percent share of Montedison (European Energy, 2001). In an attempt to deter EdF from acquiring a controlling stake, the Italian government in May 2001 issued a decree limiting the voting rights of state-owned companies not allowing reciprocal entry into their own national market. The law echoed a Spanish government response to the attempt of EnBW—subtantially owned by EdF—to gain a foothold via acquisitions in the Spanish market.[13] Both the Italian and Spanish laws reflected concerns about asymmetrical market opening—a problem that slowed postal services liberalization as well.

One year following the pronouncements of the March 2000 Lisbon European Council, in which the heads of EU states and governments called for the completion of the internal market in energy as quickly as possible, the Commission introduced a proposal for further competition in the electricity and gas sectors. The proposal pointed to the importance of achieving reciprocity between member states not only through further liberalization of demand, but also through "effective market structures" that would eliminate discrimination in network access (Commission, 2001b: 2). The proposal thus established regulated TPA as the method of granting network access; raised the minimum standard for unbundling to legal unbundling; and required that member state governments designate fully independent national regulatory authorities. As for quantitative market opening, the Commission proposal called for free choice of electricity supplier for all nonhousehold customers beginning January 1, 2003, and free choice for all customers, including households, from January 1, 2005.[14]

Although a large majority of member state governments—by some accounts, all countries other than France in the leadup to the March 2002 Barcelona summit (*The Economist,* March 9, 2002)—acquiesced to further liberalization, these governments were unwilling to impose a new directive on the French government for three reasons: (1) as the largest electricity producer in the internal market, EdF carried a certain weight in decisions about the sector; (2) closely related to (1), some member states depended on imports from France; and (3) several member states shared the overarching French concern with protecting public services (AFX European Focus, March 24, 2001). The Commission's proposal therefore was dead upon arrival. With France in essence exercising a national veto, the Commission advanced a revised proposal in June 2002.[15] The new proposal delayed until January 1, 2004, full liberalization of demand for electricity in the business sector, retaining the 2005 date for households. After fifteen years of Community-level efforts, liberalization of the electricity sector remained a halting process.

The Single Market and Postal Services Liberalization

Postal Services: Unsuited for Competition?

Specific features of the postal services sector render it inherently resistant to a competitive environment. These include the labor intensive nature of the sector and the natural dispersion of high- and low-cost areas within national borders, requiring geographical cross-subsidies. As Vincenzo Comandini points out, competition in the postal sector takes place *within* the network, in contrast with the telecommunications sector, where competition is *between* rival networks. In telecommunications, entry costs are extremely high; in postal services, barriers to entry are low, and it is relatively easy for new market entrants to supply profitable niches while refusing to supply unprofitable customers unless required to do so (Comandini, 2000: 142–143). Finally, the objective of greater competition is complicated by the "social" character of postal services; delivery of post is accompanied by other services, especially in rural areas. These include anything from the cashing of pension checks to the provision of meeting space for a municipal gathering.

When the Council of Ministers called on the European Commission in September 1989 to develop the outlines of a Community-level policy for the 80 billion euro postal services market (equal to 1.4 percent of EU GDP), the effort to develop a regulatory regime had to confront the tension between the universal service role of the public sector defended by national postal services operators and mounting pressures from postal services consumers and private competitors to introduce competition in the sector. The universal service obligation (USO)—the commitment of national postal operators to serve their entire national territory at a uniform rate—demands that some segments of the service operate at a surplus, so that they can, in effect, subsidize those areas where providing mail services are extremely costly and generate losses.

In the early stages of the policy debate, some national postal services providers took a highly protectionist position, calling for all correspondence up to 2 kg to be shielded from competition, with national governments free to extend the reserved sector beyond that limit if they wished. Protectionists justified this as necessary to ensure the supply of universal services. The fixed costs of maintaining the network required to furnish universal services were quite high; the reserved area accordingly should be extensive. Private sector firms and postal services consumers in the business sector countered that the universal service obligation was far less costly than implied by the maximally protectionist position, and that the scope of the reserved sector required to finance universal services that much smaller. Furthermore, financing the universal service obligation through protection is inefficient; competition should be maximized and universal services funded through external subsidies equal to the costs of public service provision (Commission, 1993: Annex 2, p. 10).

The debate over the extent of protection required to secure universal services was the core point of contention in the postal services liberalization debate, but national postal service operators shared three further concerns. First, since barriers to entry into profitable niches in the postal services market were low, national postal operators faced the threat that competitors could "cream off" the most profitable services, threatening the ability of national operators to fund universal services. Second, liberalization of direct mail (advertising) would raise the prospect of competitors disguising other forms of mail as "direct" mail. The inviolability of mail and consequent inability to control its content rendered this problem intractable. From the outset of European-level policy formulation, a majority of national governments therefore preferred to keep direct mail in the reserved sector. And finally, some national authorities worried about the problem of "remail" through which users of mail services could erode the national reserved area by taking advantage of differentials in national postal rates. This could be done, for example, by electronically sending bulk mailings to neighboring countries with lower mail rates, having them printed and mailed back into the country of origin at the lower rate. Accordingly, while several member states favored the liberalization of outbound cross-border mail, almost all advocated the continued protection of inbound cross-border mail (Commission, 1993: 19; 23).

Meanwhile, private sector competitors had two primary concerns. The first was cross-subsidization by national postal operators of competitive services with surpluses generated by monopolized activities. The second worry was that national operators could use their dominant market positions to attract users to competitive services by offering tariff reductions. Accordingly, private sector firms pressed for transparent accounting systems that would distinguish monopolized from competitive services, and for the separation of the regulatory function from postal operations.

Supranational Leadership: Making the Case for Competition

Studies of Europeanization often place the European Commission at the center of this process. Acting as a policy entrepreneur, the Commission draws from a variegated toolkit to advance critical issues on the Community agenda. These methods include building networks of support at both national and European levels through the consultation process, drawing on impact studies to create a rationale for and legitimate Community-level action and to help national policy makers sell the idea of Community action to their own constituents. By cultivating policy networks, the Commission affects the formation of government policy positions by strengthening subnational support for integration initiatives. Sectoral liberalization at the European Community level in telecommunications and energy illustrate this process in action.

The Commission's initial efforts to advance the single market in postal services shared common features with its early steps on behalf of liberalization of the telecommunications and energy sectors. As it launched its effort to promote telecommunications liberalization, the Commission sought during the consultation phase of the process both to soften the hostility of national service providers and to bring together user groups supportive of competition (Schneider, Dang-Nguyen, and Werle, 1994: 485). These same objectives were at the core of postal services consultation process that lasted from mid-1992 to early 1993, during which the Commission sought to assure national postal services operators that broader competition would not endanger universal service provision, and to draw together pro-liberalization business users and private sector postal services firms. As it prepared the way for its first proposed step toward opening the sector to competition, the Commission portrayed its approach as a balanced one, steering between the extremes of rapid all-out liberalization and full protection of national monopolies. In essence, the Commission sought to reduce the problem of competition to a matter of "proportionality"—a technical exercise of calculating the point at which the protected sector is exactly large enough to finance the universal service, but no larger (Commission, 1993: 9). However, it was not a simple matter to depoliticize the liberalization process.

The Commission's internal market directorate saw an opportunity to advance the cause of integration by establishing a clear rationale for liberalization that could shape internal debates as national governments formulated their preferences. The Commission identified several aspects of the postal services sector that disrupted commerce within the single market. First, wide variation in quality of postal services across member states acted as a barrier to trade. Similarly, trade within the single market was impeded by the significant "frontier effects" resulting from differences in the quality of domestic and cross-border delivery.[16] Delivery times corresponded more closely with the presence or absence of national borders than with the distances across which mail had to travel. The generally poor performance of cross-border delivery made it difficult for several types of firms—mail order, advertising, financial services—to market their products, limiting competition. Variations in standards and weight classifications across borders also represented a trade barrier. Finally, the excessively large reserved area in some member states was an obstacle to market entry by competing postal service operators (Commission, 1993: 1–2).

Despite the logic for introducing competition, the member state governments accepted only a very modest liberalization measure in 1997, which took effect in February 1999. While the European Commission's Industry DG preferred to open direct mail and inbound cross-border mail to competition, the European Parliament (EP) and Council rejected the phasing in of competition in direct and incoming cross-border mail.[17] The first market opening measure therefore would be extremely cautious, creating a reserved sector in the collection, sorting, and distribution of items of domestic correspondence costing up to five times the standard letter rate or weighing less than 350 grams. With the reserved sector defined this way, just 3 percent of postal service revenues would be opened to competition.[18]

The directive came into force in February 1999. Advocates of far more ambitious liberalization suggested that while the legislation codified maximal levels of protection of monopoly rights, it actually had the net effect of closing markets. This resulted as some national postal services that already had liberalized portions of their market in excess of that required by the 1997 directive dropped back to the minimum requirements. For example, Belgium and Italy applied the 350-gram threshold for competition to direct mail, which previously had been subject to a lower level of protection than the domestic letter monopoly. Following implementation of the directive, Belgium, France, Germany, Greece, Italy, and Spain all wound up with a higher threshold of protection on outbound cross-border mail than prior to the Community legislative measure (European Express Association, 1999).

Following the 1997 measure, efforts to advance the postal services dossier initially came from the Commission's Enterprise DG, under the political direction of European Commissioner Martin Bangemann. Bangemann pushed for a swift and complete liberalization process, with a substantial market opening by 2003 and full liberalization of the sector by 2005. In the new Commission that took over following the resignation of the College of

Commissioners in 1999, the file was picked up by the Internal Market DG, which recognized the need for a more moderate approach to this politically sensitive sector. The new proposal therefore yielded on two controversial items. The first was a retreat from the call for full liberalization of direct mail as part of the liberalization step to be introduced by 2003. Instead, direct mail would be included in the monopoly to be retained by national carriers for mail below 50-grams. With full liberalization of direct mail, 27 percent of the postal market would have been opened to competition, rather than the 20 percent to be attained via the Commission's new proposal.[19] Second, as a concession to claims of liberalization's opponents that the impact of market opening was unpredictable, the Commission refrained from specifying a final date for full liberalization of the sector. The proposal also kept incoming cross-border mail completely in the protected sector, addressing a central concern of countries such as Luxembourg and Ireland, for whom mail entering the market from outside national borders represents an inordinately large share of the postal market.[20]

As it advanced the proposal, the Commission legitimated its actions by reference to the March 2000 Lisbon European Council, at which the presidents and prime ministers of EU member governments asked the Commission "to speed up liberalisation in areas such as gas, electricity, postal services and transport," in order to "achieve a fully operational internal market in these areas" (European Council, 2000: paragraphs 16 and 17). The Commission's Internal Market DG also used the findings of several sectoral impact studies to make the case for the viability of the universal service in a competitive environment. The Commission cited studies showing that, because of their resources, customer familiarity, and market position, public postal service operators would retain 90 percent of the letter market above 50 grams if that segment of the market were opened to competition (European Report 2511, June 24, 2000). With a large majority of letters falling well below that weight, only 50 percent of postal revenues would be in the competitive sector in any case.[21] National postal services would retain the overwhelming majority of their revenues in a liberalized market. Furthermore, employment shrinkage among national postal services was likely to result from efforts to improve efficiency rather than liberalization per se. Job losses in the public sector would be offset in part by gains in private sector postal services firms (PricewaterhouseCoopers, 1998: 88).

Private Sector Competitors and the Liberalization Lobby

Dating back to the debate over the first postal services directive beginning in the early 1990s, policy initiation at the European level served as a catalyst for interest aggregation and articulation at European and national levels. The consultation process fostered organization of interests both in defense of the public sector monopoly and in favor of liberalization. These included postal service providers: national governments, national postal services administrators and regulators, private sector postal service operators, and trade unions; as well as consumers of postal services: trade associations, and both large businesses and small enterprises. PostEurop, an association of national postal services operators, formed in the course of the consultation process, just as national utilities had set up a Brussels trade association (Eurelectric) during the consultation process on electricity liberalization a few years earlier. Private firms and business associations in the postal sector, participants in competitive package delivery and express mail services, formed their own lobbying organization, the European Express Organisation (later the EEA).[22]

An accumulation of complaints by private firms and industry associations against abuses of monopoly position by national postal services—abuses that violated the competition rules of the single European market—drove postal services liberalization to the top of the European Commission's agenda in 1999/2000. These complaints dated back to 1994, when United Parcel Service approached the European Commission with evidence that the German postal service was using profits generated by its monopolized letter handling to subsidize its parcel delivery service, in which UPS and other firms competed with Deutsche Post. Additional complaints against abuses of dominant market position by national carriers piled up in the late 1990s. In February 1998, the British Post alleged that Deutsche Post was assessing surcharges and slowing delivery of bulk mailings from the UK. According to the complaint, Deutsche Post asserted that the incoming mail consisted of items originating in Germany, sent electronically to the UK, then printed and shipped as bulk cross-border mail. Since the items had originated in Germany, contended Deutsche Post, they were subject to the full German domestic rate (European Report, 2000b). DPAG was not the only target; the European Express Organization, led by UPS and Federal Express, complained to the Commission that a number of national postal services—among these the Posta Italiane,

France's La Poste, and Spain's Correo—were using their monopoly profits to curtail competition by buying up other firms (European Report, 1999).

The largest private competitors in Europe's postal services sector are UPS, FedEx, TNT, and DHL. Additional express and freight companies compete with these large "integrators," though these medium-sized firms tend to serve national markets and rely mostly on road rather than air transport. In addition, there are smaller courier companies serving regional and local markets throughout Europe. While the large integrators primarily are concerned with transport regulations (rules governing night flights, e.g.) as much as opening of national postal markets, some of the smaller firms have a stronger interest in sectoral liberalization to facilitate their efforts to capture market niches.

In the German parcels market, the main competitors of Deutsche Post (DPAG) are UPS, which entered the German market in 1976, Deutscher Paket Dienst, and German Parcel. However, DPAG has consistently held at least 85 percent of the mail order parcel market. The investigation of the UPS complaint by the European Commission's competition DG eventually revealed that Deutsche Post's commercial parcel sector had sustained losses of DM 27.5 billion from 1984 to 1996. These had been financed by Deutsche Post's other—monopolized—operations. The losses were incurred as Deutsche Post priced its parcel services below cost, using this predatory pricing to keep competitors out of parcel services in Germany.[23] But when initially confronted with the complaint by UPS, the Commission could not take decisive action until it had generated support in the Council of Ministers. In response to the resulting delay, UPS ultimately sued the Commission in the European Court of Justice for its failure to act.[24]

Faced with these antitrust and state aid complaints, the Commission in early 1999 sought to advance the liberalization of postal services. However, the draft liberalization directive prepared by the Commission was halted in its tracks when the College of Commissioners was forced to resign in March 1999. This left the problem of postal services liberalization in the hands of the new Commission, which took over in a political climate in which the Commission's very standing was at stake. When the new Commission came to office in May 1999, postal services liberalization had advanced little despite a decade of consideration at the European level.

Protectionism's Persistence

For those governments resistant to liberalization, national postal service providers were the core force behind their protectionist positions. This protectionist impulse was clearly represented in the European Parliament, which was, overall, hostile to what it considered the Commission's overzealous approach to broadening competition. As a single market measure, the proposal to increase competition in postal services would be decided through the codecision procedure, requiring parliamentary support and giving the EP important powers to amend the legislation. Given the distribution of national government positions into two roughly equal blocs, the position taken by the EP in the first reading of the proposed legislation would have an important impact on the contours of any compromise position debated within the Council.

The December 2000 debate in the EP substantially mirrored the state of national positions, with French MEPs attacking the Commission's "ultraliberal" proposal and MEPs from Portugal opposing the Commission's "unrestrained desire to liberalise."[25] In contrast, Swedish members of the Party of European Socialists (PSE) joined a Finnish MEP from the center-right PPE in calling for the establishment of a final date for full liberalization to foster modernization of national post offices and a stable investment climate in the sector. French Socialist MEP Gilles Savary argued that liberalization would render it prohibitively expensive for postal services in France and elsewhere to meet their commitments to provide a universal service. Armonia Bordes, French MEP of the GUE/NGL (Group of the United Left/Nordic Green Left), expressed total opposition to liberalization of the sector, suggesting that "whether privatisation is gradual or sudden, it will inevitably mean the destruction of the public service and will have serious consequences for postal workers."[26] The concern was shared by representatives of territories with proportionally large rural populations; as one Irish MEP asserted, post offices serving extensive rural areas would have difficulty meeting their universal service obligations while facing competition (European Report, 2000d). A large group of MEPs crafted a "European Appeal: a case for a high universal standard postal service." Of the 112 signatories as of June 2000, thirty-four were French, and just one was from Sweden, where postal services are fully liberalized (European Report, 2000d). Ultimately the Parliament voted to open only an additional 6 percent of the postal services market to competition, and to do so only in 2005, rather than the date of 2003 proposed by the Commission.

The European Parliament's stance in 2000 was consistent with its reaction to earlier efforts to introduce more competition in the postal services sector. During the consultation process initiated by the Commission in the early 1990s, the EP voiced two themes that reappear in each statement of the Parliament's position, beginning with two parliamentary resolutions passed in 1993.[27] First, as the Commission began to draft its strategy for the application of competition rules to the postal sector, the EP insisted that EC Treaty Article 100a—the foundation for the usual procedure of a Commission proposal for a single market measure submitted for the approval of the Council and Parliament—form the basis for legislation concerning the single market in postal services rather than Article 90(3) concerning the need for governments to respect competition rules in granting rights to providers of public services. Second, the EP showed a strong inclination to defend national postal service operators in several ways. These include enlarging the reserved sphere deemed necessary to protect the universal service, easing adjustment demands on the universal service operators, and calling for greater commercial freedom for national postal administrators. All these forms of defending the public sector postal operators were present in the Parliament's response to the Commission's first proposed postal services directive in 1995. At that time, the EP adopted fifty-eight amendments to the Commission's draft, generally aimed at creating a broader concept of the universal service and establishing an expansive reserved sector. The EP incorporated social protection of postal service employees in the universal service obligation, along with an anti-social dumping clause, and included in the reserved sector all direct mail and cross-border mail below the weight and price thresholds specified in the legislation. Additionally, the EP proposed easing the accounting requirements to be imposed on universal service operators, which originally were designed to eliminate cross-subsidies between reserved and competitive segments of the market.

The Commission rejected the vast majority of Parliament's amendments, accepting all or part of just sixteen of them. From the perspective of the Commission, Parliament's call for keeping all direct and cross-border mail within the reserved area was "part of a general postponement of the liberalisation process" (Commission, 1996b: 4). The greatest concession made by the Commission was acceptance of an amendment that extended the time allowed for implementation of the directive to one year from six months (Commission, 1996b). However, the position of the Council of Ministers of national governments came considerably closer to the Parliament's perspective. The Council accepted twenty-five of the EP's fifty-eight amendments.[28] Most significant, the Council adopted the Parliament's views regarding the timing of the liberalization process, and agreed that for the time being, direct and cross-border mail should be shielded from competition.[29] Ultimately, the EP position bore fairly close resemblance to the final document because of the central role of national service providers in domestic policy debates.

In January 1999, the Parliament adopted a resolution urging the Commission to slow down the liberalization process because the 1997 directive had not yet been widely implemented and its impact therefore could not be assessed, and also because the Commission had not permitted sufficient time for the completion and dissemination of impact studies. The EP asserted that Commission inaction had rendered irrelevant lapsed target dates for a new liberalization directive, and emphasized that its own evaluation of the postal services liberalization would be informed not only by the Commission's studies, but also by consultations with national universal service providers themselves.[30]

While the independent impact of the Parliament on the fate of postal services liberalization should not be overstated, the EP did interact with other actors in critical ways. First, the EP's position helped the French Council Presidency of the second half of 2000 more effectively control the bargaining process. While the French government could control the timing of the postal services debate and define the initial scope of the negotiations, it was as Council President expected to perform as a more or less neutral arbiter. By scheduling discussion of the postal services proposal in the December 2000 Telecommunications Council just after Parliamentary debate of the committee report on postal services liberalization and the EP's resounding opposition to the Commission proposal, the French government more easily could legitimate a minimalist approach to liberalization. Second, national postal operators were aware of the EP's long-standing resistance to the Commission's ambitious liberalization aspirations. Consequently, a self-reinforcing logic developed: the Parliament attracted extensive lobbying by national operators, solidifying antiliberalization sentiment in the EP.

Lobbying by the postal service operators fearing that rapid liberalization would threaten their ability to fund universal services was particularly effective for two reasons: first, national postal services were the single most important forces in domestic political debates, and, second, the European Parliament encountered relatively little countervailing pressure in favor of liberalization. National postal service providers, represented by PostEurop, strengthened their position by presenting to the EP a "common platform."[31] Basing the platform on the need to protect universal services provision,

PostEurop was able to present the EP with a strong case for a cautious approach to liberalization.[32] PostEurop claimed that the Commission had not sufficiently studied the potential impact of liberalization on finances and employment in the sector.[33] PostEurop also sought to exploit the asymmetrical nature of the liberalization debate, emphasizing the many uncertainties inherent in liberalization. The PostEurop platform warned of the low barriers to entry in portions of the postal services market and the consequent threat to universal service financing and social cohesion posed by too rapid a liberalization process.[34]

The lobbying efforts of private sector postal services companies were modest in comparison. Large delivery companies like UPS, though favoring postal services liberalization, had little interest in entering the letters market, with the exception of direct mail. Such companies were principally intent on eliminating cross-subsidies that made it more difficult for them to compete in package and express delivery. This objective, however, was most effectively pursued through their reliance on European competition law and the Community legal system, as demonstrated by the complaints lodged with the Commission against Deutsche Post and La Poste of France. Smaller firms whose dominant interest was in liberalization carried relatively little weight in the European Express Association. The European Commission, moreover, had to be cautious about pressuring the Parliament to support its position, reflecting the greater independence of the EP since the Parliament's inquiry into Commission mismanagement and the resignation of the College of Commissioners in 1999.

One potential incentive for governments to overrule national postal service providers was the threat of unilateral Commission action via EC Treaty Article 90(3). Arguably, the 1990 decision of the ECJ in *Netherlands v. Commission* laid the foundation for the Commission to use Article 90 in the postal sector. In 1988, the Netherlands passed legislation replacing its public-sector post office with a private-law firm, PTT-Post, wholly owned by the government and granted an exclusive franchise to transport all letters weighing less than 500 grams. The Commission objected to components of the law that created a set of express courier services and prohibited competitors from offering similar services below a fixed price, restricting competition from private sector international express services. The provisions thus violated Article 90 of the EEC Treaty. The government of the Netherlands defended the restriction, claiming it was necessary for PTT to fulfill its public service obligations, and therefore exempt from Article

90. When the Commission in December 1989 ruled that the Dutch law violated Article 90, the Dutch government responded by taking the Commission before the ECJ. As discussed in chapter 4, the Court in its decision upheld the Commission's right to apply Article 90(3), but nullified the Commission's decision because it had been taken without giving national postal authorities a sufficient hearing.

In the electricity sector, the prior use of Article 90 in telecommunications made the threat of resort to Article 90 credible, inducing greater flexibility in the positions of member state governments (Schneider, Dang-Nguyen and Werle, 1994: 490; S. Schmidt, 1996b). However, since the Commission clearly did not have the political authority to use Article 90 to open postal services to competition, governments taking highly or relatively protectionist stances within the Council faced less pressure to make concessions.

Europeanization

The December 2000 Council of posts and telecommunications ministers could not arrive at a common position on the Commission's modest proposal to open 20 percent of the postal services sector to competition—a proposal that private sector package delivery and express mail firms organized in the European Express Association called "the bare minimum necessary at this stage."[35] Although eight national governments supported the Commission's draft, this did not constitute the required qualified majority. The seven remaining countries preferred a minimalist measure. However, most of those national governments favoring more rapid liberalization preferred to wait for another opportunity to substantially advance postal services liberalization rather than accept a minimal agreement that would lock in high levels of protection of national postal services monopolies for several years to come. While national postal service providers organized in PostEurop were reassured by France's staunch defense of public sector postal services and the cohesion of the coalition opposing the Commission's proposed directive, private sector members of the EEA took comfort in the fact that an antiliberalization coalition had not carried the day, as it had in 1997.[36]

As for other elements of Europe's single market, the Community debate on postal services liberalization ultimately created new political opportunities, drew in new actors, and induced revisions of cost-benefit analyses on the part of existing actors. This occurred in two ways involving interaction between the European and national levels. These concern the impact of the relative timing of liberalization on the positions of national governments and the way in which initial steps toward liberalization alter the domestic political dynamics of policy formulation.

Timing

Governments that introduce competition in national markets tend to become advocates of Community-level liberalization. Allowing competition in the domestic market gives postal services in other EU member states access to the national market; Community-level liberalization reciprocates this market access. These first movers gain advantage from early liberalization, positioning themselves to compete effectively in any markets subsequently opened to competition, while opening domestic markets before later liberalizers are fully prepared to compete. This pattern is typical of small open economies, and was followed by Sweden, Finland, and the Netherlands. All these governments unilaterally opened their markets to competition and then advocated liberalization at the Community level.

In contrast, those countries that wish to protect the domestic market oppose Community-level liberalization. To the extent they are successful in blocking Community legislation, they potentially can capture benefits by using funds earned in the protected national sector to invest in acquiring market share in the open markets of unilateral liberalizers. This is the approach adopted by France.

Governments that choose to introduce competition but do so after the first wave of unilateral liberalization are more dependent on near-term reciprocal market access. For such governments, liberalization in the domestic market may be contingent on Community-wide agreement. For example, with some governments seeking to impose their preferences for liberalization at the Community level, and others hoping to secure the protection of distinctive national regulations, Germany slowed plans for introducing competition in the domestic market in response to the failure to agree to terms of liberalization at Community level in late 2000. In other words, concerns about asymmetrical market access delayed liberalization in the German market. Moreover, the option of sustained protection of the domestic market also weakened the German government's advocacy of liberalization at Community level.

Both Deutsche Post and the German government initially embraced the Commission's proposed legislation, suggesting that the next step should move toward full liberalization of postal services. While the German government has been an advocate of enhanced competition in the single market, it has at times been slow to retreat from defense of its national monopolies in public services. However, in this instance Deutsche Post invested heavily in preparation for liberalization; from the viewpoint of fall 2000, this process was to be crowned by the November sale of up to 49 percent of Deutsche Post's shares to private buyers within and outside Germany.[37] From 1998 to 2000, Deutsche Post spent more than $6.5 billion on acquisitions of European and U.S. firms in a range of areas related to postal service networks, including freight forwarding, transportation, express mail, and international mail services. In March 1998, Deutsche Post acquired a 22.5 percent stake in global express mail carrier DHL, then in December added to its holdings the world's largest air freight company, Danzas. A series of purchases followed in 1999, culminating with Deutsche Post's $1.14 billion acquisition of Air Express International, the largest U.S. air freight coordinator. This enhanced the capacity of DP to compete with UPS and FedEx in providing logistics services to large multinational corporations (*Europe,* December 1999, p. S-3). Deutsche Post therefore was in a strong position to defend their market share after liberalization.

Measures by Germany's federal Economics Ministry to override Germany's postal services regulator on the issue of timing of liberalization (Regulierungsbehörde für Telekommunikation und Post, or RTP) reflect a strategy of accumulating surpluses from monopoly operations in order to prepare for competition. According to regulations established in 1997, Deutsche Post was authorized to maintain monopoly prices on letters up to 300 grams through August 2000. In April 2000, federal Economics Minister Werner Müller preempted the decision of the telecommunications and post authority by publicly ruling out any reductions in the costs of these letters and parcels before the end of 2002, coinciding with the date for implementation of the next phase of liberalization contained in the European Commission's draft proposal for postal services competition. Klaus-Dieter Scheurle, Director of RTP, condemned this infringement on the regulator's independence, but was overriden nonetheless.[38]

The actions of the German Economics Minister must be understood in the broader context of Deutsche Post's positioning for the marketplace and the impact of EC competition law. Deutsche Post already was laboring under the uncertainty of European Commission rulings on several complaints against the German carrier. One of these was a complaint by Britain's Royal Mail against charges imposed by Deutsche Post on remailings from the UK, a procedure whereby companies transmit large quantities of mail electronically to countries with lower postal charges, and then have the letters printed and mailed from the less expensive country of origin. A second complaint initiated by private carriers alleged that Deutsche Post was using revenues from its monopoly letter service to subsidize its expansion into the private parcels sector, and that this constituted an illegal state aid that distorted competition within the single market.[39] Potential penalties stemming from Commission rulings in these cases threatened to affect the pricing of Deutsche Post shares in the public offering scheduled for November 2000. The Economics Ministry's announcement therefore was intended to diminish uncertainty in advance of Deutsche Post's partial privatization.[40]

Just a month after the Economics Ministry's decision, Deutsche Post announced a 20 percent rise in net profits over the preceding year. The profits increase was generated in part by an astonishing 50 percent increase in Deutsche Post's turnover, a direct result of its aggressive aquisitions around the globe. But the vast majority of profits came directly from Deutsche Post's monopoly position in letter delivery (*Agence France Press,* May 4, 2000). In July 2000, the RTP confirmed that monopoly pricing on letters of up to 300 grams could be maintained through 2002. This was followed by another complaint lodged against Deutsche Post—this time from within Germany—by the DVPT, the German Post and Telecommunications Federation. The federation of small and medium private courier firms charged that monopoly pricing on the protected segment of small parcel delivery was subsidizing the takeover of smaller private firms by Deutsche Post (European Report, 2000e).

Also in response to the absence of Community legislation to broaden competition, Germany's federal Economics Ministry in early 2001 unilaterally declared that the postal monopoly on letters up to 200 grams and direct mail up to 50 grams would be extended. While the German Postal Services Law had stipulated that the Deutsche Post monopoly would end after December 31, 2002, the Economics Ministry extended the monopoly for an additional five years—through 2007. This bold step came in a domestic political environment otherwise favoring sectoral liberalization. Concerns about the impact on employment held by the postal services union largely had been allayed through agreements with the union to limit job cuts to retirements and voluntary redundancies. The economics ministers of the Länder on balance favored earlier liberalization and opposed the Economics Ministry's decision to delay the process.[41] The FDP, CDU/CSU, and Greens all expressed reservations about the government's proposed delay—the former out of concern for business users, the latter for consumers—which therefore faced difficult prospects in the Bundestag (*Agence France Press*, March 7, 2001; *Frankfurter Allgemeine Zeitung*, March 15, 2001: 19). In the face of these sources of domestic opposition, the policy decision was driven by the German government's determination not to engage in asymmetrical market opening. Federal Economics Minister Werner Müller had warned in November 2000, prior to the meeting of the Telecommunications Council, that the German government would have to reconsider its planned liberalization in the absence of results at the European level. Speaking in the Bundestag in March 2001, the non-party affiliated Müller drew applause from SPD members when he asked, "Should Deutsche Post be displaced in the German market by foreign government monopolies? That would be unfair competition, to which I say simply: not with me!"[42] This German insistence on reciprocity in opening the national postal services market echoed its approach to third party access to electricity and gas markets in the mid-1990s (Schmidt, 1996b: 12–13). Interaction at the European level reinforced rather than overcoming the impulse to protect national markets.[43]

Unseating Monopoly: Shifting Domestic Political Dynamics

The French government's opposition to rapid liberalization of postal services was consistent with their reluctance to liberalize other public services, including energy markets. The British position is somewhat more perplexing, given Britain's identity as a bastion of liberalism and strong proponent of broadening the arena for competition in Europe. In 2000, British officials objected to the speed and extent of the liberalization measure proposed by the Commission. As an alternative, John Roberts, chief executive of the Post Office, suggested that enlarging the open sphere to packages above 150 grams would be more appropriate—opening a mere 6 percent of mail revenues to competition.[44] Under the Commission's proposal, competition would focus on the most profitable portion of the mail services market, consisting of business and individual services in areas of high population density—precisely the segment of the market that underwrites services to more remote areas. The step proposed by the Commission would eliminate the Royal Mail's profits, leaving it no funds for investment (AFX European Focus, May 30, 2000). Britain's Communications Workers' Union asserted that the Commission's proposed directive could cost 50,000 jobs.[45] Coinciding with the positions of the French, Greek, and Portuguese governments, the British government echoed the Post Office view that competition should only be introduced at a pace that does not endanger the universal service commitment.[46]

In the German case, the 1994 United Parcel Services predatory pricing complaint against Deutsche Post had been an added stimulus for DPAG to prepare for competition. The British government was well behind Germany in preparing its postal services sector for competition. One commentary on liberalization efforts in the sector noted that "the surprising element in the commercialisation of Europe's post office has been the slowness of the British."[47] From 1985 until the British Postal Services Act of 2000, Britain's Post Office was a statutory corporation, owned by the British government and required to make a substantial contribution to the Treasury each year.[48] Its limited access to investment resources severely constrained the Post Office's ability to prepare for competition. Demonstrating how institutions shape policy choice, this, rather than any ideological opposition to liberalization, was the ultimate source of the British position in the postal services debate. Britain's position reflected the political struggle within the UK over the commercial freedom of the Post Office. In 1999, Britain's Labour government announced plans to reduce the domestic postal monopoly, only to encounter opposition within the Labour Party. The terms of the Postal Services Act—and the primacy given to protection of the universal service—mirrored this internal battle.

The Postal Services Act converted the Post Office from a statutory corporation to a public limited company, with the British government as the sole shareholder. Prior to the reform, the Post Office was required to hand over the overwhelming majority of its after-tax profits to the Treasury. The Postal Services Act allows the Post Office to retain 60 percent of these profits for investment. Moreover, the Act permits the Post Office to borrow from government funds at a commercial rate to finance acquisitions and joint ventures.[49] The domestic political weight of the Post Office's demands for greater commercial flexibility were greatly enhanced by its need to compete with the bold market positioning of Deutsche Post. Investment resources newly placed at its disposal enabled the Post Office to begin an aggressive acquisition strategy in 1999. Since then, it has acquired companies throughout Europe and the United States. However, because its resources have been much more restricted than those available to Deutsche Post, its approach has been different. Rather than purchasing or acquiring shares in the largest market integrators, which provide the full range of services from pickup to delivery, it has sought to build a network of smaller niche firms in courier and parcel transport services by buying a number of companies in the Netherlands, Denmark, Austria, France, and Ireland. The Post Office acted most aggressively in Germany, where it acquired package delivery companies Parcel, Domberger Paket Dienst, and Deutscher Paket Dienst, sufficient to give it a capacity of 12 million parcels annually (*Agence France Press,* August 3, 2000).

An eventual shift in the British position came about as a consequence of the first highly circumscribed steps toward sectoral liberalization at the Community level—the 1997 EC postal services directive. Britain implemented the directive by creating an independent regulator, the Postal Services Commission (Postcomm). Britain's 2000 Postal Services Act charged Postcomm with recommending means to introduce competition into the sector. Postcomm was to consider the appropriate level for defining the reserved sector, as well the scope of services to be protected. In addition, Postcomm would be responsible for licensing competitors, granting access to Post Office collection or sorting facilities, and any potential restructuring of the Post Office, including separating accounting units or selling off portions of the company.[50] In addition to requiring more time to position the Post Office for competition, the British government preferred to establish a mechanism for the orderly liberalization of the domestic market before supporting liberalization at the Community level.

However, the creation of independent regulator Postcomm in compliance with the first EC postal services directive significantly altered both the domestic institutional environment and political dynamics of sectoral liberalization in the UK. Postcomm quickly became a focal point for those interests—business consumers of postal services as well as potential private sector competitors—favoring far-reaching liberalization. In September 2001, Postcomm issued the first licenses for private firms to offer services in competition with the Post Office, ending the Royal Mail's 350-year monopoly. Immediately on granting permission for Hays, part of a business services group, to collect and deliver overnight mail in the London, Manchester, and Edinburgh business districts, Postcomm met with additional applications from firms wishing to offer limited business services in competition with the Post Office.[51] Postcomm also planned a rapid general liberalization of the postal sector, with bulk mail (representing close to half of the entire mail market) to be open to competition in 2002 and full competition in letters, with no reserved sector, in 2006.

The expansion of participation surrounding the issue—the drawing in of additional private sector interests and their coalescence around PostComm—began to erode the ability of the Post Office to define the British response to pressures from the European level for sectoral liberalization. At the same time, the Post Office remained the single most important actor in the process. Faced with the transition to a competitive environment, the Post Office sought additional time to adjust to new market conditions. In response to Postcomm's ambitious competition plans, the Labour and Liberal Democratic parties, as well as the Post Office (renamed "Consignia," then restored to "Royal Mail"), urged Postcomm not to push liberalization in the UK market too far ahead of that agreed at the Community level, since the financial consequences for the Post Office of the onslaught of competition from domestic firms and foreign entrants would be devastating.[52] As in the German case, concerns about asymmetrical liberalization in the European market deterred national plans for the expansion of competition. Agreeing to give the Post Office more time for restructuring, Postcomm called for the phasing in of competition in bulk mail in 2003 and 2005, and delayed full liberalization of the letters sector to 2007.[53]

Liberalization Delivered: A Modest Package

With liberalization of the domestic market under way, the UK joined the proponents of Community-level liberalization. In October 2001, the Council of telecommunications ministers agreed on a liberalization package. The deal was approved by the European Parliament in March 2002 and adopted as a new postal services directive by the Council of Ministers in May 2002. The directive opens to competition beginning in 2003 the delivery of all letters weighing more than 100 grams and all outgoing cross-border mail.[54] A second phase of liberalization opens delivery of letters of more than 50 grams to competition in 2006.

The directive does not establish a date for full liberalization of the postal services market. Instead, the legislation charges the European Commission with the task of evaluating the impact of liberalization and proposing any further market opening in 2009; any such proposal will require the support of the European Parliament and the Council of Ministers. Even with British reluctance overcome by the force of private sector interests invited into policy formulation by initial steps toward sectoral liberalization and critical changes in British institutional structures, three-quarters of the letters market will still be protected in the European Community until 2006. Ultimately moved forward by virtue of broader participation in the policy making process, postal services liberalization is hardly a story of rapid delivery.

7

CHALLENGING THE SOCIAL MARKET ECONOMY? EUROPEAN COMMUNITY COMPETITION POLICY AND GERMANY'S PUBLIC LAW BANKS

Chapter 5 demonstrated that competition in a sector may be legislated at the European level, but not achieved in practice. Chapter 6 showed that interactions of national governments and EU institutions, while often promoting sectoral liberalization, also can stimulate protectionist impulses at the national level. The chapter also illustrated how EC regulations may prompt critical changes in the domestic regulatory and political environment of a pivotal country. This chapter echoes that lesson. The chapter portrays a protracted standoff between EC law and preferences of dominant domestic political actors. But just as changes in the regulation of the postal services sector at the European Community level created conditions that eventually fostered support for liberalization in the UK, so too did interactions between the national and European levels lead to the transformation of the regulatory regime for Germany's public sector banks as these interactions altered domestic political alignments.

Overview

The conflict that erupted in the early 1990s between Germany's system of public law financial institutions and Europe's single market process represents a rigorous test of the conditions for extension of Community competition rules to the public sector. As outlined in the book's introduction, the dispute brought the institutional apparatus of the EC into confrontation with deeply institutionalized elements of German federalism and the social market economy. From the perspective of their proponents, the public sector banks represented the type of innovative institutional solution to the deficits of the market characteristic of the social market economy, ensuring the provision of critical public services without undermining—and arguably enhancing—competition in the sector. Moreover, the close ties with local and regional party organizations enjoyed by the public law banks ensured their support across the political spectrum and safeguarded their legitimacy. In essence, the public law banks were thoroughly insulated from any genuine domestic political challenge; only the progressive extension of Community competition rules to the public sector and the existence of European Community institutions armed with significant enforcement powers in the realm of competition policy made a challenge to these structures possible.

Two aspects of the ensuing competition policy process offer insight into the impact of single market competition on public sector activities. First, political pressure from the German government did not stop the European Commission from pursuing the case. At the same time, the Commission's competition policy enforcement powers did not lead directly to a resolution of the conflict, which required a long process of negotiation in which institutionally powerful actors in the German Länder played a central role. Only at the end of 2001, the better part of a decade after the private sector banks originally lodged a complaint with the European Commission regarding the status of the public sector financial institutions, did Germany's Land governments, Landesbank officials, the federal government, and the European Commission arrive at the terms of a solution that would bring the public law banking system into compliance with Community competition rules.

Reflecting the enhanced political mobility of capital resulting from European economic integration, the challenge to the public law banking system emerged from Germany's commercial banks, which saw in Community competition policy an opportunity to challenge the privileges that accrued to their competitors in the public sector by virtue of their public law status. Failing at the federal level to make their case that the public law financial institutions enjoy unfair advantages that distort competition, the commercial banking federation took its claims outside Germany's domestic arena, to the European Commission. In response, the European Commission had by the mid-1990s staked out a position that identified arrangements governing the public law segment of Germany's banking system as a violation of Community competition law. Germany's federal government, facing pressure from state governments through the Bundesrat, asked the European Commission to drop its scrutiny of the public law financial institutions. The Commission did not do so. Yet, as in the cases of public procurement and postal services liberalization, the expansion of competition did not follow automatically from the application of competition rules. The legal authority of European Union institutions notwithstanding, the infusion of greater competition into areas of public sector activity was mediated by domestic political processes.

The Public Law Banks: Public Services and Political Support

Characteristic of the German system of organized capitalism, the German banking sector incorporates a functional division of labor between different types of financial institutions. The banking system is composed of three "pillars"—the profit-minded commercial banks, member-oriented cooperative banks, and a network of public law banks. The public law network includes a system of state banks (Landesbanken) as well as local savings banks (Sparkassen). Several factors have fostered deep institutionalization of the public law banks. First, within the three pillar structure of the German banking system, the different types of financial institutions have throughout much of the history of the Federal Republic engaged in activities that complement one another. For example, by providing banking services to Land and local governments and financing local and regional economic development, the public law banks lend stability and dynamism to the entire banking environment. Second, the public sector banks can claim a high degree of historical continuity for the public service functions they perform, dating back to Imperial Germany. And, finally, the close relationship between public law banks and their local and regional governments has fostered political support for the Landesbanken and Sparkassen that is independent of political ideologies and therefore spans the party system. This support reflects the degree to which the public law banks are a critical instrument of the policy autonomy of the Länder (Deeg, 1999: 32).

The savings banks trace their roots to the early nineteenth century, when they emerged to fulfill functions in an industrializing economy that were not met by the large-scale investment activities of the private banks. These included the provision of rural credit, financing for urban housing construction and small businesses, and banking services for lower- and middle-income households (Tilly, 1994: 305). As Richard Tilly points out, the savings banks developed as "municipal institutions linked to the local welfare administration" (Tilly, 1994: 305). As the banking system was reconstituted in the Federal Republic, the savings banks continued to perform these functions, growing in importance along with the sharp increase in private household savings (Edwards and Fischer, 1994: 97–105; Tilly, 1994: 308). The Landesbanken were established to serve as clearing banks for the networks of Sparkassen and provide financial services to their state governments. The Landesbanken, which are owned by their state governments and regional savings bank associations,[1] comprise some of the largest banking institutions in Germany—half of the twenty largest as of the mid-1990s (Deeg, 1999: 82, Table 4; Sinn, 1999: 12, Table 2.1).

The twelve Landesbanken and 600 or so Sparkassen collectively operate more than 20,000 offices and employ approximately 375,000 workers.[2] Together, the Landesbanken and savings banks account for two-fifths of all banking business in Germany—roughly one-fifth each (Sinn, 1999: 4, Figure 2.1). From the 1970s to the mid-1990s, the savings banks and Landesbanken held approximately one-third of all loans to firms, with a slight upturn in this figure in the second half of the 1990s; commercial banks held 30.7 percent of such loans (Deeg, 1999: 83, Table 5). Within the European Union, public banks have a larger share of all banking system deposits in Germany than in any other member state except Spain. At 38 percent, this figure far exceeds the market share of savings banks in the UK (approximately 2 percent), France (16 percent), and Italy (23 percent) (Sinn, 1999: 18, Figure 2.5).

The public law banks provide a diverse range of public services derived from the fundamental principles of German federalism and the social market economy. These include commitments to finance and advise small and medium enterprises and to support local and regional economic development and cultural projects. Even as international capital mobility has increased, the network of public sector savings banks (Sparkassen) has remained attentive to the long-term financing needs of Germany's *Mittelstand* (Deeg, 1999: 19 and 32). The Sparkassen are the primary "relationship" banks for the small- and medium-enterprises vital to the German economy. This means that the Sparkassen not only provide a large share of the financing for the *Mittelstand*—about half—and fund about half of Germany's new business start-ups, but also that the savings banks provide services such as small business advising and collective goods like technology centers and regional company networks.[3] The Sparkassen and Landesbanken perform similar services for Germany's local governments, providing the majority of municipal loans, offering investment consulting to public administrations, and, especially in the case of the larger Landesbanken, acquiring shares in the interests held by individual Länder.[4]

The public law financial institutions also facilitate constitutionally mandated government efforts to equalize living conditions across regions. The Landesbanken are intimately involved in regional economic development and restructuring.[5] Each of the German Länder pursues structural policies intended to promote selected economic activities, such as investment in new technologies, housing construction, or environmental protection. The Landesbanken provide the financial services required to implement these policies. In essence, the Landesbanken have furnished the financial means for the execution of political objectives at the Land level (Johnson, 1998: 45).

Given the role played by the savings banks and Landesbanken in state and local government policy implementation, it is unsurprising that the public law banks benefit from broad political support from state and local political leaders. The public law banking system is even further interwoven with political leadership by the presence of government officials—from whichever parties govern at the regional or local level—on the boards of their Landesbanken or local savings banks.[6] Government officials, typically from state finance ministries, often move into top positions at the Landesbanken when they leave government service. In sum, the political ties of the public law banks are territorial rather than partisan. Since governing coalitions tend to be stable across localities and regions in Germany, but display substantial variation across the national territory, political support is deeply institutionalized, particularly across the two largest political parties, the SPD and CDU/CSU.

As implementation of Europe's single market accelerated in the early 1990s, then, Germany's public law banking system appeared to be well insulated from the reach of EC competition policy. The public law banks were extensively involved in the provision of public services critical to individual households, small businesses, municipal and state governments, and regional economic development, and had deeply rooted political support from senior regional and local party officials. Moreover, while the European Commission in its application of Community state aid rules often had demanded the restructuring of entities dependent on subsidies to keep them in operation, the public sector banks did not rely on state subsidies to meet their operating costs, but were in fact profitable, even as they provided public services.[7]

Mobilization of Private Sector Competitors and Germany's Public Law Banks

The public law status of the savings banks and Landesbanken carries important benefits designed to compensate these financial institutions for their public service obligations and to ensure that they will be able to carry out these functions. The three-pillar structure of the German banking sector facilitates public service provision within a competitive market environment. Conflict between the different types of financial institutions in theory is muted, provided that the activities of the three pillars remain complementary. However, the public law banks and commercial banks clearly compete with one another, and this competition has intensified since the 1980s with the liberalization of Europe's financial markets. The Landesbanken, in fact, are not only the primary financial institutions of their state governments and the central institutions of the regional savings banks, but are also universal commercial banks. The Landesbanken and their Land governments view earnings from commercial banking activities as crucial to their financial capacity to execute their public service functions. Conflict between different types of banking institutions is driven by this competition. But the conflict that burst forth in the 1990s was not entirely new. During the debate over a new banking sector law in the early 1960s, for example, the private banks attacked the favorable regulatory and tax treatment of the savings banks as an unfair competitive advantage. While the tax-exempt status of savings banks was eliminated in the late 1960s as savings bank profits grew in response to the rapid rise in private household savings in the Federal Republic, the conflict was hardly resolved, and commercial banks continued to complain about the privileged treatment of the public law institutions (Deeg, 1999: 49–50).

Even as implementation of Europe's single market proceeded in the late 1980s and early 1990s, Germany's Landesbanken and Sparkassen continued to enjoy substantial regulatory advantages. There were three dimensions to these benefits. First, state and local governments guaranteed both the institutional functions and the liabilities of their public law banks. This means that Land governments were committed to providing their public sector banks with the resources necessary to fulfill all their functions. The full guarantee of bank liabilities meant that both depositors and creditors could be certain that their funds were protected. As Hans-Werner Sinn points out, the liability guarantee essentially represented a second line of defense, since the institutional guarantee ensured that deposits and the investments of creditors never were endangered (Sinn, 1999: 28). As a direct consequence of these guarantees, the public sector banks obtained higher credit ratings. This, in turn, lowered their borrowing costs.[8] Indeed, in 2000 there were twenty-two public sector credit institutions in Germany that garnered a "Triple A" rating from credit agencies. Only nine additional banks in the entire EU matched this rating.[9]

A second benefit accruing to the public sector banks also relates to their liability guarantee and consequent high credit ratings. Because they did not have to fear the impact of investment risk on their credit ratings and costs of raising capital, the public sector banks could engage in higher-risk investments than financial institutions in the commercial sector. This enabled the Landesbanken in particular to extend their influence far beyond their regions. Westdeutsche Landesbank, for example, the largest of the Landesbanken, does more than one-third of its business abroad, and earns two-fifths of its returns there.[10] It is particularly strong in East Asia, a high-risk investment market, though in addition to branches in Hong Kong, Tokyo, and Singapore, it has branches in London and New York, and representative offices in Sydney, Peking, Rio de Janeiro, Osaka, and Toronto (Pohl and Freitag, 1994: 480). Under its politically powerful chief executive, Friedel Neuber, WestLB also pursued ambitious expansion plans in London financial markets, in French banking and insurance, and, after 1989, in East European markets. In short, in response to financial market liberalization, the Landesbanken, beginning in the late 1980s, became deeply involved in corporate lending and international investment banking, competing directly with large commercial banks in Germany and other European Union countries.[11]

Finally, governments demanded far lower returns on their equity from public sector banks than private shareholders expect from the commercial banks. As Sinn argues, government capital invested in public sector banks should on economic grounds earn higher returns than equity in private banks precisely because of the liability guarantee carried by that capital. In fact, the public sector banks consistently provide lower returns on capital than the private banks.[12] Moreover, the public law status of the Landesbanken, coupled with their intimate role in the implementation of Land-level policies, makes them a natural destination for state resources earmarked for regional development functions. This is illustrated by the 1991 decision of the state parliament of Nordrhein-Westfalen to integrate into the Westdeutsche Landesbank its Housing Promotion Agency (Wohnungsbauförderungsanstalt, or Wfa), which had operated as an independent public law institution from its founding in 1957. This step ultimately brought the internal German conflict between different types of financial institutions to the European level and triggered the application of European Community competition law to Germany's public law banks.

The government of Nordrhein-Westfalen justified the transfer of Wfa assets totaling DM 5.9 billion (approximately $3.6 billion at then prevailing exchange rates) to WestLB as a means of reducing the cost of administering the Land's low-cost housing development programs.[13] According to the Land government, plans to achieve greater administrative efficiency in the housing promotion program had been under discussion since the 1970s (Commission, 2000a: paragraph 111). But the transfer also accomplished an increase in capital needed by WestLB to comply with capital adequacy rules established in the 1988 Basel Convention.[14] Indeed, five additional state governments—Lower Saxony, Berlin, Schleswig-Holstein, Hamburg, and Bavaria—emulated the Nordrhein-Westfalen maneuver as a means of meeting the new capital requirements. Transfer of the housing program assets therefore was an alternative to privatization, a new issue of shares by the bank (a step WestLB's private sector competitors had to take to achieve capital adequacy), an injection of capital from the state budget in a time of fiscal scarcity, or a contraction of the bank's business in order to restructure its risks. But the transferred assets also exceeded the amount needed by WestLB for capital adequacy, and therefore permitted WestLB to expand its commercial activities.[15] Germany's commercial banks, which had hoped in vain that the Bundesaufsichtsamt für das Kreditwesen, Germany's banking supervisory body, would not permit the public sector banks to treat the housing development assets as core capital, viewed this as a serious threat given the aggressive expansion WestLB had embarked on.

In response, WestLB's private sector competitors sharpened their attack on the benefits accruing to the public sector banks. The Bundesverband deutscher Banken (BdB), Germany's federation of commercial banks (representing approximately 300 privately owned banks, including the giants Deutsche Bank and Dresdner Bank), argued with increasing vehemence that the privileges of the public law banks limited the growth potential of the commercial banks in the domestic German market, while public resources subsidized the far-flung investment banking and corporate lending activities of the Landesbanken abroad. Lodging a complaint with the European Commission in 1993, the commercial banks initially sought to have the integration of the Wfa declared invalid based on the capital adequacy directive adopted by the European Community in the wake of the Basel Accord. However, the Commission's internal market Directorate General was reluctant to overrule the approval of the measure by Germany's federal banking supervisory authority. The BdB then took a different approach, complaining to the European Commission's competition policy DG that the increase in the bank's equity capital constituted an illegal state aid that distorted competition in the single market because WestLB had not paid an adequate rate of return on the capital.[16] The BdB sought to exploit the political opportunity opened by the increasingly assertive enforcement of state aid rules from Brussels by the European Commission. In lodging its state aid complaint, the BdB did not refer to the liability and institutional guarantees extended to the public law banks, a step that would have been fraught with risk given the potential for state governments to retaliate by altering the regulatory environment—for example, by requiring commercial banks to sustain higher equity ratios.

Acutely aware of the intensely political nature of the issue, the Community's Competition Policy Commissioner, Karel van Miert, encouraged Land NRW, WestLB, and the commercial banking federation to resolve the issue internally. Such an approach also was favored by Germany's federal Finance Ministry, which wished both to prevent conflict with Brussels and avoid tension with the Länder. As one German government official described the impact of the multiple tensions at work, "no one wanted to put a finger in this hornets' nest."[17] Hoping to facilitate a German solution to the problem, the Commission participated in sixteen meetings with German federal and state authorities, representatives of WestLB, and of other Landesbanken between July 1994 and June 1997.[18] However, confident that it could justify the rate of return paid to the Land government and in the power of its political support, WestLB was not willing to offer enough of an increase in its return to the state to satisfy the BdB.[19] After several rounds of discussion facilitated by the federal government and including the Bundesverband Oeffentlicher

Banken (VOeB), the association of public sector banks, the BdB announced that it was no longer prepared to participate in talks at the national level, and that it would pursue the issue exclusively in Brussels.[20]

In January 1997, the Commission's competition DG informed the Landesbanken and commercial banks of its intention to open a formal investigation of the Wfa case. The public law banks were outraged. The VOeB, whose chairman, Friedel Neuber, also served as chairman of the WestLB, argued that in pursuing their complaint, the commercial banks were simply reacting to the growing market presence of the public sector banks. The VOeB joined the smaller DSGV, the Federation of German Savings and Giro Banks, in a threat to withdraw support for European monetary union (*Frankfurter Allgemeine Zeitung*, April 25, 1997: 19). However, the threat was counterproductive and opened the first cracks in the political defense of the public law banks. The position not only came under widespread attack in the German press, but the parliamentary party of the FDP (the Liberal Democrats, junior partners in the coalition government with Helmut Kohl's CDU) labeled the effort "attempted blackmail," calling it "a typical example of the inclination of the public law sector to block competition." The FDP declared that "the interests of the public law banks cannot be placed before that of Germany's competitive position and before the goal of European integration."[21] Germany's commercial banks, on the other hand, now hoped that the Westdeutsche Landesbank case would draw the European Commission's attention beyond the matter of the state housing development funds to the much more significant issue of state loan guarantees extended to the Landesbanken. Unwilling to take on this politically sensitive issue directly, the BdB hoped the Commission would embark on a more far-reaching scrutiny of the German banking system.[22]

Guarantees under European Scrutiny

At the June 1997 intergovernmental summit, German representatives secured the agreement of other member state governments to a "Declaration of Public Credit Institutions" annexed to the June 1997 Amsterdam Treaty. The statement acknowledged that Germany's public credit institutions are entitled to full compensation for the public service functions they perform. While there was debate within Germany about the significance of the document, many supporters of the public sector banks believed they had built a fire wall against any possible Commission intervention on competition policy grouds. In a press release, the DSGV presented its interpretation of the declaration, asserting that "the European Commission acknowledges that the member states have the right to self-determination in the structuring of their financial infrastructure." From the perspective of the savings bank federation, the declaration confirmed that "the organizational form and activities of the Sparkassen and Landesbanken are fully compatible with European Community competition rules."[23]

Why wasn't this declaration, accepted by the national governments of all EU member states, sufficient to protect the public law banks against the reach of Community competition policy? The declaration in fact represented an egregious defeat for the public sector banks and for the German Länder. In seeking an intergovernmental agreement to protect Germany's unique public law banks, the German federal government was acting at the insistence of the Länder. Concern among the Land governments about the application of Community state aid rules to the public law banks was heightened by the European Commission's January 1997 decision to open a formal investigation into the transfer of housing development resources to WestLB. In February 1997, the Land government of Schleswig-Holstein, occupying the rotating Bundesrat presidency, introduced a draft resolution concerning the broader question of state guarantees. The resolution called on the federal government to seek agreement in the intergovernmental conference to a protocol to Article 222 of the EC Treaty (which establishes the Community's neutrality regarding public versus private ownership) that would declare that state aid rules do not apply to the guarantees extended to the public law banks (Bundesverband deutscher Banken, 1997: 4–5). The resolution was adopted unanimously by the Bundesrat. In short, the Länder sought to preempt any threat to the status of the Landesbanken and Sparkassen by explicitly excluding them from Community competition rules. The resolution sought legitimacy by basing its defense of the public law banks on the need to preserve the diversity of governing structures and forms of public sector enterprise throughout the European Union. The Kohl government had been reluctant to take up this initiative because of its broader support for the Community state aid regime and its fear of losing political credibility within Europe in the area of competition policy.[24] But Chancellor Kohl came under severe pressure from the Minister-Presidents of several Länder to pursue the idea of writing protection of the public law banks into the Treaty revision.

The protocol sought by the Länder would have had legal force. However, the German government was unable to obtain support for such a measure in the European Council.[25] The declaration obtained by the German government at Amsterdam, which is not attached to a Treaty article and has no legal significance, simply states that compensation should be strictly limited to that required by public service duties.[26] Moreover, the declaration refers to the Commission's view that Community competition rules permit compensation for services of general economic interest performed by Germany's public law credit institutions. The statement therefore left open the question of the admissability of state guarantees of bank liabilities. Ultimately, the German government's effort to secure protection of the public law banks was important by virtue of its perverse consequence: it publicized the guarantees (the liability guarantee, or Gewährträgerhaftung; and Anstaltslast, the guarantee of institutional functions provided by the state) behind the Sparkassen and Landesbanken, until then a feature of the social market economy little-known outside Germany, and made the system a focus of scrutiny at the European level. Representatives of the German government and of individual Länder describe this as a case of the German government having "shot itself in the foot."[27] As officials depict the impact, after the Amsterdam declaration, "there were experts on Gewährträgerhaftung and Anstaltslast not only in Berlin, but also in Paris, London, Amsterdam and New York."[28]

After the Amsterdam declaration, opposition remained to the benefits granted to the Landesbanken from other member state governments and from the European Commission, which expressed concern about the ability of the large Landesbanken to use state guarantees of their liabilities to obtain more favorable credit ratings.[29] Competition Commissioner Karel van Miert had expressed the view as early as 1996 that the system of guarantees was inconsistent with EC competition policy. The Commission had come under heavy political pressure from the German government not to pursue this issue, and again called on the Landesbanken, Länder, commercial banks, and federal government to resolve the matter internally. In order to intensify the pressure for a German resolution to the guarantees problem, the Commission in November 1998 presented before the Council of member state Economics and Finance Ministers (ECOFIN) its report on public service provision in the banking sector, which indicated that the guarantees represented illegal state aid (Commission 1998b).

The report was designed to address the claim that the Landesbanken and Sparkassen were exempt from Community state aid rules by virtue of their provision of services of general economic interest—in other words, according to Treaty article 90(2). In the report the Commission challenged the justification for the guarantees furnished to the public law banks on three fundamental grounds. First, simply providing a national financial services network across all regions does not by itself constitute a service of general economic interest. Where a service offered can be provided by a market actor, any compensation provided by the government violates EC competition rules. The report contrasted the German public law banking system with that in Sweden, where a public credit institution set up under the auspices of the postal service is required to serve sparsely populated areas not served by any other credit institution, and is justly compensated for performing this public service function. As for financial services for regional and local economic development, the Commission asserted that these must be evaluated on a case-by-case basis. Were the states and municipalities to allow all financial institutions to offer these services on a fee basis, some would in fact be offered by profit-motivated commercial banks. Moreover, in cases where state assistance is provided to institutions set up for exclusively public functions, such as raising capital for state governments, government support "may not spill over in any way into competitive activities of the institution" (Commission, 1998b: section 3.3). Invoking the same regulation that was to constrain Deutsche Post in its competition with private package delivery companies, as discussed in chapter 6, the Commission indicated that compensation for public services can not cross-subsidize commercial activities.

The Commission's report also purposefully noted that state aid to savings banks with purely local impact does not come under state aid rules when the activites of local banks do not affect trade between member states. This point gave the politically important signal that the dispute over state guarantees could be resolved with minimal disruption to the small and medium Sparkassen. However, hoping to sustain maximal political support, German political leaders seeking to defend the public law financial institutions repeatedly underscored the unity of the system, encompassing Sparkassen and Landesbanken alike. It was only two years later, in the context of discussions over reform of the public law banks, that supporters of the local Sparkassen began to perceive a clear difference of interests from the Landesbanken.

Domestic Resistance Provoked: The WestLB Ruling

By mid-1998, the European Commission in the course of its formal investigation of the Housing Promotion Agency (Wohnungsbauförderungsanstalt, or Wfa) transfer to WestLB had received comments from two additional national banking associations—the French and the British—in support of the BdB complaint. The Association Française des Banques pointed specifically to the boost given by the asset transfer to WestLB's presence in France's municipal finance sector (Commission, 2000a: paragraph 96). Meanwhile, the European Commission staked out a clear position on the issue of state guarantees, indicating that those provided to the Landesbanken violated EC competition rules. Significant support for the Commission's position emerged among EU member state governments; at the November 1998 ECOFIN Council, the German government was isolated in its opposition to the Commission's report.[30]

The Commission's investigation provoked adamant opposition from pivotal actors supportive of Germany's federal structures. The Director of Schleswig-Holstein's Landesbank called the Commission's involvement a "frontal attack" against the existence of Germany's public credit institutions (*Der Spiegel*, 10/1997: 106). The Sparkassen and Landesbanken were able to draw on extensive cross-party political support in the early stages of the controversy. Helmut Kohl voiced his support for the integral role of public banks in Germany's federal system, particularly after the public credit institutions threatened to withhold their support for the single currency (*The Economist*, February 15, 1997: 69). The Minister-Presidents of the Länder also rallied to the defense of the public sector banks. Following a January 1997 meeting in Brussels with European Commission President Jacques Santer, Nordrhein-Westfalen Minister-President Johannes Rau (SPD), claiming to speak for the executives of all the Länder, expressed the view that the German banking system would be "unimaginable without the Sparkassen and Landesbanken."[31] Heide Simonis, Minister-President of Schleswig-Holstein, accused the private banks of "treachery," and warned EU Competition Commissioner Karel van Miert against conducting a one-sided investigation in the interest of the private banks (*Süddeutscher Zeitung*, April 2, 1998).

Despite this high-level political opposition, the European Commission in July 1999 ruled that WestLB would have to repay nearly DM 1.6 billion ($868 million) of aid to the Land of North Rhine Westphalia. The Commission reasoned that a market investor would have demanded a higher rate of return than that received by the Land government for the housing development funds transferred to West LB. The kernel of the Commission's position was that while member states are free to use public assets to achieve policy objectives, market economy rules apply once those assets are used for commercial activities. As phrased in the Commission's decision, "as soon as the State decides to assign public-purpose assets to a commercial use, it should seek a remuneration corresponding to market terms" (Commission, 2000a: paragraph 178). According to the Commission's assessment, the state of Nordrhein-Westfalen did not seek such remuneration in the case of the Wfa asset transfer; the repayment demanded reflects the difference between a market rate of return and that paid by WestLB, plus interest.[32]

The Commission's decision had significance far beyond the immediate case of the transfer of capital to WestLB in 1992. Within months after the new Commission assumed office in May 1999, the competition directorate under Commissioner Mario Monti announced that as a matter of general principle, state guarantees are incompatible with the single market when they improve the terms on which enterprises acquire funds.[33] In late 1999, the Commission began investigating cases involving similar infusions of capital into six additional Landesbanken (*Süddeutsche Zeitung,* November 25, 1999: 25). Germany's Federation of Public Banks (VOeB) reacted with outrage, asserting that the Commission's objective was to alter Germany's institutional structures and system of property ownership (*Vereinigte Wirtschaftsdienste,* October 29, 1999). The VOeB insisted that since the banking structure is a core part of the social market economy, and essential to funding local and regional development, it lies outside the jurisdiction of the European Commission. Invoking core EU norms of subsidiarity and a "Europe of the regions," the VOeB called on the European Parliament and the German Bundestag to impose tighter controls on the activities of the European Commission. Arguing along similar lines, and reflecting an unusual cross-party political alliance with the CSU's Bavarian Premier, Edmund Stoiber, Henning Scherf, SPD leader of the Bremen government, called the progress of European integration a danger for federalism.[34] And in defiance of Brussels, the Bundesrat on the day following release of the Commission's decision in the WestLB case passed a resolution defending Germany's public sector banking system.[35]

WestLB and the state of Nordrhein-Westfalen adopted a two-track response to the Commission's decision. First, both WestLB and Nordrhein-Westfalen challenged the Commission's decision in the European Court.

However, since a legal challenge does not have a suspensive effect according to EC law, WestLB was required to comply with the Commission's decision unless and until it is anulled by the courts. Accordingly, the government of Nordrhein-Westfalen offered to remedy the situation by taking a larger equity stake in WestLB in lieu of a cash repayment of the aid. But the Commission ruled out this approach, asserting that it would not compensate for the advantages accruing to the Landesbank from the use of state funds.[36]

In late 1999, Germany's federal government also filed a complaint with the ECJ against the European Commission's decision on the transfer of Wfa funds to WestLB.[37] Given the SPD/Green coalition's reliance on the opposition-controlled Bundesrat to endorse its program of tax and pension reforms, and the fact that the threat to the Landesbanken and Sparkassen affected every Land government, the federal government had little choice but to support the legal action of Nordrhein-Westfalen and WestLB. Furthermore, the Commission's rejection of the offer of Land Nordrhein Westfalen to increase its equity stake in WestLB created the need for a horizontal coordination mechanism to resolve the incompatibility between the structure of the public law banks and EC competition rules in a way that would not severely damage the competitiveness of the Landesbanken and Sparkassen and which would be acceptable to the regionally diverse Landesbanken. The result was the formation of the Koch-Weser group, led by the federal government's deputy finance minister and including representatives of the savings banks and Landesbanken.

But the public sector banks remained determined to use their political leverage to force the Commission to back down. Several political leaders at the state level threatened in the year immediately following the decision on the WestLB case to use their power in the German Bundesrat to block any proposed institutional reforms designed to prepare the EU for enlargement. Noting that some EU issues still require unanimous support from member state governments, Detlev Samland of the SPD, Nordrhein-Westfalen's Minister for European Affairs, warned that "The Commission must consider very precisely if it really wants a legal confrontation with Germany" (*Süddeutsche Zeitung*, July 24, 2000: 21). Samland's threat to veto institutional reforms was seconded by Henning Scherf, premier of Bremen, and Edmund Stoiber of Bavaria.[38] As of late 1999 and through the first half of 2000, the conflict between European Community competition rules and central elements of German federalism and social market economy appeared irremediable.

Domestic Interests Divided: The Koch-Weser Group

Although the decision on the WestLB state aid case directly involved only a single Landesbank, the decisive classification of the transfer of housing development assets as an illegal state aid clearly affected additional Landesbanken. Moreover, the emerging scrutiny of the entire system of state guarantees provided to all Landesbanken further indicated the need for a coordinated response. At a formal level, Community state aid rules identified the federal government as the partner of the European Commission responsible for implementation of a state aid decision. In the months following the WestLB decision, the Minister-Presidents of the Länder called on the federal government to coordinate negotiations over a solution to the problems faced by the Landesbanken. The result was the formation, in fall 1999, of the Koch-Weser group, an informal roundtable led by Caio Koch-Weser, State Secretary at the federal Finance Ministry. The purpose of the Koch-Weser group was to facilitate discussions between the public law banks of measures that could resolve the conflict between state guarantees and EC competition rules and to carry out negotiations with the European Commission.

From the outset, there were critical cleavages within the Koch-Weser group. One ran between the federal and Land governments. The federal government accepted the legitimacy of the Commission's involvement, preferred to minimize conflict with Brussels, and therefore wished to find a way to rapidly resolve the issue. The Länder rejected Brussels' authority and believed that Germany's public law structures were outside the competence of the Commission. Officials from the Länder hoped to achieve a new understanding about the scope of Community competition law rather than redefining the structure of the Landesbanken, to which they intended to make no more than marginal adjustments. Despite this divide, the federal government recognized that it would be very costly politically to impose its will on the Länder, and did not attempt to do so. A second cleavage ran through the Länder themselves, a product of the varying levels of dependence of their Landesbanken on commercial activities to fund their public service functions; this cleavage deepened as market conditions intensified pressures, especially on WestLB, for decisive steps toward reform. As a consequence of these cleavages, discussions in the Koch-Weser group during its first year of existence were largely exploratory, and the group struggled to find a common approach to the problem of state guarantees.

The Landesbanken view that it was still possible to satisfy the demands of Community competition rules with minimal adjustment costs for the public law banking system was reflected in WestLB's initial response to the Commission's decision concerning the Wfa funds. The state of Nordrhein Westfalen and WestLB proposed that WestLB repay to the Land government the amount fixed by the Commission, with the Land simultaneously increasing its equity stake in WestLB by an equivalent amount. In essence, WestLB would return DM 1.6 billion to the state of Nordrhein Westfalen, and the state would hand it back to WestLB. There would be no net transfer of funds, only an issue of additional shares to the Land government. The Commission quickly rejected this as inadequate. Several months later, NRW and WestLB offered an alternative that relied on fundamentally similar accounting mechanisms: the bank would repay the amount identified by the Commission by writing back general reserves, and the Land government would simultaneously make a capital contribution of the same amount that would then be notified to the European Commission as a state aid and subject to Commission scrutiny.[39] This, too, was rejected by the Commission, leaving supporters of the Landesbank with a dilemma: both the bank and the Land government were relying on the European Courts to annul the Commission's decision, but interim implementation of the decision, required by EC law, would now entail measures with irreversible consequences.[40]

Meanwhile, the Koch-Weser group considered several options for addressing the incompatibility of state guarantees with Community competition rules. One possible resolution, supported by some CDU/CSU politicians at the federal level, was for the public sector banks—both Landesbanken and Sparkassen—to pay a market rate of interest to state governments for the capital to which they have access and a market rate of return on the guarantees provided to them. The CDU/CSU parliamentary group's competition policy spokesman, Hartmut Schauerte, argued that such an approach would not only improve competition in the banking sector, but would also carry fiscal benefits for state governments and improve the international reputation of the German financial sector (*Frankfurter Allgemeine Zeitung*, July 29, 2000: 13). Ironically, some of Germany's commercial banks had suggested at an early stage of the dispute over the Wfa transfer that they would be willing to drop their case if the Landesbanken would agree to pay a premium on the capital from state housing development funds to which they have access (*The Economist*, February 15, 1997: 69).

But this proposed resolution of the tension between state guarantees and EC state aid rules ultimately proved unviable. Since the guarantees provided to the Landesbanken were for an unlimited amount and duration, determining a market premium would prove difficult. The potential for controversy over the amount paid would prolong market uncertainty; as discussed later, the value of certainty increased over time for WestLB and the other Landesbanken.

Splitting commercial activities from public service functions represented a more definitive solution. Operationally separate, the latter would continue to benefit from state guarantees; the former would no longer be underwritten by the state. Such a breakup of the bank's operations might or might not be accompanied by privatization of the commercial unit. Though careful to emphasize that it had nothing to say about the ownership structure of Germany's public banks, the European Commission encouraged a comprehensive and final resolution of the conflict through the splitting off of private from public functions. While notifying the German government officially in January 2001 that state guarantees of the Landesbanken constituted a state aid incompatible with Community law, the Commission also underscored that since the system of public law banks predated the EC Treaty, the guarantees would be treated as "existing aid." Consequently, the Landesbanken were not liable for repayment of the value of past state guarantees, and the guarantees provided on any debt already issued would remain in place. Despite these incentives to comply with Community competition rules, both the Landesbanken and Land governments remained hesitant to fundamentally restructure the public law banking system.

The Interests of the Public Sector Banks Redefined

Until fall 2000, the official position of the Koch-Weser group reflected an unwillingness of the Land governments to yield to the Commission. The Länder continued to wage a positional war against the application of Community state aid rules, insisting both that the Commission's assault on the Landesbanken was inconsistent with the principle of a "Europe of the regions" and that the guarantees did not in any case constitute state aid. As state and local politicians declared their defiance of the Commission in the months following the WestLB decision, no one, including Germany's BdB, had yet lodged a formal complaint about the liability and institutional guarantees. In December 1999, this changed. The European Commission received a formal complaint from the European Banking Federation (EBF) alleging that "state guarantees gave public banks an unfair advantage in the highly competitive euro-zone."[41] The complaint specifically named three of Germany's public law institutions: Westdeutsche Landesbank, Stadtsparkasse Köln, and Westdeutsche Immobilienbank, and chose these institutions from different segments of the public law sector in order to target the entire system of guarantees. The EBF essentially served as a vehicle through which the BdB channeled its complaint to the Commission. The Commission itself had encouraged the complaint, by repeatedly admonishing the BdB that it would not proceed in the absence of a formal complaint. With the complaint in hand, the Commission could claim that it had no choice but to apply state aid rules to the guarantees provided to the public law banks. Recent European Court cases in which third parties had won judgments against the Commission for failing to act on their state aid complaints—as in Telecinco, the Spanish public broadcasting case discussed in chapter 4—lent credibility to the Commission's claim.[42] And since the complaint came from the European level rather than directly from the BdB, it signaled that this was not simply a matter of Germany's commercial banks attempting to gain competitive advantage. Rather, the case involved a breach of Community competition rules with Europe-wide implications.

At the federal level, the governing SPD publicized its view that the Landesbanken could not legally defy Brussels, and tried to craft a compromise solution. In a July 2000 meeting with respresentatives of the states, Chancellor Gerhard Schröder proposed that the public credit institutions establish a barrier between public functions and commercial activities (with the former backed by state guarantees). The reactions to this general approach did not break neatly along party lines; the concept of splitting Landesbank activities was rejected by Henning Scherf, SPD leader of the Bremen government, Edmund Stoiber (CSU), Minister-President of Bavaria, and Bernhard Vogel (CDU), premier of Thuringia. Others, including Peter Steinbrück (SPD), Nordrhein Westfalen's finance minister, and Sigmar Gabriel (SPD), premier of Lower Saxony, were more supportive of Schröder. The Federal government informed the Commission that it could not reach a compromise formula, and Schröder pronounced that the issue could now only be settled in the courts, although he remained anxious "to avoid straining the already tense political relationship between the federal states, the Berlin government, and Brussels."[43]

As the federal/Land cleavage became more pronounced, pressure on the Koch-Weser group intensified. The Commission's decision in the WestLB case and its formal announcement that state guarantees constituted illegal state aid created market uncertainty for WestLB, which began to experience a small but observable impact on its cost of raising capital. This, as much as the threat of Commission action on the EBF complaint, provided WestLB with a powerful incentive to seek a final resolution of the conflict with the Commission.[44] The Commission's investigation of capital transfers to other Landesbanken had a similar impact, concentrating the attention of the Landesbanken on a decisive settlement. In this context, discussions in the Koch-Weser group advanced. In February 2001, a delegation led by Koch-Weser and Peter Steinbrück, proposed to the Commission a plan for splitting the public service and commercial operations of WestLB—the latter representing about four-fifths of the bank's assets. The Commission raised several doubts about the proposal, including questions about where the line between the two portions of the operation would be drawn and whether there might remain possibilities for the commercial segment to subsidize the public service portion of the business. The WestLB plan called for a parent public sector institution to provide a letter of unrestricted guarantee to its commercial subsidiary, for which the subsidiary would not provide any remuneration.[45] But most of the Commission's reservations came in response to efforts of the Land government to protect the state's system of Sparkassen. The restructuring proposal was limited to the Landesbanken and did not address the situation of the Sparkassen, for which it sought to maintain preferential financing terms and to secure an exemption from the EC public sector transparency directive, which in July 2000 had been extended to cover the banking sector.[46]

At the same time, officials of the larger Sparkassen recognized that, with Sparkassen Köln mentioned specifically in the EBF complaint, the savings bank sector would not remain untouched by the application of Community competition law. Local level politicians initially had been stunned by the prospect of EC constraints on the use of Sparkassen resources for local political objectives.[47] It also became increasingly clear to supporters of the Sparkassen that, in the absence of nearly a decade of intransigence by the Landesbanken, they might have escaped the reach of Community state aid rules. But the Sparkassen were less dependent than the Landesbanken on liability guarantees because they raised capital primarily through customer deposits rather than through capital markets.

Therefore, rather than undergo the sort of scrutiny and uncertainty experience by the Landesbanken, officials of the large Sparkassen came to favor reforms that would remove any doubts about the compatibility of their activities with Community state aid regulations. The smaller Sparkassen, focused exclusively on local or regional markets, still hoped to emerge from the conflict intact.

In May 2001, the European Commission informed the German government that it had two months to accede to the requested reform of its guarantee scheme for public law banks—which, according to the Commission, conferred on the public sector financial institutions an economic advantage of approximately 1 billion euro annually (Moser, Pesaresi, and Soukup, 2002: 3)—and until the end of September 2001 to inform the Commission about how it would accomplish this. Germany would then have until March 31, 2002, to implement the specific measures agreed to achieve compliance (European Report, 2001). The solution that emerged from the Koch-Weser group involved the elimination of the liability guarantee (Gewährträgerhaftung). The institutional guarantee (Anstaltslast) is provided to undertakings of the public law form as a matter of German law. But according to the measures adopted to establish compliance between public sector banks and Community law, Anstaltslast would operate with the provision that if the guarantee is used, it will be informed to the Commission as a state aid and subject to the Commission's approval according to the terms of EC competition rules. Reflecting the varying perspectives of the Landesbanken, this arrangement would form the basis of a "platform model" around which the different Landesbanken could structure their own arrangements.[48] Finally, in June 2001, the German delegation to the European Commission abandoned the insistence on providing a guarantee to WestLB's commercial division, clearing the way for a final settlement of the conflict between Germany's public law banking system and EC state aid rules. The principal issue remaining for negotiation concerned the transition period for eliminating the liability guarantee. The Bavarian state government proposed a period of ten years; in July 2001, the Commission and the Koch-Weser group reached an understanding which provides for a four-year transition period lasting to July 18, 2005. Existing liabilities will be grandfathered in; liabilities created during the transition period may be backed by Gewährträgerhaftung (guarantee of liabilities) provided their maturity does not extend beyond the end of 2015 (Moser, Pesaresi, and Soukup, 2002: 9–10).

Conclusion: Identifying Domestic Intermediaries of Change

Reflecting a widely shared view of the magnitude of the change involved, Bavaria's Finance Minister has called the reform of Germany's public law banking sector "a revolution."[49] It is likely that the rump public service components of the Landesbanken will be substantially depoliticized. It also is not clear that, without the profits obtained from commercial activities, the Landesbanken will be able to provide as extensive an array of public goods as they have in the past.[50] Nonetheless, with the system of local and regional Sparkassen intact, the social market economy model endures, and is perhaps invigorated by the purging of the increasingly internationalized and commercial components of the large Landesbanken (Smith, 2001b). At the same time, it also is clear that, as predicted by defenders of Germany's public sector institutions (see the introductory discussion in chapter 1) the struggle over state guarantees in Germany's public banking sector has had implications that reach beyond Germany. Late in 2002, the European Commission announced that state guarantees extended by the French government to establishments with EPIC status (Etablissement Public Charactere Industrial et Commercial), including Électricité de France, were incompatible with internal market competition rules. As a consequence, the Commission called for the French government to end guarantees of EdF's debt and demanded that EdF repay to the French government a sum equal to the financial benefit it had garnered from past guarantees and other state subsidies. The Commission's actions threatened the newly elected French government's plans to sell off shares of EdF as part of its effort to combat a mounting fiscal deficit.[51] In response, the French government in late 2003 pledged to withdraw EdF's unlimited guarantee by the end of 2004; in June 2004, the French National Assembly passed the government's bill altering the statute of EdF and preparing for partial privatization.[52]

The dramatic restructuring of Germany's public sector banks, so deeply rooted in German political and economic development and intricately embedded in German federalism, would not have been possible without the emergence of the European level as an alternative arena of interest articulation and a supplementary regulatory mechanism. At the same time, the application of European Community regulatory instruments was hardly mechanical. The process was protracted and involved extensive bargaining both between the European and German levels and within the German political arena.

The application of Community competition law to Germany's public sector banks was a product of two factors: the aggressive expansion of the business of the public sector banks into commercial activities, intensifying direct competition with the private sector; and enhanced opportunities for private sector actors—in this case the BdB, the association of Germany's commercial banks—to challenge at the European level restraints on competition emerging from domestic institutional arrangements.

Even though the European Commission, charged with enforcing single market competition rules, found potential merit in the BdB complaint, it encouraged resolution through a domestic political process rather than a European one. Futhermore, as discussed in chapter 8, even after the process shifted to the European level, involving the European Commission and the formal application of Community competition law, the dimensions of reform did not fully emerge until politically central actors in German politics began to recast their conceptions of the nature and role of the Landesbanken and Sparkassen in the political economy of the Federal Republic. Once the process began to operate at the European level, the pressures faced by the Landesbanken to resolve the incompatibility with EC competition rules were directly proportional to their involvement in international markets. WestLB thus faced the most intense pressures, and became anxious to comprehensively resolve the EC competition policy cases pending against it. Additionally, beginning from a conception of the Landesbanken and Sparkassen as tightly knit components of a unitary, inviolable public sector element of the social market economy, first federal-level leaders of the major political parties, then regional politicians, began to distinguish the Landesbanken from the Sparkassen, identifying the latter as the vital core of the public law banking system. In this sense, while the European single market was the force driving change, those national party leaders who viewed the restructuring demanded from the European level as consistent with the values of Germany's social market economy served as critical intermediaries in the process of adaptation.

8

LIBERALIZATION AND ITS LIMITS

This book began from the premise that the forces of liberalization set in motion by the European integration process have the potential to fundamentally alter the role of the public sector in the societies of EU member states. To what extent has the provision of public services and the decision making of public authorities come to be guided by economic efficiency rather than political expediency? And how broadly has competition been imposed on unwilling public service operators reluctant to give up their protected status? To what degree is Europeanization undermining the traditional discretion of West European states to use the public sector to pursue diverse political objectives?

The empirical material reviewed in chapters 5 through 7 indicates that, for the countries of the European Union as a whole, the protections traditionally accorded markets served by the public sector have been eroded significantly, and governments and public service providers that seek to sustain restrictive practices face further challenges. Public services in numerous sectors now operate in a competitive environment that would have been unthinkable a decade ago. Governments cannot freely subsidize state-owned public service providers and thereby keep markets closed to foreign-owned or domestic private sector competitors. But the case studies also indicate that European economic integration has not created a liberalization steamroller that simply "flattens" the public sector across EU governments, rendering it an apolitical mechanism for the pursuit of economic efficiency. Nor has liberalization advanced without accommodating the interests of protected public service providers.

The prima facie case for expecting European economic integration to translate into unrestrained liberalization of markets served by the public sector derives from several sources. First is the the overarching policy objective of state hardening shared by governments that agreed to create the single

European market and single currency. Abetting pursuit of this goal is the authority over competition policy exercised by the European Commission, whose competition unit operates with a pronounced liberal policy bias. Chapter 2 discussed the development of a European-level competition policy. This policy has had a transformative potential for public services markets due to the steady extension of European Community competition rules to the public sector, documented in Chapter 4. The legal mechanisms available to private sector market entrants to seek enlargement of the competitive realm have amplified the impact on the public sector. The consequence of these forces has indeed been the infusion of a significant degree of competition into activities that for decades had been subject to protection. Nonetheless, as discussed in chapter 1 (Table 1.1), across several sectors liberalization has been an uncertain and highly uneven process. Indeed, the aspiration of advocates of European integration—established in the European Union's "Lisbon Process" initiated at the March 2000 Lisbon summit—to make the EU the world's most competitive and dynamic economy through liberalization of services markets, remains largely unfulfilled. Progress toward this objective has been disappointing, as expressed as early as 2002 in EU Internal Market Commissioner Frits Bolkestein's pronouncement that the process to that point consisted of "more poetry than motion" (*The Economist*, March 9, 2002: 52).

How do we make sense of the juxtaposition of powerful market-making mechanisms with the relatively halting advance of competition? A response demands that we address three questions: (1) How extensive are efforts of potential competitors of protected public sector monopolists to invoke European Community competition rules in order to advance sectoral liberalization?; (2) to what extent do protected public service providers and their political supporters revise their assessments of the costs and benefits of liberalization?; and (3) to what degree does the interaction between European and domestic political processes reduce the weight of protectionists in policy formulation?

Chapter 3 proposed two sets of explanatory hypotheses for the scope and timing of liberalization. The first suggests that liberalization is driven largely by the behavior of competitors and potential competitors of public enterprises who have found in EU institutions new opportunities to seek access to markets. As posited in chapter 3, hypothesis I(a) states the proposed relationship:

The scope and timing of liberalization are a function of European-level pressures for adaptation—in particular, the extent to which private sector competitors of protected public enterprises employ EU channels to combat restrictive practices of governments.

Table 8.1 shows the relationship between the exploitation of political opportunities at the European level (the political mobility of capital) and liberalization outcomes (the pace and scope of liberalization) in each sector studied.

As reflected in the table, political mobility of capital is not tightly correlated with the timing (pace) of liberalization. There are cases in which multiple appeals to EC legal channels by private sector competitors of public service providers—or even a single competition policy complaint that represents a sharp departure from prior political opportunities for competitors—is associated with a slow pace of liberalization, as in postal services or in Germany's banking sector. Complaints from private sector competitors of public service providers don't necessarily speed liberalization, but appear to be associated with an ultimate increase in competition. In the case of the telecommunications sector, liberalization was rapid, despite a low level of political mobility of capital, but this may be an exception reflecting technological factors peculiar to the sector. In general, higher political mobility appears to increase the likelihood of more extensive sectoral liberalization. In German banking, political mobility ultimately led to a

TABLE 8.1: **Political Mobility of Capital and Sectoral Liberalization**

Sector:	Public Procurement	Postal Services	Public Sector Banking (Germany)
Extent of competition complaints to European Commission or ECJ from competitors/ potential competitors in sector	Few, especially relative to the vast number of transactions in the sector	Significant number of cases involving allegations of far reaching violations of Community competition rules	Complaints from major competitors—German and European banking federations
Liberalization outcome	Infusion of competition in the sector highly constrained; progress slow	Introduction of competition moderate in both pace and scope	Slow but ultimately extensive rollback of constraints on competition

wide scope of sectoral change, even if the process was slow. While a high degree of political mobility of capital is associated with only a modest scope of sectoral liberalization in European postal services, private complaints did foster preparation for far-reaching liberalization in Germany's postal services, where most complaints were focused.

Since political mobility therefore helps translate EC legislation into broader competition, it is essential that we explain the behavior of actual and potential competitors of protected public service providers. How and under what conditions do prospective market entrants and firms competing in portions of the market served by a public enterprise use European-level mechanisms to seek market opening?

Mobilizing Private Sector Competitors

The political mobility of capital provides an opportunity for broader participation in the formulation of policy regarding protection and competition in public services. As chapter 7 demonstrates, domestic political resistance to sectoral reform was overwhelmed as the structure of German public law banks became more highly politicized over time, culminating with the European Banking Federation's December 1999 competition complaint. As politicization progressed, opportunities expanded for both private sector banking interests and their political supporters to participate in policy making.

However, the availability of legal means to seek enhanced market access does not by itself ensure that market entrants or existing competitors of public sector service providers will deploy these instruments. Therefore, the crucial question about the political mobility of capital is this: under what conditions do private sector actors face sufficient incentives to use the legal mechanisms at their disposal? The empirical evidence from the public procurement, postal services, and German public sector banking cases indicates that the decisions of firms and business associations to complain about violations of EC competition rules are shaped by the costs and benefits these actors perceive. These, in turn, are determined by the relative dependence of private firms on the good will of public authorities, the extent of barriers to market entry in the sector, and possibilities for seeking remediation of competitive distortions in the national setting relative to those available in the EC context.

Chapter 5 revealed that in the euro 1.5 trillion market for purchases of goods and services by governments across the EU, the promise of open competition largely has been unfulfilled. Despite opportunities for firms competing for public sector contracts to challenge perceived violations of Community rules, relatively few market participants or new entrants have done so. As discussed in chapter 5, the explanation for this relies on strong disincentives for competitors to lodge complaints. These derive from the prospect of being punished in future competitions for public contracts and from the low expected private benefits of a successful complaint (i.e., the expected results of the reopening of a public tender and the difficulty for disgruntled competitors to obtain awards for any damages stemming from the loss of a contract opportunity).

Second, the existence of a public sector monopoly is, of course, the most significant barrier to market entry. Aside from this, entry barriers vary across sectors. The lower these barriers, the more private sector actors have to gain from seeking the end of public sector monopoly. In postal services, the costs of entry into market niches is low, so that ending the public sector monopoly produces a steady stream of market entrants. In other sectors, in contrast, there is little incentive for firms shut out of markets served by public enterprises to pursue legal redress when even a reduction of political barriers leaves potential competitors economically unable to enter the market.

Finally, incentives for private sector competitors and potential competitors to invoke EU competition law in response to violations of competition rules tend to be high in sectors in which a protected public service provider already has competitors in a segment of the market. This is the case for package delivery services in the postal services sector, and for a wide range of commercial services in German banking. In such instances, competitors will seek to improve the conditions for competition in the market segments open to competition; some may seek to broaden the competitive realm. Private sector competitors will take action at the European level to the extent that they have few opportunities to gain redress at the national level. This explains why Germany's highly organized federation of commercial banks, which had failed to penetrate the political insulation surrounding the public sector financial institutions, complained to the European Commission, as well as why UPS took its complaint against Deutsche Post to the Commission and, eventually, the European Court of Justice.

Whatever the state of EC law, the cost-benefit calculus of private sector actors accounts for the extent to which capital takes advantage of the opportunity to exploit the EC competition regime. This calculus produces the following relationships:

1. The extent of complaints from competitors/political mobility of capital is inversely related to the extent to which private actors can be punished by public authorities for challenging their regulatory authority.
2. Political mobility also is inversely related to the extent of barriers to market entry in the sector in question.
3. Pursuit of redress at the Community level by competitors of public sector monopolists is inversely related to opportunities for redress that exist at the national level.

Having established the incentives for potential market entrants and the implications of their behavior, we turn to the attitudes toward liberalization of actors in dominant market positions and their relative weight in policy formulation.

Liberalization and Dominant Market Actors

The second set of hypotheses presented in chapter 3 concerns the degree to which dominant market actors embrace or resist pressures emanating from the European level. While the first hypothesis concerning the behavior of potential competitors considers the extent to which liberalization is "imposed," this second set of hypotheses focuses on processes of accommodation. However forceful the drive to deepen European integration and fill in the single European market, the liberalization process may well stagnate as long as market incumbents perceive a fundamental conflict between their objectives and Community-level liberalization. On the basis of this hypothesis, critical questions relevant to the fate of liberalization initiatives concern the impact of the Europeanization process on protected public service providers and their political supporters. Can European-level interactions induce dominant market and political actors initially averse to competition to adjust their evaluations of the relative costs and benefits of sectoral liberalization? This is the dynamic addressed by Hypothesis II(a):

> Where incumbent public service monopolists oppose European-level liberalization initiatives, liberalization's prospects depend on the extent to which the Euro-

peanization process induces incumbents to revise their assessments of the relative costs and benefits of competition.

We know from examples of unilateral liberalization by some governments that public sector monopolists may recast their strategies independently of the European integration process. As previously discussed, governments whose public service providers have sought a competitive environment in order to capture first-mover advantages will become advocates of liberalization at a European level. But Europeanization may also be a cause of a strategy shift.

The empirical evidence gathered in this study suggests a range of objectives pursued by public undertakings. Some public sector entities focus on defending their share of the domestic market and sustaining employment levels. Others may embrace the opportunity to expand international market share; public service operators in countries with smaller domestic markets often are the first to pursue such opportunities. Almost all public service providers are concerned with maintaining the financial resources required to meet public service obligations, though there are varying interpretations of how best to achieve this goal. Given these objectives, shifts in incumbent positions toward sectoral liberalization can come about through any of three adjustment paths involving reassessments of the costs and benefits of enhanced competition:

1. *Response to market opportunities.* Public service providers may actively promote reform in response to market opportunities. Technological changes in a sector (telecommunications is a useful example) may create opportunities for first-mover advantages; the opening of a previously monopolized public service market in another country within Europe's single market might provide an opportunity for gains in market share that can be captured through reform of the public undertaking and reciprocal liberalization.
2. *Reassessment of benefits of reform.* A public service provider initially opposed to sectoral liberalization may subsequently revise their position based on a reassessment of the potential gains of sectoral reform. This recalculation may reflect cognitive change following the introduction of new information such as a sectoral impact study or the decision of other EU member governments to open their national market to competition, or it may reflect changes in the substance of a proposed European Community reform measure, such as a slowdown in the

pace of liberalization or reduction in the scope of market opening. Reassessment also can lead in the opposite direction: as we've seen in the postal services case, public service providers favorably disposed toward sectoral liberalization may revert to a protectionist stance if it appears that public service providers in other member states will be laggards in implementing a Community-level agreement to open markets to competition.

3. *Increase in costs of status quo.* In contrast to a revision of potential gains, a public service provider may reassess the costs of resisting reform. Resistance to reform might undermine political support for the public service provider, intensify complaints from business consumers of the public service, or prompt legal action by proponents of freer competition. The case of Deutsche Post (DPAG)—and its response to the UPS complaint to the European Commission concerning DPAG's predatory practices—illustrates the point. While Deutsche Post already faced demands from business users for more efficient services, the UPS competition complaint indicated that pressures would soon mount to accomplish this in a competitive environment. Rather than waiting for EU competition authorities or the ECJ to impose reform, Deutsche Post adopted its aggressive strategy of global acquisitions to prepare for a competitive environment.

EU institutions may be pivotal in how public service providers assess the costs and benefits of enhanced competition. The EU may affect these assessments in three ways: policy flexibility, shifting the domestic political balance, and threatening ECJ action. First, the European Commission may trigger revisions of costs and benefits through flexibility in the design of reform proposals. Jacoby's study of institutional transfer in Germany emphasizes that flexibility on the part of those seeking to achieve transfer is critical to success.[1] A similar point applies here. Liberalization measures proposed by the European Commission typically are complex bundles addressing the extent of competition to be introduced, the segments of the relevant market to be opened to competition, the timing of the liberalization process, and arrangements for additional phases of liberalization. Bargaining over liberalization, whether between a national government and the European Commission or among national governments in the EU's Council of Ministers, is likely to include all these dimensions. Where the issue at stake is Community-wide sectoral liberalization, the

European Commission has an interest in flexibility due to its desire to complete Europe's single market and promote economic integration. In the formulation of legislation, if the Commission in its consultations with national governments has not been able to secure a sufficient majority from the Council, it will seek the support of additional governments without jeopardizing the support of backers of a proposal. This will require successive marginal revisions of a liberalization proposal. Even in instances where the Commission is seeking to apply competition rules in a single country rather than to an entire sector across the Community—as in the German Landesbanken case—the Commission still has an interest in minimizing political confrontation and facilitating compliance through flexibility.

Finally, in cases when neither flexibility in the design of liberalization nor the sharing of information at European level alter the domestic political balance, the threat of ECJ action may raise the potential costs to public service providers of resisting the introduction of more competition in the sector.

Table 8.2 depicts the empirical relationship between liberalization—both its pace and scope—and gains in the receptiveness of public sector monopolists to liberalization in each of the sectors studied.

TABLE 8.2: Responses of Public Sector Monopolists to Liberalization Pressures

Sector:	Public Procurement	Postal Services	Public Sector Banking (Germany)
Increase in receptiveness of public sector monopolists to liberalization?	Overall, no; continued adherence to restrictive practices	UK: Initially, no; modest increase in receptiveness over time Germany: yes. Aggressive attempt to prepare for competition through acquisition strategy; partial pullback following failure to reach liberalization agreement at European level	No (some eventual increase in receptiveness on the part of local Sparkassen, but not larger Landesbanken)
Liberalization outcome	Infusion of competition in the sector highly constrained; progress slow	Introduction of competition moderate in both pace and scope	Slow but ultimately extensive rollback of constraints on competition

The stunted liberalization of the public procurement sector is overdetermined, for it is consistent both with the constrained exercise of capital mobility analyzed earlier and the lack of support from public authorities discussed in chapter 5. One of the sources of success of EC regulation generally is that while rules are agreed at a European level, implementation costs accrue at the national level. One reason for the disjuncture between the formal success of the single market in public procurement and the absence of substantial competition in practice is that public authorities have sought to elude what are perceived to be high social and political costs of implementing a fully competitive public procurement regime. Additional costs imposed by Community public procurement regulation include those associated with onerous procedures for publicizing contracting opportunities and tendering procedures. Moreover, governments have resisted the European Commission's urging that they emulate the Swedish model by creating independent regulatory authorities at the national level. In this case, that is, the European Commission has not been able to fully convince national governments to absorb the costs of enforcing the single market public procurement regime. In addition, officials in these public authorities may be opposed to their loss of control over technical standards and their loss of discretion in using procurement as an instrument of local or regional development or of social policy. As suggested by scholars who have conducted intensive study of the EC public procurement regime, Community public procurement policy has upset the balance between efficiency criteria critical to the internal market and social criteria valued by public authorities (Arrowsmith, 1995; Fernandez Martin, 1996: 55–57).

In Germany's postal services sector, relatively far-reaching liberalization has followed from Deutsche Post's shift toward support for a competitive environment, although, as explained in Chapter 6, the process was slowed by the delayed agreement of a sectoral liberalization regime at the European level.

As the table shows, there are two anomolies—extensive liberalization despite only partially diminished opposition from public sector monopolists in the British postal services sector and essentially unyielding opposition of German public sector Landesbanken. The following section, which examines shifts in the relative weight of public sector monopolists and their supporters in domestic policy making, explains these two cases.

Liberalization and Participation Expansion

EU institutions may have a critical impact on the domestic political balance. This may occur, for example, as political leaders gain information at the European level—either through interaction with members of other governments or with EU officials—that they subsequently bring into domestic political debate, shifting the positions of government ministries or political parties. Might this impact of Europeanization restructure interests in domestic politics such that public sector monopolists are less able to defend protectionist practices? This is the relationship captured by hypothesis II(b):

> Where public service monopolists oppose European-level liberalization initiatives, liberalization's prospects depend on the extent to which Europeanization fosters a shift in domestic interest aggregation that reduces the weight of market incumbents in national policy formulation.

Table 8.3 arrays outcomes in the pace and scope of liberalization for each sector according to whether or not there have been changes in the relative weight of protected public service providers in the policy formulation process.

TABLE 8.3: Liberalization and Participation Expansion

Sector:	Public Procurement	Postal Services	Public Sector Banking (Germany)
Reduction in weight of protectionists in policy formulation?	Only marginal	UK: yes, following the creation of an independent regulator in response to 1997 Community Postal Services Directive Germany: no (but as noted, increased receptiveness to sectoral liberalization)	Yes, in the aftermath of split between Landesbanken political supporters at national and state levels
Liberalization outcome	Infusion of competition in the sector highly constrained; progress slow	Introduction of competition moderate in both pace and scope	Slow but ultimately extensive rollback of constraints on competition

The relationships depicted in the table reveal that a reduction of the relative weight of the market-dominant public service provider in policy formulation has been critical to the liberalization of British postal services and German public sector banking. In the case of Germany's Landesbanken, this shift in domestic political alignments, characterized by the ascendance of national political party leadership over local and regional leadership, evolved over a protracted period, explaining the deliberate pace of change in that instance. In the electricity sector, broader bargaining in policy formulation in response to European-level processes interacted with small shifts in public sector monopolists' evaluations of liberalization to foster gradual, partial liberalization of the sector. What unites all three cases is the role of "participation expansion"—a process of politicization and activation of latent support for policy change among actors previously excluded from policy determination—as an explanation for the scope of liberalization.[2]

European-level processes had a dramatic impact on domestic political constituencies in the cases of both British Post and Germany's public sector banks. In the former, implementation of the EU's first postal services liberalization directive broadened the range of actors involved in determining the fate of the sector. As discussed in chapter 6, the most significant change was the creation of an independent regulator, Postcomm, in compliance with the 1997 EC Postal Services Directive. Charged with managing the orderly introduction of competition in British postal services, Postcomm provided both business consumers seeking improved service and potential market entrants with a vehicle for advancing the cause of competition. This broke the monopoly of British Post not only on mail services, but also on defining the terms of the policy debate in Britain.

In the case of the Landesbanken, the BdB complaint to the European Commission concerning Westdeutsche Landesbank did not by itself induce a shift in WestLB's strategy. As discussed in chapter 7, WestLB executives and political supporters believed their political insulation was beyond the penetration of EC competition rules; accordingly, WestLB and the other Landesbanken did not take preemptive action to prepare to compete with commercial banks on an equal footing. Indeed, without the European Banking Federation's (EBF) December 1999 complaint to the European Commission, political institutions supportive of the state banks throughout Germany may well have been able to continue to resist pressures from the European Commission for fundamental sectoral change.

The EBF action completed a nearly decade-long process of participation expansion that began with private banks in the early 1990s.

In contrast with the public procurement regime, where participation has not expanded significantly, this case is especially illustrative of the process of participation expansion and how it can redefine the dynamics of policy formulation at the national level. As the European Commission intensified its scrutiny of the system of state guarantees protecting the Landesbanken, regional political elites redefined their understanding of the relationship between the public law banks and the social market economy. And, critically, national political elites found it politically possible to choose Europe over domestic protectionism. These changes followed developments during the course of 2000, which weakened the political base undergirding the Landesbanken. A shift in perceptions of the Landesbanken and Sparkassen among German political elites created the necessary conditions for the withdrawal of arrangements that advantaged the Landesbanken in their competition with commercial banks. However, some accommodation also was required even in these circumstances of diminished political support, exhibited in the relatively comfortable pace by which the Landesbanken would lose their state guarantees.

How was this fundamental change in the status of the public law banks possible at all given the deep institutionalization of Landesbanken and Sparkassen political support? The support for Germany's private banks provided by the European Banking Federation further undermined the position of the Landesbanken and contributed to an erosion of their support from the political parties at the federal level. Unsurprisingly, the German liberal democrats (FDP), freer to take up the cause of the commercial banks both because of their programmatic commitment to liberalism and weaker institutionalized political ties to the fate of the Landesbanken and Sparkassen, were first to condemn the position of the public sector institutions. Otto Graf Lambsdorff, former Economics Minister, who had called for privatization of the public law banks as early as 1993,[3] asserted that the Landesbanken and Sparkassen were doomed to fail in a confrontation with Brussels. A few years later, in the wake of the WestLB state aid decision, Lambsdorff argued that "there is no reasonable basis" for taxpayers in Nordrhein Westfalen to finance the activities of the WestLB abroad.[4] Baden-Württemberg's Economics Minister, Walter Doering, also of the FDP, called for a partial privatization of the Landesbanken, agreeing with Lambsdorff's assessment and suggesting that "it is proper that the European Commission no longer tolerate the constriction of competition by the Landesbanken."[5]

But the critical blow to the Landesbanken came when the national leadership of the large parties began to view their position as untenable. In July 2000, the European Affairs spokesperson for the CDU/CSU parliamentary group, Peter Hintze, asserted that the Landesbanken had far overstepped their initial mission, and had become "overly large, internationally active investment banks." Hintze called for full privatization of the Landesbanken. Most significant of all, he justified the European Commission's case in terms of Germany's domestic political needs: "fair competition is a central requisite of the functioning of the social market economy."[6] This marked the full-blown development of a reform discourse grounded in values of the German political economy.[7] Similarly, the CDU/CSU parliamentary group's competition policy spokesman, Hartmut Schauerte, argued that "From the perspective of competition, the European Commission can not decide otherwise than to prohibit these privileges."[8] Schauerte criticized the high degree of political influence in Germany's financial sector, and pronounced it "shocking" that public law institutions constitute 50 percent of the sector. Schauerte concluded that "the time for privileges that narrow competition has passed," and that "the complaint of the private banks is fundamentally justifiable."[9] And Friedrich März, leader of the CDU/CSU Bundestag delegation, argued that the Federal Republic lacks an instrument of national subsidy control; by providing effective control of subsidies for Germany's public sector banks, Brussels was filling in this gap.[10]

In Nordrhein-Westfalen (NRW), Christian Democrats on WestLB's executive committee began to promote splitting of the public and private functions of the Landesbanken and partial privatization as a solution in 2000. Following a series of municipal election victories that gave the CDU control of local savings banks with seats on WestLB's supervisory board, the CDU gained control of the board. Jürgen Rüttgers, NRW's CDU leader, in November 2000 announced the board's support for breaking up and partially privatizing WestLB (*Business Week*, November 20, 2000: 59). But CDU leaders were clear to distinguish the fate of the Landesbanken from that of the Sparkassen.[11] The CDU's Peter Hintze argued that the legitimacy of the regional responsibilities of the Sparkassen must be fully distinguished from the case of the Landesbanken, and that their role should be determined by local political leadership.[12] Moreover, some state level political leaders began to rally around the Sparkassen at the expense of the Landesbanken. Wolfgang Clement, Minister-President of Nordrhein-Westfalen, argued before a forum of the German Banking Federation that the European Commission must make it clear "that the German savings bank system—as we know it today—remains."[13] The president of the federation representing the small and medium enterprises of the Mittelstand (Bundesverband mittelständische Wirtschaft) endorsed this position, while deriding the Landesbanken for "juggling currency and shares in the Far East" (*Süddeutsche Zeitung*, July 29, 2000: 26). These comments offer further evidence of the rise of a reform discourse consistent with valued elements of the social market economy.

Had the threat of Community-level action been perceived as credible at an earlier stage by those actors in the most powerful institutional and market positions—particularly the Finance Ministry of Nordrhein Westfalen and top officials of the Westdeutsche Landesbank—a bargain might have emerged within the German political arena. However, the domestic bargaining environment was highly asymmetrical, with Land governments and Landesbanken officials confident that the public law banking system was politically immunized against the application of EC competition rules and therefore facing few incentives to make concessions to the claims of the commercial banks. Within the main political parties, national level leaders that might have preferred a domestic resolution to conflict with the European Commission were, until the broader scrutiny triggered by the late 1999 EBF complaint, constrained by their political need to support the Länder and their own regional party leadership.

EC electricity liberalization provides another illustration of the impact of participation expansion. Electricity liberalization has moved more slowly than suggested by a model of the EC decision-making process in which: (1) governments that open their own markets become proponents of European-level liberalization; and (2) the Council decides by weighted majority vote. Developments in the electricity sector seem to offer supportive evidence for intergovernmentalist theories of European integration, which suggest that the degree of integration is determined by exogenous preferences of national governments. However, there has been a significant—if halting—advance of sectoral liberalization, and European institutions and policy debate have had a formidable influence on actors that are at the center of national policy formation. Therefore, in order to capture the dynamics—both possibilities and limits—of the liberalization process driven by Europe's single market, we need to explain how European-level interactions both generated greater support for liberalization in some countries and abetted reluctance elsewhere, as in France. Why initial German hesitance, then support, for introducing competition into the electricity sector? And why the shift in the French position from initial support for liberalization, to outright opposition, then measured acceptance? What can this tell us about the role of participation expansion in the evolution of sectoral competition regimes?

The German case powerfully illustrates how efforts toward a single European electricity market altered the domestic politics of electricity liberalization. At the outset of the 1990s, Germany's peak association of electric utilities, despite its otherwise highly diverse composition, was unified around the benefits of closed markets. And Germany's CDU/CSU-FDP coalition government met with skepticism initial proposals for liberalization of European electricity markets (Eising and Jabko, 2000: 16). But, as for other EU member countries, the European-level debate created new opportunities for some actors in the German electricity sector, fostered reevaluation of costs and benefits by pivotal government ministries, and drew additional actors into the policy process.

First, the unity of Germany's producer alliance around protected markets was shattered by the prospect of sectoral liberalization. Faced with the possibility of market opening, local utilities sought to defend their protected status; the larger utility companies saw in liberalization both the prospect of moving into protected local markets and the chance to expand internationally (Eberlein, 2000: 86). While municipal, regional, and larger utilities agreed that any market opening involving other EC countries must be reciprocal, given the vulnerability of Germany's relatively fragmented industry structure, the larger utilities recognized that a purely national liberalization initiative would reflect the political ties of the municipal utilities to local government and would be likely to sustain their protected status; they therefore preferred a Community-level liberalization process (Eising and Jabko, 2000: 18).

Germany's federal Economics Ministry, meanwhile, revised its own estimation of the potential benefits of electricity liberalization for the German economy. Evidence of possible gains from liberalization—including lower energy costs for industry without a serious threat to the security of supply—

was readily available to the government, but the European-level debate altered the Ministry's assessment of that evidence and of the legitimacy of demands for sectoral change from smaller industrial electricity consumers (Eising and Jabko, 2000: 16–17). Still, the choice for liberalization was not uncontested. Just as Germany's local savings banks—as discussed in chapter 7—could rely on extensive political protection, so, too, could the municipal utilities draw on substantial political support in the opposition-controlled German Bundesrat (representing the Länder). Ultimately, discussion at the European level in the Council of Ministers was a vital force that tilted the German debate in favor of accepting a revised Community-level liberalization program (Eising and Jabko, 2000).

In France, while EdF executives hoped to penetrate other European markets, there was serious concern that sectoral liberalization would challenge the comprehensive EdF monopoly on electricity production, transmission, and distribution. This fear was shared by the French government, which had made a massive investment in nuclear energy capacity; the Finance Ministry viewed EdF as an important revenue source (Eising and Jabko, 2000: 12). But the overriding priority of the French government was to defend the French model of public service; ultimately what was required for liberalization to move forward at the Community level was for the French government to reassess the compatibility of this objective with the Community initiative.

Three factors contributed to the required reevaluation. First, there remained the potential for unilateral Commission action through Article 90. In contrast with this worst-case outcome that could seriously threaten the French government's concept of *service publique,* a gradual, controlled liberalization of the sector might be negotiated in the Council of Ministers (Conant, 2002: 126; Schmidt, 1996: 12). Second, the European-level policy debate affected decision making within crucial ministries. For example, the process taking place at the European level strengthened the influence of the Finance Ministry's competition directorate, which was less protective of the EdF monopoly (Eising and Jabko, 2000: 13). And, third, as in Germany and other EU countries, the push for competition in the electricity sector at the European level induced important shifts in the alignment and weights of domestic political forces. As Eising and Jabko assert, a range of electricity consumers, including large industrial users, as well as potential market entrants, began to push their agenda more aggressively in France in response to developments at the European level (Eising and Jabko, 2000: 13).

These developments in the interaction between the European-level quest for an internal market in electricity and France's domestic political dynamics explain why the French government agreed to a limited electricity liberalization proposal in 1996. France's position is most likely to evolve with the capacity of EdF to withstand further competition. This, in turn, may be enhanced as EdF expands its foothold in European markets in the wake of its campaign of acquisitions—an approach that bears a strong resemblance to the preparation undertaken by Deutsche Post in advance of sectoral liberalization of postal services in the European Community.

What these cases demonstrate is that the EC liberalization project is at root a project of participation expansion. When public sector monopolists are unprepared for competition, they can slow down processes of sectoral change; however, to the extent that European-level bargaining processes expand participation in domestic policy formulation, protected public service providers are unlikely to wield the capacity to block liberalization outright. A case such as public procurement, in which competition has advanced only marginally, ultimately reflects the weak incentives for participation expansion in the sector.

Domestic Political Change in Comparative Perspective

This book began by situating the study of EC competition policy and Europe's public sector in the context of the comparative political economy debate on convergence and diversity of capitalist democracies. As noted in the book's introduction, European integration exposes domestic political economies to external forces for change in an especially "concentrated" form. Economic integration is both far-reaching and voluntary, endorsed by domestic political coalitions that generally favor expansion of competition. This is the basis for conceptualizing the EU as an efficient engine of liberalization, and for the expectation that forces of convergence should be especially powerful in the EU context. Does the evidence confirm this expectation? What lessons does it generate for our understanding of processes of change in domestic policies or institutions in response to pressures from the international economy?

We have found that forces of European economic integration create intense pressures for the infusion of competition into markets served by the public sector in West European countries; these have pared back restrictive practices. But, as shown by Table 8.4, this has occurred only to the extent that (a) domestic actors initially occupying dominant market positions have adjusted their assessments of the compatibility of sectoral liberalization with their objectives; and, of most significance, (b) efforts at the European level to advance the cause of sectoral liberalization have altered domestic political dynamics, resulting in a reweighting of the various actors in policy formulation. These actors include public sector monopolists, their political supporters, government ministries, private sector competitors, and consumers. Building on the work of scholars of comparative and international political economy such as Jacoby and Schoppa, these findings further clarify the precise mechanisms by which domestic political institutions mediate forces for change of policies and institutions.

The process of participation expansion has followed different paths in different polities, illuminating how domestic institutional structures shape the path, timing, and scope of domestic policy change. In Britain, participation expansion in the postal services sector consisted of the redistribution of power *across market actors*, as the creation of an independent regulator for the sector empowered competitors wishing to enter the market

TABLE 8.4: Factors Mediating States of Liberalization

Sector:	Public Procurement	Postal Services	Public Sector Banking (Germany)
Competition complaints from competitors?	Relatively few	Significant number	Small number of major complaints
Increased receptiveness to sectoral liberalization?	No	UK: No Germany: Yes	No
Participation expansion?	Only Marginal	UK: Yes Germany: No	Yes
Liberalization outcome	Slow and constrained	Moderate pace and scope	Delayed but extensive

and demanded that British Post prepare for greater competition. In the banking sector in Germany's federal system, participation expansion involved a shift in the balance of political debate *across levels of government.* Local and regional elites closely tied to the Landesbanken and their public service functions controlled the debate for the first several years of the standoff with the European Commission; as pressure for change mounted at the European level, national elites were drawn into coordinating negotiations between Europe, the public sector banks, and the Land governments. Where modest participation expansion took place in the determination of policy for the French electricity sector, the public sector monopolist, EdF, retained a preeminent position, but there was a relative shift in policy-setting roles *across government ministries*. These different paths of participation expansion may also help explain why policy change, although late in coming relative to processes taking place at the European level, was nonetheless rapid in the UK's postal sector; why it was delayed, negotiated, and gradual, even if far-reaching, in the case of Germany's public sector banks; and late, slow and only partial in the French electricity sector.

The EU: Always an Efficient Engine of Liberalization?

The book has treated the extension of EU competition policy as a driving force behind both the mobilization of private sector competitors of public enterprises and the unilateral reform of some public service providers. The examination of states of liberalization has demonstrated that private sector actors do not always face sufficient incentives to act at the European level, and that protected public service providers and their political supporters have substantial capacities to resist, or at least retard, sectoral change. Furthermore, as we have seen, the tendency toward participation expansion varies across sectors.

As we contemplate ultimate consequences for the role of the public sector, a final question concerns the forces for intensified competition emerging from the European level: can we assume that the "self-reinforcing liberal bias" described in chapter 2 will persist? Is there any prospect of systemic change that may alter the liberalizing thrust of the European integration project itself? This thrust is justified by the hegemonic premise—promoted by the European Commission since the early implementation of the 1986 Single European Act, and embraced by governments that agreed to create the single market and then the single currency—that *the external competitiveness of European states is best served by internal competition.* According to this premise, the single market project and the competition policy undergirding it are not ends in themselves, but means to the higher objective of global economic competitiveness: a well-functioning internal market will produce more efficient European firms. Although EU member state governments have at various times resisted instances of implementation of single market competition policy, this fundamental premise has remained unchallenged since the late 1980s.

In the first decade of the new century, there are nascent indications that this can change. For some national governments looking outward toward the international economy—especially Germany and France—the benefit of Europe's competition regime is not beyond question. These governments are asking whether the single market competition policy disadvantages EU countries relative to competitors with more vigorous sectoral policies, especially the United States. The result is an emergent dialogue on the development of an EU industrial policy involving selective application of competition rules across sectors. This raises the spectre of a refocused European competition policy whose liberalizing edge may be blunted.

The German position has evolved from a series of conflicts between Community competition policy and German industry,[14] including a Community plan to open the European autos market to greater competition and a new regulatory framework for the chemicals sector. In the months before Germany's September 2002 parliamentary elections, Chancellor Gerhard Schröder stepped up his criticism of the European Commission's competition and internal market directorates for failing to consider the needs of German industry in developing and applying competition rules. While this public effort certainly was related to the impending German electoral contest, tensions between the German government and the Commission over industrial policy were a constant throughout the SPD-led coalition's second term.

Schröder's concerns were publicized in an April 2002 article in the *Financial Times,* which made the case that the "new economy" (services) should not be promoted at the expense of the old economy (manufacturing, in which, Schröder contended, Europe remains highly successful) and that strategic sectoral policies would boost economic prosperity in Europe. Critical of the "hardline" Commission approach to competition policy,

Schröder's essay underscored that competitiveness is not always served by a rigid competition policy:

> policy-makers should take more account of the global dimension to their decisions. For European companies to succeed internationally over the long term we need to create the right policy framework. That raises questions about the global implications of single market regulations.[15]

These concerns resonate with issues involving global competition—particularly vis-à-vis the United States—raised in the European Commission's 2002 report on European competitiveness (Commission, 2002). While the report hews to the premise dominant in EU institutions that competition and competitiveness are mutually reinforcing, it also notes that some dimensions of European competition policy are far more stringent than for their American counterparts. For example, while control over subsidies—state aid to industry—is a core element of the competition regime enforced by the European Commission, subsidies granted by local, state, or federal government do not fall under U.S. competition law. Furthermore, as the Commission's report notes, "US subsidy policy is oriented towards strategic industrial sectors" (Commission, 2002: 87). This includes extensive public support for small business startups, especially high-tech ones, both through direct public funding and guarantees provided to financial institutions in the venture capital sector (87–88). Also included is research and development subsidization of strategic industries, such as aerospace and electronics, typically through defense spending (88).

Adding to the pressure for a new approach to competition policy, Chancellor Schröder in September 2003 joined forces with Tony Blair and Jacques Chirac to submit a letter warning Commission President Romano Prodi of the danger of deindustrialization and urging that the Commission assess the impact of its policies on industrial competitiveness. Conditions appeared to be developing for a challenge to longstanding competition policies. However, in contrast to the Commission's 2002 report on competitiveness, a follow-up report on industrial policy in enlarged Europe issued in 2004 leaves much less room for expectations of a shift in the tenor of EU industrial or competition policies. The 2004 document emphasizes the need to export the EU's successful regulatory approaches rather than to alter those approaches in response to the policies of governments of industrial competitors (Commission, 2004b: 3). The paper underscores that attention to better regulation in highly competitive sectors "does not indicate a return to the interventionist policies of the past"; instead, pursuing sectorally-sensitive policies means examining whether a sector's problems are the consequence of insufficient incentives to innovate, anti-competitive practices of other governments (requiring action through transnational institutions), or inadequate internal market integration (Commission, 2004b: 37 and 38).

Any movement toward a redefined industrial policy and concomitant changes in competition policy will face extensive opposition from within EU institutions and from several national governments that have invested heavily in processes of state hardening. These proponents of a rigorous competition policy are particularly loathe to allow eastward enlargement of the EU to provide opportunities for the softening of the competition policy regime. For well over a decade, competition as the most effective means to competitiveness has held hegemonic status within the European Community. As this book has demonstrated, sectoral liberalization has advanced significantly during that period, even if under critical constraints. It remains unlikely that a new conception of industrial policy will supplant the hegemonic position of competition, or fundamentally alter Europe's state of liberalization.

NOTES

Notes to Chapter 1

1. Socialist MEP Wilhelm Piecyk, in debate over postal services liberalization, European Rpt. no. 2511, June 24, 2000.
2. Linda Weiss, *The Myth of the Powerless State* (Ithaca: Cornell University Press, 1998). Taking the position that the ability of states to adjust to external pressures for adaptation may have become more differentiated across states rather than simply declining for all, Weiss (p. 9) argues that "where states appear weak in responding to international change, we should view this as a sign less of the power of 'global' forces than of pre-existing frailty in the institutions governing domestic linkages."
3. Numerous others also take this view, including Richard Deeg, who finds that the German financial system retains its distinctive characteristics despite substantial transnational harmonization of financial market regulation. See *Finance Capitalism Unveiled: Banks and the German Political Economy* (Ann Arbor: University of Michigan Press, 1999).
4. Scholars not explicitly part of the regulation school share this conclusion: as Pempel writes of the impact of global economic forces on domestic institutions, "even the most rapidly adjusting countries have continually adapted in accord with established domestic political and economic arrangements." See T. J. Pempel, *Regime Shift: Comparative Dynamics of the Japanese Political Economy* (Ithaca: Cornell, 1998), p. 219.
5. Interview with director of the regional banking federation for North-Rhine Westfalia, Cologne, May 17, 2001. Author's translation.
6. Westdeutsche Landesbank, "The Decision of the European Commission on the Integration of the Wfa," p. 2. The briefing paper adds (p. 7) that "If the historic structures of Germany's public sector banks were to be changed as a result of the decision at hand, public-sector companies in other industries and member states could sooner or later be affected too."
7. From here I will use "European Community" to refer to the regulations governing the Single European Market, and "European Union" to designate the institutions and member states.
8. Statement of Peer Steinbrück, Economics Minister of Nordrhein-Westfalen, to the Bundesrat, July 9, 1999, reprinted and translated in Westdeutsche Landesbank Girozentrale, "The Decision of the European Commission on

the Integration of the Wohnungsbauförderungsanstalt NRW (Wfa) into WestLB," p. 19.

9. See, for example, John Vickers and Vincent Wright, eds, *The Politics of Privatization in Western Europe* (London: Frank Cass, 1989); Ezra N. Suleiman and John Waterbury, eds, *The Political Economy of Public Sector Reform and Privatization* (Boulder: Westview, 1990); Nikolaos Zahariadis, *Markets, States, and Public Policy: Privatization in Britain and France* (Ann Arbor: University of Michigan Press, 1995); and Vivien A. Schmidt, *From State to Market? The Transformation of French Business and Government* (Cambridge: Cambridge University Press, 1996).

10. For a systematic case that the political logic of social welfare policy reform resists sweeping transformation, see Paul Pierson, "The New Politics of the Welfare State," *World Politics* 48 (January 1996), pp. 143–179. Jonah D. Levy, "Vice into Virtue? Progressive Politics and Welfare Reform in Continental Europe," *Politics & Society,* Vol. 27, No. 2 (June 1999), pp. 239–273, supports the case for revision rather than retrenchment. On the other side of the debate are scholars who believe that domestic and international economic pressures have fostered a fundamental recasting of social welfare systems, such as Richard Clayton and Jonas Pontusson, "Welfare-State Retrenchment Revisited," *World Politics* 51 (October 1998), pp. 67–98; and Martin Seeleib-Kaiser, "A Dual Transformation of the German Welfare State?" *West European Politics* 24, 4 (Oct 2002), pp. 25–48.

11. Thomas Risse, Maria Green Cowles, and James Caporaso agree, asserting that "much of the literature on European integration . . . treats the process of integration as the end point of a causal process beginning with domestic and transnational societal interests and ending with European outcomes." See "Europeanization and Domestic Change: Introduction," in Risse, Cowles, and Caporaso, eds, *Transforming Europe* (Ithaca: Cornell University Press, 2001), p. 12.

12. See Simon Hix and Klaus H. Goetz, "Introduction: European Integration and National Political Systems," special issue on "Europeanised Politics? European Integration and National Political Systems," *West European Politics* 23, No. 4 (October 2000): 1–26; Tanja A. Börzel and Thomas Risse, "When Europe Hits Home: Europeanization and Domestic Change," European University Institute Working Paper RSC No. 2000/56 (San Domenico, Italy: 2000); Christoph Knill and Dirk Lehmkuhl, "How Europe Matters. Different Mechanisms of Europeanization," *European Integration online papers* (EioP) Vol. 3 (1999), No. 7; http://eiop.or.at/eiop/texte/1999-007a.htm. For one of the earliest efforts to assess the impact of integration on domestic political institutions and policies, see Y. Mény, P. Muller, and J-L. Quermonne, eds, *Adjusting to Europe* (London: Routledge, 1996).

13. Andrew Moravcsik argues that the pooling of sovereignty is a strategy for governments to make their policy commitments credible and "to lock in future decisions against domestic opposition." See Andrew Moravcsik, *The Choice for Europe* (Ithaca: Cornell University Press, 1998), p. 73. Wayne

Sandholtz analyzes this potential explanation for "choosing (monetary) union," but points out that only the impact of the single European market and the fact that preference formation by member state governments is endogeneous to the integration process can explain why member state governments chose this particular means of tying their hands. See "Choosing Union: Monetary Politics and Maastricht," *World Politics* 47, No. 1 (1993), 1–39. The concept of state hardening is developed by Vincent Della Sala, "Hollowing Out and Hardening the State: European Integration and the Italian Economy," *West European Politics* 20, No. 1 (January 1997), pp. 14–33.

14. On systems of industrial relations, see Kathleen Thelan and Ikuo Kume, "The Future of Nationally Embedded Capitalism: Industrial Relations in Japan and Germany," in *The End of Diversity? Prospects for German and Japanese Capitalism*, Kozo Yamamura and Wolfgang Streeck, eds (Ithaca: Cornell University Press, 2003), pp. 183–211. Steven K. Vogel, "The Re-Organization of Organized Capitalism: How the German and Japanese Models Are Shaping Their Own Transformations," in Yamamura and Streeck, eds, pp. 306–333, considers corporate governance in Germany and Japan; while Vivien Schmidt, *The Futures of European Capitalism* (Oxford: Oxford University Press, 2002), evaluates the impact of globalization and Europeanization on British, French, and German models of capitalism.

Notes to Chapter 2

1. As Kenneth Dyson describes for the French case, "EMU provided an opportunity to provide France with an institutionalised discipline, surpassing in efficacy the ERM as an external anchor for domestic economic policy." See Dyson, 1999: 37.
2. Numerous analysts have observed this policy of acceding to binding constraints on economic policy making for political reasons. Wayne Sandholtz, "Choosing Union," p. 35, cites the decision of policy makers to tie their own hands in order to make credible their commitment to monetary discipline. Both Kenneth Dyson, 1999, who refers to a strategy of "binding Leviathan," and George Pagoulatos, who writes of a "self-binding" strategy of governments, focus on the objective of fiscal discipline and fending off demands of domestic interest groups. See Pagoulatos, "Financial Repression and Liberalization in Europe's Southern Periphery: From 'Growth State' to 'Stabilization State'," paper presented at the Sixth Biennial Conference of the European Community Studies Association, June 1999.
3. This remains true, the March 1999 resignation of the Commissioners of the European Commission notwithstanding. The failings that led to the fall of the Commission revolved around poor management and oversight of programs, particularly when the Commission subcontracted tasks to third parties. While the inquiry leading to the mass resignation certainly damaged the reputation of the Commission, its regulatory function remains crucial to the

objectives of elites in the member states, and, if anything, may have been reinforced by the trauma of March 1999.

4. On the general significance of policy networks, see Peterson, 1995, and Schneider et al., 1994.
5. European Court of Justice (1990), Case C-21/88, Dupont de Nemours Italiana SpA v. Unitá Sanitaria Locale No. 2 di Carrara, ECR I-889. The distributional consequences of this decision are highly significant, since 30 percent of public procurement contracts would bring southern Italy in excess of $20 billion annually. See Fernandez Martin and Stehmann, 1991.
6. Sbragia emphasizes the importance of this "budgetary poverty," pointing out that "The lack of money means that the Community can only provide a very limited set of side-payments compared to the side-payments which many national governments have routinely paid either labor or capital (or both), for instance." See Sbragia, 1998b: 19.
7. On the entrepreneurial qualities of the European Commission in regulatory policy making, see Laura Cram, "The European Commission as a Multi-Organization: Social Policy and IT Policy in the EU," *Journal of European Public Policy* 1, No. 2 (1994): 195–217; Majone, 1993; and Nugent, 1995.
8. For a thorough account of the multilevel governance framework, see Marks, Hooghe, and Blank, 1996; also see Liesbet Hooghe and Gary Marks, *Multi-Level Governance and European Integration* (Oxford: Rowman & Littlefield, 2001).
9. European Commission, *Growth, Competitiveness, Employment: The Challenges and Ways Forward Into the 21st Century* (Luxembourg: Office for Official Publications of the European Communities, 1994), pp. 63 and 79.
10. As Della Sala illustrates, for the two decades from 1975 to 1994, Italy's annual public deficits hovered between 9 and 12 percent of GDP before assuming a sharp reduction beginning in 1995. Accumulation of deficits lifted public debt to more than 120 percent of GDP. See Della Sala, 1997, p. 23, Table 1.
11. Herman Schwartz writes about reforms pursued in several smaller advanced industrial economies sharing the objective of shielding state resources from rent-seeking by numerous interests, including public sector employees. See Herman Schwartz, "Small States in Big Trouble: State Reorganization in Australia, Denmark, New Zealand, and Sweden in the 1980s," *World Politics* 46, No. 4 (July 1994): 527–555.
12. This role of the European Commission as leverage for national policy makers depends on its credibility as a rigorous regulator. While the Treaty of Rome gives the Commission exclusive competence in the area of competition policy, the wording of the relevant Treaty articles leaves open the precise powers of the Commission. Until the mid-1980s, the Commission's authority remained fairly circumscribed. In concert with the implementation of the single market program, the Commission stepped up the rigor of the state aid regime, bolstered by European Court of Justice decisions sanctioning both

broader use of Commission investigatory authority and powers to compel member states to provide information, as well as the capacity to order recovery of aid granted in violation of the Treaty. For a detailed discussion of this process, see Smith, 1998.

13. Focusing on national traditions and party structures, Nancy Bermeo points to the ascendance of technocrats within the PSOE in the 1980s as a critical source of public sector reform in Spain. See Nancy Bermeo, "The Politics of Public Enterprise in Portugal, Spain, and Greece," in Ezra N. Suleiman and John Waterbury, eds, *The Political Economy of Public Sector Reform and Privatization* (Boulder: Westview Press, 1990), pp. 137–162.
14. Dyson, "The Franco-German Relationship and Economic and Monetary Union," p. 37. According to Dyson (p. 37), the commitment to EMU elevated the role of the Finance Ministry and Banque de France, by "rejuvenating . . . a domestic tradition of conservative liberalism" in these institutions.
15. Carsten Steevens, "Bankenstreit: Schuss for WestLB-Bug erst der Anfang?" *Vereinigte Wirtschaftsdienste*, November 23, 1999; and *Neue Zuercher Zeitung*, November 15, 1999: 23.

Notes to Chapter 3

1. On the rigidities and prospects for reform of the institutional structures of the German political economy, see Lauk, 1994; Streeck, 1997; and Wolfgang Streeck and Kozo Yamamura, "Introduction: Convergence or Diversity? Stability and Change in German and Japanese Capitalism, in Streeck and Yamamura, eds, *The End of Diversity? Prospects for German and Japanese Capitalism*. (Ithaca: Cornell University Press, 2003), pp. 1–50.
2. Scharpf (1999: 104) refers to this possibility of free-riding in the implementation stage of liberalization measures.
3. The Netherlands, for example, was prepared to respond in this way in late 2000 if the Commission's proposed postal services directive became too watered down by the Council. Author's interview with official of the Dutch permanent representation to the Council, Brussels, November 14, 2000.
4. Technically, UPS's case is against the Commission for failing to act on its complaint against DPAG.
5. Referring to this as a "divide-and-conquer" strategy of the European Commission in its effort to advance the cause of economic integration, Schmidt (2000: 47) writes that "Once the targeted countries have . . . incurred the costs of domestic reform, they are themselves interested in comparable community-wide changes."
6. Examining the period from 1975 through 1998, Patterson and Beason (2001: 518–519) find that "a formal meeting between a Japanese prime minister and a U.S. president raises the odds of a package being announced by approximately 11.6 times."

Notes to Chapter 4

1. The relevant EEC Treaty Articles governing state aid regulation are 92 and 93; these became Articles 87 and 88 in the October 1997 Amsterdam Treaty, which took effect on May 1, 1999. However, the chapter adheres to the original numbering, since most of the documents and cases described in the chapter took place prior to the effective date of the Amsterdam Treaty and therefore refer to Articles 92 and 93.
2. The relevant treaty articles are EEC 85 and 86; these became 81 and 82 with the Amsterdam Treaty revisions. As for Articles 92 and 93 governing state aid, the chapter uses the original numbers.
3. This corresponds with the argument made by Conant (2002).
4. When a new Commission took office in 1985, Competition Commissioner Peter Sutherland responded to the paucity of aggregate data on state aid levels by setting up a task force to begin compiling such data. This task force became institutionalized administratively as the state aid directorate's analysis unit and procedurally in the form of biannual state aid surveys.
5. This does not apply to undertakings involved in "non-economic" activities, such as provision of social security and compulsory education.
6. In other words, Article 90 is, as described by Aurelio Pappalardo, a "reference provision" that is only infringed when another provision of the Treaty, such as that relating to the free movement of goods (Article 30), freedom to provide services (Article 59), the freedom of establishment, or the abuse of dominant market position, is infringed. See Pappalardo (1991).
7. Commission Directive of 25 June 1980 on the transparency of financial relations between Member States and public undertakings," OJ 1980 L195/35.
8. This paragraph draws on Smith (1997).
9. For a discussion of these telecommunications sector directives, see Conant, 2002: Chapter 4.
10. For example, in 1989, the Commission required that the Italian government terminate restrictive practices that favored Italy's public sector international express service, Corriere Accelerato Internazionale della Poste. See Commission of the European Communities, *Nineteenth Report on Competition Policy* (1989), p. 201, point 228.
11. Report for the Hearing, Criminal proceedings against Paul Corbeau, Reference for a preliminary ruling from the Tribunal de Premiere Instance, Liege, [1993] ECR I-2534.
12. Judgement of the Court of 19 May 1993, Case C-320/91, [1993] ECR I-2563.
13. *Official Journal of the European Communities* C 281/3, September 26, 1996.
14. See "Services of general interest in Europe" (1996), paragraph 23. In an October 1996 speech to the International Forum on Public Utilities, Liberalization and Consumers, Competition Commissioner Karel Van Miert cited the problem of uneven quality and high price of public services, and the extent to

which recently liberalized services, including air transport, express delivery, and telecommunications, had demonstrated that competition improves quality and reduces prices. See Karel Van Miert, "Public Utilities, Liberalization and Consumers: Comprehensive explanation of the Commission's position," Rome, October 4, 1996.

15. Treaty Establishing the European Community, consolidated version (1999), Part One, Article 16 (previous article 7d).
16. Kurzer argues that social concertation collapsed in Belgium and the Netherlands prior to Austria and Sweden because in the former countries the European Monetary System and single market accelerated the gain in power resources of capital relative to labor.
17. The data, compiled from several Commission annual reports on monitoring of the application of Community law, include complaints about alleged violations of all aspects of Community law—including most prominently environmental law (comprising 587 of the 1,300 complaints received in 2001) and internal market rules (351 of 1,300). The next largest category of complaints came in the area of health and consumer protection, which accounted for 86 of 1,300 third-party complaints received by the Commission. The figures represent complaints from all parties, including governments.
18. The Commission's review indicated that little interpenetration of national procurement markets had resulted from the public works and supplies directives of the 1970s. See Arrowsmith and Fernandez Martin, 1993: 324.
19. Private sector French firms providing security services filed a case against the European Commission for failing to rule that the French government had infringed EC Treaty Articles governing internal market competition when it set up a state-owned commercial company to furnish security and other services for the French post office. In a decision on an appeal lodged by the Commission, the European Court of Justice in April 1998 confirmed the decision of the lower court that the Commission must provide "clear and unequivocal" reasoning for reaching the conclusion that arguments put forward by complainants fail to demonstrate the existence of illegal state aid (Judgment of the Court of Justice, 2 April 1998, Case C-367/95, paragraph 63).
20. Sytraval is the acronym for Chambre Syndicale Nationale des Enterprises de Transport de Fonds et Valeurs.
21. In taking this action, Sytraval and Brink's France used the provisions of Article 173 of the EC Treaty, which permit any "natural or legal person" to institute Court proceedings against a decision by one of the EU institutions addressed either directly to themselves or which affects them directly.
22. As amended by the 1993 Maastricht Treaty, Article 190 states that "Regulations, directives and decisions . . . adopted by the Council or the Commission, shall state the reasons on which they are based and shall refer to any proposals or opinions which were required to be obtained pursuant to this Treaty."
23. Judgment of the Court of Justice, 2 April 1998, Case C-367/95, paragraph 63. Beginning with Sytraval, a struggle over the nature of third party rights

developed between the Tribunal (Court of First Instance) and Court of Justice. In its rulings, the Tribunal has sought to make rights of third-party complainants in state aid cases similar to those in cases of anticompetitive practices (governed by Articles 85 and 86), including the right of complainants to have access to case files; the Court of Justice, whose interpretation has prevailed, takes the narrower view that state aid investigations are conducted between the Commission and a member state government, with the Commission simply required to provide third parties with an "adequate explanation" of its reasoning.

24. The Court of First Instance, set up in 1989 to alleviate the backlog of cases experienced by the European Court of Justice (ECJ), is the venue for state aid cases unless they are appealed to the ECJ.
25. The CFI announced its decision in the BP Chemicals case (case T-11/95) on September 15, 1998. In the decision, the CFI annulled a Commission decision not to investigate a complaint about capital injections into EniChem, a subsidiary of the Italian state holding company ENI. For a description of the BP Chemicals ruling, see Case T-11/95, *Competition Law in the European Communities* 21, 10 (October 1998): 229–230. A critical distinction between the political significance of this case and Sytraval is that the complaint lodged against EniChem came from a company in another member state, while in Sytraval private firms were challenging the policies of their own government.
26. Judgement of the Court of First Instance, Case T-127/98, UPS Europe SA v Commission of the European Communities, September 9, 1999.
27. Judgment of the Court of Justice of the European Communities of May 7, 1998, joined cases C-52/97, C-53/97, and C-54/97. Reported in *Competition Law in the European Communities*, 21, 8 (August 1998): 184–187.
28. This was how a Commission official described these developments in an interview with the author in Brussels on January 19, 1999.
29. Whether or not the European Court, unlike the Commission fundamentally a legal rather than a political institution, is similarly constrained has been the subject of scholarly debate. See Geoffrey Garrett, "The Politics of Legal Integration in the European Union," *International Organization* 49, 1 (Winter 1995): 171–181.

Notes to Chapter 5

1. The relevant directives include Directive 89/440/EEC on public works; 88/295/EEC on supplies; 92/50/EEC on services; and, updating and consolidating the earlier legislation on public works and public supplies, Directives 93/36/EEC and 93/37/EEC, respectively. Directives governing procedures for the award of public works and supplies contracts were legislated in the 1970s, but were largely ineffectual because public authorities typically circumvented them either by splitting contracts into smaller amounts so that

they would fall below the thresholds at which the directives took effect or by liberally interpreting the conditions allowing for closed public tenders in order to negotiate with favored local, regional or national suppliers. See Commission (1986).

2. Several cases of non-transposition remained into the late 1990s, with Germany and Austria among the worst offenders. For details, see Commission (1996a: 51); and Commission (1997).
3. For example, in the Commission's May 2002 Internal Market Scoreboard (No. 10), p. 13, the Commission cites atop a list of "Targets missed" failure to agree proposed public procurement reforms that could capture savings of up to 50 billion euros.
4. Such objectives have been included in Italian and British public procurement policies. Italian Law No. 64 of 1986, "System of rules governing special aid for Southern Italy," required all public authorities and bodies to purchase at least 30 percent of their supplies from undertakings established in the Mezzogiorno; as discussed later, this was nullified by an ECJ preliminary ruling following a case brought against an Italian authority by a German firm excluded from competing for a contract. See European Court of Justice, *Judgement of the Court of 20 March 1990,* Judgment C–21/88, paragraph 3; and Fernandez Martin and Stehmann (1991). In the UK, government procurement rules granted a 5 percent "price preference" to tenders that created jobs in Northern Ireland (Arrowsmith, 1995: 272).
5. In April 1994, coinciding with the Uruguay GATT accord, the EU signed a new agreement opening up government contracts in the areas of supplies, works, and services at all levels to international competition, effective January 1, 1996. The Government Purchasing Agreement also covers ports, airports, water, electricity, and urban transport sectors and is based on the principles of nondiscrimination and national treatment of foreign competitors.
6. According to the Commission, the figure was 11.5 percent, or ECU 721 billion in 1994. See "The impact and effectiveness of the Single Market," Communication from the Commission to the European Parliament and Council, COM(96) 520 final, 30 October 1996, p. 21. Winter (1991: 742) put the figure at 9 percent for central and local governments, and up to 15 percent if public undertakings are included. The Checchini Report on the costs of non-Europe also placed the total figure at 15 percent (Crauser, 1993: 69). The higher figures typically include procurement by private law-governed public enterprises that falls outside state budgets. The Commission's Internal Market Directorate revised its estimate to 16.3 percent of EU GDP, in 2002. See Commission (2004a), p. 5.
7. Public sector purchasing as a percentage of GDP was 18.8 percent for Denmark, 17.0 percent for Germany, 21.5 percent for the Netherlands, 20.5 percent for Sweden, and 18.4 percent for the UK. The figure was lowest for Italy, at 11.9 percent. See Commission (2004a, p. 5, Table 1).
8. The difference is explained by the numerous authorities whose purchases of goods and services fall below the minimum threshholds established in the EC

directives. However, these authorities are in theory still obliged to respect Treaty provisions on the free movement of goods and services.

9. See Swann (1992: 61, Table 3.2). Foreign penetration of government procurement markets is lowest in Italy.
10. Principal sectors for which public procurement represents a very significant portion of total sales include power generation equipment, computers and office machinery, aerospace equipment, railway rolling stock, and telecommunications equipment (Commission, 1991b: 16).
11. Of 3,307 advertised contracts, 817 followed open competition procedures. French public authorities, advertising the largest number of contracts, intended to award 48.6 percent by open tendering (437 of 900); the UK 13.1 percent (113 of 849); and Italy 1.5 percent (11 of 713). See Commission (1986: Annex, p. 12). For several member states, foremost among these Italy, the low proportion of contracts awarded by "open" tendering procedures reflected regional preference schemes. Additionally, these numbers may be disproportionate to the relative value of the contracts involved.
12. The largest number of contracts, in descending order, were in Italy, the UK, and France. In Italy only 1 percent of contracts were by open procedure (11 of 1,157); the UK 0.8 percent (8 of 1,071); and France, which was considerably less open than for public supply contracts, 21.1 percent (157 of 743). In Germany, on the other hand, with the next highest total number of contracts, the open procedure was followed 86.3 percent of the time (623 of 722 contracts). See Commission (1986: Annex, p. 11).
13. In its November 1996 Green Paper, DGXV points out that "Public procurement is one of the internal market areas where there are the most problems both in terms of communication of the implementing measures and in terms of the quality of implementation." See Commission (1996a: 7).
14. Examining 1,184 suspected breaches of the public procurement rules from July 1, 1990 to April 18, 1991, Arrowsmith found that only 10 percent came to light through complaints by contractors; the remaining 90 percent were uncovered by Commission monitoring. See Arrowsmith (1993: 6).
15. Nine of these fifteen cases involved Italy; two Greece, and one each for Ireland, Spain, Portugal, and Denmark. See Bovis (1997: 79).
16. For example, it is a matter of national law whether a contract award can be set aside in the event of a breach of the rules, or whether remedies are limited to damages. There also are likely to be significant national differences in how damages are assessed. On these points, see Arrowsmith (1993) and Bovis (1997: 102–108).
17. In 1994, the Commission dealt with a total of 206 infringements, of which 66 were settled before the procedure ran its full course. Report from the Commission to the Council and European Parliament, The Community Single Market, 1994 Report, paragraph 260.
18. Author's interview with officials of the European Commission's Internal Market DG (then DG XV), Brussels, June 11, 1997.

19. On possible explanations for the Court's relative caution, see Garret, Kelemen, and Schulz (1998).
20. The European Commission's Single Market Scoreboard, No. 4 (June 1999), Part B, p. 8, Figure 7, shows 74,232 notices published in the Official Journal for 1998 by 13,595 public entities. As a percentage of GDP, these range from 1.10 percent for the Netherlands and 1.12 percent for Germany to 3.29 percent for Luxembourg and 3.20 percent for the UK.
21. To place this in a broader perspective, though, economists have found a strong in-country bias in trade in goods even where trade barriers between countries are removed and adjustments are made for linguistic differences and geographical distance. See Jeffrey Frankel, "Globalization of the Economy," in Joseph S. Nye and John D. Donahue, eds, *Governance in a Globalizing World* (Washington, D.C.: Brookings, 2000), p. 55.
22. The relevant directives set these thresholds at ecu 5 million for public works contracts; ecu 200,000 for supplies and services contracts from local governments; ecu 400,000 for such contracts from utility companies, except for those in the telecommunications sector, for which the threshold was set at ecu 600,000.
23. Such barriers existed in 816 of 1,184 cases, or 68.9 percent. See Arrowsmith (1993: 9).
24. See the European Commission's Public Procurement infringements website at http://www.europa.eu.int/comm/internal_market/en/publproc/infr; press release of April 5, 2001.
25. Announcements of July 31, 2001 and October 4, 2001, respectively, on the European Commission's public procurement infringements webpage.
26. Announcements of July 31, 2001 and July 22, 1997, respectively, on the European Commission's public procurement infringements webpage.
27. Sue Arrowsmith (1995) makes a similar point.
28. The European Commission's most recent study of the impact of competitive public procurement markets indicates that public authorities following Community public procurement rules pay prices approximately 34 percent less than those who do not follow the rules. Italy reportedly saved 3.7 billion euros in 2003 out of 23 billion euros of public purchases by virtue of competitive public procurement practices. In order to demonstrate the beneficial impact of following these rules, the Commission points out that a savings in procurement spending of 10 percent would bring all 15 older EU member states within the Stability and Growth Pact's fiscal deficit limits. See Commission (2005: 9).
29. See Communication from the Commission, "Public Procurement: Regional and Social Aspects," COM (89) 400 final, Brussels, July 24, 1989, p. 3, which notes that "the concern with implementing the internal market in public procurement in a way that takes fully into account the needs of economic and social cohesion has been a consistent concern of the European Parliament."

Notes to Chapter 6

1. Deutsche Post asserted that the incoming mail was subject to the full German domestic rate because it consisted of items originating in Germany, sent electronically to the UK, then printed and shipped as bulk cross-border mail. See European Report (2000b).
2. Visco Comandini identifies forty-nine acquisitions by European universal service providers between 1994 and 1998; thirty-four of these were in the express courier, parcels, and letters market. Of the thirty-four, half are acquisitions in the domestic market, half abroad. See Comandini (2000: 146, Table 1).
3. Schneider (2001: 75) makes a similar argument about "self-stimulating feedback" in the telecommunications sector.
4. For a rigorous statement of this point, see Schmidt (1996a: 45).
5. For details of the timing of liberalization, I have relied on Volker Schneider, "Europeanization and the Redimensionalization of the Public Sector: Telecommunications in Germany, France and Italy," draft (07–05–98), p. 7, Table 1; and Schmidt (1996b: 9).
6. The need for political consensus despite the availability to the European Commission of powerful legal mechanisms is the central theme of Conant (2002). As Conant argues (p. 123), "reforms that defy political consensus cannot simply be legally imposed."
7. On the infringement proceedings, see Conant (2002: chapter 5); and Schmidt (1998: 177).
8. Directive on common rules for the internal market in electricity, 96/92/EC, in OJ L 27, 30.01.1997.
9. These percentages corresponded to the grant of the right to choose their supplier to industrial consumers of over 40 GWh annually (February 1999)—the level of use of a large factory in an energy-intensive sector, such as a shipyard; consumers of over 20 GWh (February 2000), corresponding to the usage level of a sizeable factory in a sector that is not especially energy intensive; and, in the final step provided for in the directive, consumers of more than 9 GWh (February 2003), which would include users such as hospitals and large hotels. These levels do not reach down to household consumers.
10. As the largest exporter, France in 1999 exported a net of 62,197 Gigawatt hours (GWh) of electricity; Italy, in contrast, *imported* a net of 42,012 GWh. See Commission (2001b: 9). National export and import totals exclude trade within Scandinavia and between Ireland and the UK.
11. See Orla Ryan, "Not in France's Back Yard," Reed Business Information Ltd., *Utility Europe,* August 1, 1999, p. 9; and "Relinquishing Control Reluctantly," *Petroleum Economist,* August 26, 1999, p. 19.
12. By 2002, EdF accounted for more than 10 percent of electricity generation and supply in the UK. See Ross Tieman, "Europe Pulls the Plug on French State Aid for EdF," *The Business,* October 20, 2002, p. 11; (Lexis-Nexis Academic Universe).

13. In 2002, the European Commission took steps to end these restrictions on competition in the Italian and Spanish markets, but only after initiating action to end the French government's guarantees of EdF's debts, a product of EdF's status as an Etablissement Public Charactere Industrial et Commercial (EPIC). See Ross Tieman, "Europe Pulls the Plug on French State Aid for EDF," *The Business,* October 20, 2002, p. 11 (Lexis-Nexis Academic Universe). As noted in chapter 7, the Commission's scrutiny of state guarantees in France followed from the Commission's struggle to eliminate state guarantees extended to public sector banks in Germany.
14. European Commission, "Proposal for a Directive of the European Parliament and of the Council amending Directives 96/92/EC and 98/30/EC concerning common rules for the internal market in electricity and natural gas," COM(2001) 125 final, Brussels, March 13, 2001, Article 19.
15. Commission of the European Communities, "Amended proposal for a Directive of the European Parliament and of the Council amending Directives 96/92/EC and 98/30/EC concerning rules for the internal markets in electricity and natural gas," COM(2002) 304 final. Brussels, 7 June 2002. Lisa Conant points out how French objections to initial proposals to open up network access in the early 1990s, coupled with the reluctance of Germany and other member state governments to isolate France on such a critical issue, rendered the decision rule for Community legislation "*de facto* unanimity." See Conant (2002: 132).
16. According to the Commission's report following the Green Paper consultation process, the Community-wide delivery time for internal mail averaged between one and a half and two working days, while the average for cross-border mail was four days. See Commission (1993: 2).
17. The Council's position deferred a decision on these segments of the market to 1999, at which point the EP and Council would make a decision on the basis of a Commission proposal for further liberalization to be presented by the end of 1998. As it turns out, neither of these deadlines was met.
18. Directive 97/67/EC of the European Parliament and the Council of 15 December 1997 on common rules for the development of the internal market of Community postal services and the improvement of quality of service, Official Journal of the European Communities L 015, January 21, 1998, pp. 0014–0025, paragraph 17.
19. Neil Buckley, Deborah Hargreaves, and Cathy Newman, "UK and France unite to oppose Brussels plan for postal reforms," *Financial Times* (London), May 31, 2000, p. 1.
20. 36.5 percent of Luxembourg's mail volume involves cross-border flows, the highest in the EU. But Luxembourg is a net mail exporter, with 21.7 percent of its mail volume comprised of outbound cross-border mail, and 14.8 percent of inbound mail. Ireland has the largest share of inbound cross-border mail in the EU (17.8 percent of total mail volume); 27.6 percent of its mail volume consists of cross-border flows. See Pricewaterhouse Coopers (1998: 26, Table 2.7).

21. According to the November 1998 "Study on the Weight and Price Limits of the Reserved Area in the Postal Sector" commissioned by the European Commission and authored by CTcon, 77.1 percent of all letter and direct mail revenues would remain in the reserved sector if direct mail and letters were liberalized above 50 grams. With direct mail fully liberalized and only letters up to 50 grams protected, 65.2 percent of these revenues would still be reserved for the national operators.
22. In 1999, the European Express Organisation merged with the Association of European Express Carriers (AEEC) to create the European Express Association (EEA).
23. European Report (2000a); and Commission of the European Communities, RAPID Press Release IP: 00/919, "Commission initiates proceedings against Deutsche Post AG for abuse of a dominant position," August 8, 2000.
24. The European Commission's investigation of the case eventually revealed that DPAG was keeping competitors out of the market through both predatory pricing and loyalty agreements that encouraged customers to rely on DPAG for their package services. Infringments lasted from 1974 to 2000; the gravity of these intensified from Nov 1997 to Oct 2000. Ultimately the Commission found that from the mid-1970s until mid-1995, DPAG operated under cooperation agreements with large mail order customers, providing discounts in exchange for commitments of these companies to send all of their parcels up to a certain weight (typically 10 or 20 kg) with DPAG. In subsequent agreements during the second half of the 1990s, DPAG offered volume incentives to large parcel customers as well as incentive discounts tied explicitly to transfers of their parcel services from a competitor, presumably UPS, to DPAG—both of these constituting "fidelity rebates," which are illegal under EC competition law, according to which these constitute an abuse of DPAG's dominant market position. The Commission ultimately required DPAG to structurally separate its commercial parcel services, which DPAG did by spinning off Newco to handle all business-to-business and business-to-consumer mail-order parcel services from December 31, 2001. In addition, the Commission in June 2002 ordered Deutsche Post to repay an astonishing 572 million euros ($540 million at the prevailing exchange rate) in illegal state aid received from the German government to offset losses in its parcel operations.
25. MEPs generally reflected national positions, though one Swedish MEP from the GUE/NGL (Group of the United Left/Nordic Green Left) cited Swedish postal services liberalization as a negative example that had exacerbated regional equalities, and one GUE/NGL Dutch MEP criticized both the "extreme" liberalization proposal of the Commission and the more moderate EP compromise generated by a "secret deal" between the Christian Democrats and Socialists. Verbatim text of the debate of the European Parliament of December 14, 2000 (European Parliament website, http://www.europarl.eu.int/plenary/default_en.htm).

26. Verbatim text of the debate of the European Parliament of December 14, 2000, http://www.europarl.eu.int/plenary/default_en.htm.
27. The 1993 actions include European Parliament, "Resolution on the Green Paper on the development of the single market for postal services," January 22, 1993, OJ C 42, February 15, 1993, pp. 240–245, and a resolution of June 25, 1993 (OJ C 194, July 19, 1993, p. 397). Subsequent measures echoing these themes include the October 25, 1995 "Resolution on the implementation of a single market for postal services," OJ C 308, November 20, 1995, p. 60.
28. Explanatory statement, Report on the joint text approved by the Conciliation Committee, for an EP and Council Directive on common rules for the development of the internal market of Community Postal Services, 13 November 1997, p. 5.
29. Common Position (EC) No. 25/97, adopted by the Council on 29 April 1997, OJ C 188, June 19, 1997, p. 9.
30. European Parliament, Resolution on European postal services, January 14, 1999, OJ C104, 14 April 1999, p. 134.
31. PostEurop's internal rules stipulated that support of ten of its fifteen voting members, corresponding to the member states of the EU, was required for agreement on a common platform.
32. PostEurop's February 2000 platform was supported by ten countries: Austria, Belgium, Denmark, France, Greece, Ireland, Italy, Luxembourg, Portugal, and the UK.
33. Common Platform of PostEurop, February 18, 2000, para. 7.
34. Common Platform of PostEurop, February 18, 2000, paragraphs 9, 13, 14.
35. Press release of the European Express Association, 12 May 2000. The same position is presented in European Express Association (2000).
36. Author's interviews with officials of the EEA and of PostEurop, Brussels, March 2001.
37. One-quarter of the shares of Deutsche Post were sold in an initial public offering on November 20, 2000. The German government garnered approximately $5.6 billion from the sale.
38. Scheurle, a CSU member appointed to the post by Chancellor Helmut Kohl, resigned in November 2000. Named as his successor was the RTP vice-president, SPD member Matthias Kurth.
39. Deborah Hargreaves, "Probe into Deutsche Post pricing," *Financial Times* (London), May 30, 2000, p. 4.
40. Ralph Atkins, "German minister attacked over mail cost ruling," *Financial Times* (London), April 4, 2000, p. 4.
41. AFX News, "Regierung beharrt auf langerem Postmonopol—Bedenken bei Grunen," March 8, 2001, web.lexis-nexis.com/universe.
42. AfX News Limited, "Wirtschaftsminister Mueller will Postmonopol nach 2002 nicht volling aufgeben," November 24, 2000, web.lexis-nexis.com/universe.

43. Confirming that the German government's fears about asymmetrical liberalization were well-founded, the French government continued to resist market opening in the sector long after the adoption of a new postal services liberalization measure in May 2002. In December 2003, the European Commission referred France to the European Court of Justice for two instances of failure to implement EU postal services Directives. First, the French government had not established an independent postal services regulator as required by the 1997 postal services Directive, instead appointing the Minister for Economic Affairs, Finance and Industry—who also exercises some operational authority over the French postal service—as the regulatory authority. Second, the French government had not opened its postal services sector to competition in accordance with the 2002 Directive. In bringing France before the ECJ, the Commission simultaneously ended infringement proceedings against Belgium, Greece, and Austria, all of which had come into compliance with the postal services Directives. See Rapid Press Release IP/03/1754, "Postal services: France before the Court over the non-implementation of two postal Directives," December 17, 2003, http://europa.eu.int/rapid.
44. "Europe's last post," *The Economist,* U. S. Edition, May 13, 2000, web.lexis-nexis.com/universe.
45. Christine Buckley and David Lister, "Ministers fight EU plans to end postal monopoly," *The Times* (London), May 31, 2000.
46. Alan Jones and Geoff Meade, "Post Office Alert on EU Threat to Deliveries," *The Scotsman,* May 31, 2000, p. 2.
47. Charles Batchelor and William Hall, "Germans first past the post," *Financial Times* (London), December 11, 1998, p. 29.
48. These dividends totaled approximately pounds 2 billion. See Jonathan Walker, "Hands Off Our Post," *The Birmingham Post,* June 6, 2002; and Robert Budden et al., "In the post," *Financial Times* (London), June 14, 2002, p. 18.
49. Though the government, as the Post Office's only shareholder, still must grant permission for any transaction exceeding 75 million pounds. See "First Annual Report to Parliament on the Progress of the Reforms Set Out in the White Paper on Post Office Reform," Department of Trade and Industry website, http://www.DTI.gov.uk/por.
50. See "Promoting effective competition between postal operators: A consultation document," 29 September 2000, http://www.DTI.gov.uk/por.
51. See Christine Buckley, "Licence awards leave Royal Mail facing death by a thousand cuts," *The Times* (London), September 18, 2001; and Kevin Brown, "Trouble in the post for Consignia," *Financial Times* (London), September 10, 2001, p. 21.
52. See Jonathan Walker, "Hands off our post, says Euro MP Lynne," *The Birmingham Post,* June 6, 2002 (lexis-nexis/Financial Times Information, Global News Wire—Europe Intelligence Wire).

53. Christopher Adams and Sarah Laitner, "Mail Competition Deferred," *The Financial Times* (London), May 29, 2002, p.1; and Sophie Barker,"Consignia wins year breathing space," *The Daily Telegraph*, May 30, 2002, p. 34.
54. The directive contains a clause allowing governments to keep this segment of the market closed to competition if they deem that the revenues are vital to providing the universal service. See EU Press Release IP/02/671, "Postal services: Commission welcomes adoption of a new Directive fostering competition," Brussels, May 7, 2002.

Notes to Chapter 7

1. For example, Westdeutsche Landesbank, the largest of the public law institutions, was at the outset of the conflict described in the chapter owned 43.2 percent by the state of North Rhine-Westphalia; 11.7 percent each by the regional Associations of the Rhineland and Westphalia-Lippe, and 16.7 percent each by the Savings Banks and Giro Associations of the Rhineland and Westphalia-Lippe. See "WestLB in Brief," http://www.westlb.com/overview; also see Tilly (1994: 479).
2. *Der Spiegel,* 10/1997: 106; and "Information on the Economic and Social Commitment of the Savings Bank Finance Group," Deutsche Sparkassen- und Giroverband.
3. See DSGV (2000); and DSGV and Verband der Öffentliche Banken (VOeB), "Public-Law Credit Institutions."
4. See DSGV (2000: 5); and Westdeutsche Landesbank, "Strengthening the Regions Through Structural Change," p. 2.
5. On the role of Westdeutsche Landesbank in regional development and restructuring activities in Nordrhein-Westfalen, see Deeg (1999: 133–145). For example, Deeg finds (127) that "the most important institutional development in the regional economic policy network was the utilization, beginning in the early 1970s, of the Landesbank of North Rhine-Westphalia (the Westdeutsche Landesbank) as a major instrument of state industrial policy. By developing and using the capacities of the WestLB, including its ability to purchase large holdings of industrial firms, the Land government has been able to influence directly adjustment in particular firms and sectors."
6. To cite one example of many, Ernst Schwanhold, Nordrhein-Westfalen's Minister for Economics, Energy and Transport, became a deputy member of the Westdeutsche Landesbank supervisory board in February 2000, and head of the board in June 2001. See "Minister Schwanhold ist Vorsitzender des WestLB-Verwaltungsrates," *Die Welt,* June 5, 2001: 13 (Lexis-Nexis Academic Universe).
7. See Sinn (1999: 12, Table 2.1 and 38, Table 3.4). These tables show an average pre-tax return on equity for the period 1980 to 1994 ranging from 4.9 percent for WestLB to 10.5 percent for Südwestdeutsche Landesbank.

8. The high ratings given to the Landesbanken by rating agencies such as Fitch, S & P, and Moody's contrast with their much lower financial strength ratings, suggesting that their credit ratings are a direct product of state guarantees. Moreover, the substantial exposure of some Landesbanken to the financial crises in Asia and Russia provide a "test" of this proposition—their credit ratings did not suffer. See *Financial Times,* July 10, 1999; and Tony Barber, "Privileged Status Under Threat," *Financial Times Survey of German Banking and Finance,* October 25, 1999: 6. Sinn (1999: 36) finds that the benefits of higher ratings lower borrowing costs by something like 15–20 basis points, depending on the financial instrument and maturity.
9. Four of these are in Austria, three in France, and two in the Netherlands. See "Brüssel will schnell über Beschwerde gegen Sparkassen entscheiden," *Frankfurter Allgemeine Zeitung,* July 28, 2000: 13.
10. See Sinn (1999: 29–30). From a presence in twenty-four countries in 1991, WestLB achieved a presence in thirty-five countries by 1997. See Commission (2000a: paragraph 19).
11. From 1987 to the end of 1991, WestLB's assets grew by more than half. See "Upward Bound: WestLB," *The Economist,* May 16, 1992: 109–110. Sinn (1999: 105–106, Appendix 2), documents some of the activities of public law banks in the mid-1990s, including Westdeutsche Landesbank's expansion of investment banking in London and its acquisition activity and increased market presence in France. The *Financial Times* in 2000 noted the formative role of WestLB's Director, indicating that "Over the past 10 years Mr. Neuber, a former Social Democrat politician, has transformed a once-humble provincial lender into a global universal bank with offices in almost 40 countries." See Tony Major, "WestLB split may provide model for German banking," *Financial Times* (London), November 10, 2000: 36.
12. According to Sinn (1999: 38, Table 3.4), compared with the average return on equity capital from 1980 to 1994 of the five largest Landesbanken of between 4.9 percent (WestLB) and 10.5 percent (SüdwestLB), the five largest private banks returned between 12.0 percent (Dresdner) and 18.3 percent (Deutsche Bank).
13. Wfa funds come from annual contributions from the state budget as well as income from housing loans.
14. The Basel Convention harmonized international bank capital regulations throughout the twelve leading industrial countries, ostensibly with the aim of curbing excessively risky lending and creating conditions for fair competition. The rules called for international banks to achieve a ratio of capital to assets of 4 percent for core capital and 8 percent overall by December 31, 1992 (see *Bank Management* 67, 8 (August 1991): 6–7). Without the Wfa capital, WestLB's core capital would have been approximately 2 percent of assets, far below the required level.
15. The excess capital on which WestLB could expand its commercial activities amounted to DM 2.5 billion. As the European Commission concluded in its subsequent investigation of the transaction (following the complaint described

in the next paragraph), "by way of the transfer, the Land enabled WestLB, which was operating at the very edge of its equity base, to avoid reducing its business activities and even to expand those business activities open to risk." See Commission (2000a: paragraph 74).

16. The rate paid by WestLB was 0.6 percent annually. Moreover, the agreement between Land Nordrhein-Westfalen and WestLB establishing the terms of the transfer stipulated that this would be paid only if WestLB earned profits. See Commission (2000a: paragraph 69). Also see *Financial Times,* January 14, 1997: 2; and *The Economist,* "Germany's Protective Wings," May 22, 1999: 81. The BdB complaint named the five additional Länder that had transferred housing development funds to their Landesbanken, but focused on the WestLB transaction because it was by far the largest.
17. Author's interview with official of the German Permanent Representation to the EU, Brussels, May 16, 2001.
18. Commission (2000a: paragraph 3). Representatives of the Commission subsequently participated in a meeting with German government officials, WestLB representatives, and the BdB in November 1998.
19. WestLB asserted consistently during the two years imediately following the decision on the Wfa state aid case that the Commission in its calculations had confused pretax and after-tax returns, and that the 0.6 percent rate of return actually corresponded to a pretax return of 9.4 percent, close to the prevailing market rate of 10.3 percent achieved by German banks during the period in question. Moreover, WestLB argued that the investor (the state of NRW) contributing the Wfa assets incurred a lower risk than that associated with an investment of share capital in a commercial bank, accounting for the difference between the 10.3 percent market rate and the 9.4 percent rate of return paid by WestLB. See Westdeutsche Landesbank, "The Decision of the European Commission on the Integration of the Wohnungsbauförderungsanstalt NRW (Wfa) into WestLB." During discussions with the BdB while the complaint was under consideration by the European Commission, WestLB did offer to increase the return by a relatively small but nonetheless significant amount, adding by some accounts a half percentage point.
20. "Bankenverband dringt auf puenktlichen," *Süddeutcher Zeitung,* March 18, 1997. One columnist pointed out the episode highlighted the contradiction of a government that supported the construction of the single European market yet which sought special status for public credit institutions. According to this German commentator, the private banks would have to pursue their rights outside the national level, since in German domestic politics, the complaints of the private banks "have no chance." See Winfried Muenster, "Das Thema des Tages: Nur Brüssel sichert den Wettbewerb," *Süddeutsche Zeitung,* September 25, 1997.
21. Paul K. Friedhof, "Öffentlich-rechtliche Banken gegen den Euro?" Tagesdienst der FDP-Bundestagfraktion Nr. 272, May 7, 1997. Reprinted in Bundesverband deutscher Banken (1997: 7). Author's translation.
22. Author's interview with European Commission official, January 21, 1999.

23. DSGV Press release, June 18, 1997, reprinted in Bundesverband deutscher Banken (1997: 13). Author's translation.
24. Jeffrey Anderson argues that the vast flow of aid to the eastern Länder following unification, as well as a number of additional high-profile cases (including an illegal aid to VW in Saxony and aid to the Bremer Vulkan shipbuilding group, in which aid approved for the east was siphoned off to the west), already had damaged Germany's credibility as a proponent of a rigorous Community state aid regime. See Anderson (1999: Chapter 5).
25. It is likely that the federal government was unwilling to push too heavily on this issue, and that its efforts merely were sufficient to credibly inform Land representatives that the government had made the case but could not win over its European partners.
26. Declaration 37 of the Amsterdam Treaty, which states that "the Conference notes the Commission's opinion to the effect that the Community's existing competition rules allow services of general economic interest provided by public credit institutions existing in Germany and the facilities granted to them to compensate for the costs connected with such services be taken into account in full." While recognizing that the organization of its financial infrastructure to deliver financial services to the regions is a matter for the German government, the declaration concludes that "such facilities may not adversely affect the conditions of competition to an extent beyond that required in order to perform these particular tasks and which is contrary to the interests of the Community." It is, of course, the Commission that is responsible for assessing the compatibility of national arrangements with Community interests.
27. Author's interviews with officials from the Representation of Land Nordrhein-Westfalen to the EU and from the German Permanent Representation to the EU, Brussels, May 15 and 16, 2001.
28. Author's interviews, Brussels, May 15, 2001.
29. Bettina Schragl, "EU: Kompromiss Bei Banken-Privilegien," *Wirtschaftsblatt*, June 19, 1997, p. 3.
30. Confirmed in author's interviews with EU officials, Brussels, January 20 and 21, 1999.
31. Press release, Düsseldorf, January 24, 1997 (www.NRW.de). Calling for the European Commission to preserve the status quo, Rau emphasized the high level of public trust garnered by the three pillar system of German credit institutions, composed of the public, cooperative, and commercial banks. He credited the public sector banks with facilitating structural adjustment and numerous local and regional cultural and social projects.
32. See "Commission Decision of 8 July 1999;" and Mario Monti, "Competition Policy and Financial Services," speech to the European Banking Congress, Frankfurt, November 19, 1999.
33. Informed largely by the case of the Landesbanken, the communication establishes that a state guarantee may be considered aid even when the guarantee is never invoked, and that this aid distorts competition in the single market to the extent that state guarantees enable enterprises to gain higher credit

ratings and more favorable loan terms. See "Commission notice on the application of Articles 87 and 88 of the EC Treaty to State aid in the form of guarantees," November 29, 1999, paragraphs 2.1.2 and 2.1.3.

34. However, Scherf's position was rejected by the SPD's state party organization. See "Nur Porzner für Scherf," *die tageszeitung*, October 19, 2000 (Contrapress media GmbH, Lexis Nexis Academic Universe).

35. In a veiled threat of opposition to the introduction of Europe's single currency, the resolution asserted that "An intact banking system with efficient public-law banks and the resulting guaranteed availability of financial services to all strata of the population is an indispensable precondition for the success of the monetary union." See Westdeutsche Landesbank Girozentrale, "The Decision of the European Commission on the Integration of the Wohnungsbaufoerderungsanstalt NRW (Wfa) into WestLB," p. 27.

36. See *Financial Times*, December 2, 1999, p. 16. In December 2002, the ECJ ruled in favor of an action by the European Commission against the Federal Republic of Germany for failing to fulfill its Treaty obligations by adopting measures required for WestLB to repay illegal state aid. See Judgment of the Court, Case C-209/00, 12 December 2002.

37. In March 2003, the Court of First Instance upheld the complaint by WestLB and the state of Nordrhein Westfalen (NRW), supported by the German government, against the decision of the European Commission (supported by the BdB) in the WestLB case. The ruling annulled the Commission's decision on the grounds that the Commission had not fully justified the rate of return it used to calculate the amount that WestLB would have to return to the state of Nordrhein Westfalen. While the Court's decision requires that the Commission either provide more compelling reasoning or reach a different agreement (based on a lower rate of return on Wfa funds) with NRW and WestLB, it does not affect the phasing out of state guarantees to the Landesbanken, which is a separate issue. See Judgment of the Court of First Instance, Joined cases T-228/99 and T-233/99, March 6, 2003. In October 2004, the European Commission announced that the amount to be repaid by WestLB would be 979 million euros. Six other Landesbanken would have to make similar repayments to their state governments of benefits garnered from the transfer of state housing development funds in the early 1990s; the total repayment for the seven Landesbanken reached 3 billion euros. The settlement remained disputed, however, because of the conditions placed on the repayment by the EU's new Competition Commissioner: that the repayment take place by the end of 2004; and that recapitalization of the Landesbanken be at a level less than the repaid amounts, that recapitalization be delayed until after the lapse of state guarantees in July 2005, and that private investors be permitted to take part in the recapitalization. See "EC Landesbank settlement under threat," *European Banker*, December 31, 2004, p. 5 (http://web.lexis-nexis.com/universe).

38. Deborah Hargreaves, "Landesbank issue could hit EU reform, *Financial Times*, January 28, 2000, p. 9; and Thomas Hanke and Haig Simonian,

"States resist Schröder's solution to banks dispute," *Financial Times,* July 19, 2000, p. 12.

39. "Implementation tallies with EUR Treaty," WestLB website, May 26, 2000.
40. According to the West LB website, the "tax implications would cause permanent damage to the bank . . . that could not be reversed in the event that the outcome of the main proceedings is positive as is currently expected." See "WestLB: Implementation tallies with EUR Treaty," May 26, 2000.
41. Deborah Hargreaves, "Brussels to act on German bank guarantees," *Financial Times,* July 28, 2000, p. 8.
42. This instance suggests the dual implications of recent gains in the rights of third parties alleging competition infringements. On the one hand, the Commission's ability to control the state aid agenda is diminished; on the other, its ability to act vis-à-vis reluctant governments by claiming that its hands are tied is enhanced.
43. Thomas Hanke and Haig Simonian, "States resist Schröder's solution to banks dispute," *Financial Times,* July 19, 2000, p. 12.
44. Interviews with officials of the European Commission, Brussels, May 15, 2001; officials from the German Permanent Representation to the EU, Brussels, May 16, 2001; and representatives of Westdeutsche Landesbank, Düsseldorf, May 17, 2001.
45. See "Berlin Outlines Full Plans for "New" WestLB Public-Sector Banking," (Global News Wire, Lexis-Nexis Academic Universe) *Handelsblatt* (English Version), May 14, 2001.
46. European Commission Online (http://www.europa.eu.int/rapid/start/cgi), "Commission and Germany start focused discussions on guarantees to public banks," IP/01/187, February 9, 2001.
47. Author's interview with official of Brussels representation of Land Nordrhein-Westfalen, May 15, 2001.
48. See European Commission Online (http://www.europa.eu.int/rapid/start/cgi), "Commission requests Germany to bring state guarantees for public banks into line with EC law," IP/01/665, May 8, 2001.
49. "Germany Concedes Ground in Landesbank Dispute," *Handelsblatt* (English version), June 15, 2001; Lexis-Nexis Academic Universe.
50. In preparation to compete without state guarantees, WestLB engaged in extensive cost-cutting in 2003 and 2004, including sharp cuts in its work force. The bank's supervisory board also developed a new business strategy focused on three areas of activity: a consolidated international presence, assistance to small and medium German companies, and financial product development guidance for public savings banks (Sparkassen). See "WestLB unveils new 3 pillar strategy, to retain international presence," *AFX European Focus,* July 2, 2003 (http://web.lexis-nexis-com/universe).
51. Ross Tieman, "Europe Pulls the Plug on French State Aid to EdF," *The Business,* October 20, 2002, p.11 (Lexis-Nexis Academic Universe).
52. The European Commission in December 2003 called for EdF to repay more than 1 billion euros to the French government related to subsidies it

had received in the form of underpayment of taxes from 1986 to 1997. The 2004 bill passed by the National Assembly permits the sale of up to 30 percent of EdF. See Commission of the European Communities, RAPID Press Release IP: 03/1737, December 16, 2003; and Marion Bywater, "French legislature sticks to task in hand," *Platts Power in Europe,* July 5, 2004, p. 8 (http://web.lexis-nexis.com/universe).

Notes to Chapter 8

1. Jacoby thus argues that institutional transfer is more likely to succeed when the effort is to achieve "functional equivalence" rather than exact transfer, allowing for indigenous input in the design of institutional change. Consistent with his argument about the role of societal actors in "pulling in" institutional change, Jacoby points out that while exact transfer is design-oriented, functional equivalence is actor-oriented. See Jacoby (2000: 17).
2. As discussed in chapter 2, the concept is developed by Leonard Schoppa in his study of the Structural Impediments Initiative pursued by the United States to obtain greater access to Japanese markets (Schoppa, 1993); the idea also coincides with the notion of institutional transfer and policy change developed by Wade Jacoby (2000).
3. Reflecting the reaction of the commercial banks to the 1992 decision of Germany's banking supervisory authority to allow the Landesbanken to count Wfa assets as core capital, Lambsdorff, then FDP economics spokesman, asserted that the public law banks had outgrown their original function of reconstructing the German economy; their functions could now be assumed by the private sector. Furthermore, estimates at this time of difficult government finances indicated that privatization could raise DM 100 to DM 150 billion. See David Waller, "Raw nerve of Germany's state banks," *Financial Times* (London), September 28, 1993: 2.
4. The quote is from a Lambsdorff interview in the *Berliner Zeitung,* cited in AP Worldstream—German, July 20, 2000; http://web.lexis-nexis.com/universe.
5. Thomas Widder, "Doering (FDP) für Teilprivatisierung von Landesbanken," *Financial Times Deutschland.* Reported by *Vereinigte Wirtschaftsdienste* GmbH, August 8, 2000; http://web.lexis-nexis.com/universe.
6. CDU/CSU Bundestagfraktion, "Hintze: Landesbanken fit machen für Europa—Privatisierung sauberste Lösung," *News Aktuell,* OTS Originaltextservice, July 20, 2000; http://web.lexis-nexis.com/universe.
7. Developing his argument in the context of welfare state reform, Robert Cox identifies the need for governments to cast a path-shaping reform discourse in terms that resonate with national norms and values. See Robert Henry Cox, "The Social Construction of an Imperative: Why Welfare Reform Happened in Denmark and the Netherlands but Not in Germany," *World Politics* 53, No. 3 (April 2001): 463–498.

8. Beate Preuschoff, "Unionspolitiker: Klage der Privatbanken im Grundsatz berechtigt," *Vereinigte Wirtschaftsdienste* GmbH, August 3, 2000; http://web.lexis-nexis.com/universe.
9. CDU/CSU Bundestagfraktion, "Landesbanken und Sparkassen müssen öffentliche Garantien marktgerecht verzinsen." *News Aktuell*, OTS Originaltextservice, August 3, 2000; http://web.lexis-nexis.com/universe.
10. "NRW will Sparakssen erhalten—Niedersachsen: Gemeinsame Strategie," Deutsche Presse-Agentur—Europadienst (Lexis-Nexis Academic Universe), November 23, 2000.
11. Especially prior to the December 1999 EBF complaint to the European Commission, which included Stadtsparkasse Köln among the three named institutions, distinguishing between the Landesbanken and Sparkassen had the advantage of creating a solution acceptable to the Commission. EU law provides a basis for differentiating between the Landesbanken and Sparkassen due to the greater impact of the former on commerce between member states. In addition, in contrast to the large Landesbanken, the Sparkassen do not raise most of their funds on the capital markets (an activity that invokes the benefits of the higher credit ratings generated by state guarantees), relying instead on savings deposits. Reflecting the possibility for smaller, regional Sparkassen to retain their structures even after the EBF complaint, Competition Commissioner Mario Monti raised the prospect of such a distinction in a March 2000 speech before Economic Affairs Ministers of the Länder. See Mario Monti, "The Community's State Aid Policy," Speech before the Conference of the 16 Ministers of Economic Affairs of the German Länder, March 30, 2000. Speech 00/113; http://europa.eu.int /rapid/start.
12. CDU/CSU Bundestagfraktion, "Hintze: Landesbanken fit machen für Europa—Privatisierung sauberste Lösung." News Aktuell, OTS Originaltextservice, July 20, 2000; http://web.lexis-nexis.com/universe.
13. "NRW will Sparakssen erhalten—Niedersachsen: Gemeinsame Strategie," Deutsche Presse-Agentur—Europadienst (Lexis-Nexis Academic Universe), November 23, 2000.
14. For a discussion of many of these conflicts, and the argument that they emerged due to a redefinition of German interests in the wake of unification, see Anderson (1999).
15. Gerhard Schröder, "Shaping industry on the anvil of Europe," *Financial Times* (London Edition), April 29, 2002, p. 21.

BIBLIOGRAPHY

Books, Book Chapters, Journal Articles, and Documents

Alter, Karen J. 2001. *Establishing the Supremacy of European Law.* Oxford: Oxford University Press.

Anderson, Jeffrey. 1999. *German Unification and the Union of Europe.* Cambridge: Cambridge University Press.

Arrowsmith, Sue. 1993. "Enforcing the Public Procurement Rules: Legal Remedies in the Court of Justice and the National Courts," in Sue Arrowsmith, ed., *Remedies for Enforcing the Public Procurement Rules, Public Procurement in the European Community:* Volume IV. Winteringham, UK: Earlsgate Press: 1–90.

Arrowsmith, Sue. 1995. "Public Procurement as an Instrument of Policy and the Impact of Market Liberalisation," *The Law Quarterly Review* 111 (April): 235–284.

Arrowsmith, Sue, and José M. Fernandez Martin. 1993. "Developments in Public Procurement in 1992," *European Law Review* 18, 4: 323–345.

Börzel, Tanja A., and Thomas Risse. 2000. "When Europe Hits Home: Europeanization and Domestic Change," European University Institute Working Paper RSC No. 2000/56. San Domenico, Italy.

Bovis, Christopher. 1997. *EC Public Procurement Law.* London: Longman.

Buendia Sierra, Jose Luis. 1999. *Exclusive Rights and State Monopolies under EC Law.* Oxford: Oxford University Press.

Bundesverband deutscher Banken (Federation of German Banks). 1997. "Daten, Fakten, Argumente: Die Amsterdamer Erklärung zu den öffentlich-rechtlichen Kreditinstituten." Köln, November.

Bundesverband deutscher Banken. 1998. "Daten, Fakten, Argumente: Wettbewerbsuntersuchung der EU-Kommission." Köln, March.

Caporaso, James A. 1996. "The European Union and Forms of State: Westphalian, Regulatory or Post-Modern?" *Journal of Common Market Studies,* 34, 1: 29–52.

Cerny, Philip. 1997. "International Finance and the Erosion of Capitalist Diversity," in Colin Crouch and Wolfgang Streeck, eds., *Political Economy of Modern Capitalism.* London: Sage: 173–181.

Cini, Michelle, and Lee McGowan. 1998. *Competition Policy in the European Union.* New York: St. Martin's.

Comandini, Vincenzo Visco. 2000. "Postal Services," in Damien Geradin, ed., *The Liberalization of State Monopolies in the European Union and Beyond.* The Hague: Kluwer Law International.

Commission of the European Communities. 1985. *Completing the Internal Market: White Paper from the Commission to the European Council.* Luxembourg: Office for Official Publications of the European Communities.

Commission of the European Communities. 1986. Communication by the Commission to the Council, "Public Procurement in the Community." COM(86) 375 final.

Commission of the European Communities. 1988. Research on the "Cost of Non- Europe" Volume 1: Basic Findings, Executive Summary of "The Cost of Non- Europe in Public Sector Procurement," WS Atkins Management Consultants.

Commission of the European Communities. 1989a. "Re-examined proposal for a Council Directive amending Council Directive 71/305/EEC concerning the coordination of procedures for the award of public works contracts." COM(89) 141 final.

Commission of the European Communities. 1989b. *Public Procurement: Regional and Social Aspects.* COM(89) 400 final.

Commission of the European Communities. 1991a. "XXth Report on Competition Policy," Luxembourg: Office for Official Publications of the European Communities.

Commission of the European Communities. 1991b. "European Industrial Policy for the 1990s," Bulletin of the European Communities, Supplement 3/91.

Commission of the European Communities. 1993. Communication from the Commission to the Council and the European Parliament, "Guidelines for the Development of Community postal services." COM(93) 247 final.

Commission of the European Communities. 1994a. Internal Market: Public Procurement, Services, Capital Movements, Cooperation. National Implementing Measures. Situation at April 30, 1994.

Commission of the European Communities. 1994b. *Growth, Competitiveness, Employment: The Challenges and Ways Forward Into the 21st Century.* Luxembourg: Office for Official Publications of the European Communities.

Commission of the European Communities. 1996a. Green Paper, "Public Procurement in the European Union: Exploring the Way Forward."

Commission of the European Communities. 1996b. "Amended proposal for a European Parliament and Council Directive on common rules for the development of the internal market of Community postal services." COM(96) 412 final, July 31.

Commission of the European Communities. 1996c. "Services of general interest in Europe." Brussels, September 11. OJ 1996 No C 281: 3.

Commission of the European Communities. 1997. Special Sectoral Report No. 1: Public Procurement. Brussels, November.

Commission of the European Communities. 1998a. "Public Procurement in the European Union," Brussels, March 11. COM (98) 143.

Commission of the European Communities. 1998b. Report to the Council of Ministers, "Services of general interest in the banking sector." Adopted by the Commission on 17 June and presented to the ECOFIN Council on 23 November. http://www.europa.eu.int/comm/competition/state_aid/others/report_bank/report_bank_en.html.

Commission of the European Communities. 2000a. "Commission Decision of 8 July 1999 on a measure implemented by the Federal Republic of Germany for Westdeutsche Landesbank Girozentrale (WestLB). Official Journal L 150, 23/06/2000: 1–37.

Communication from the Commission. 2000b. "Services of general interest in Europe," COM 2000(0580) final.

Commission of the European Communities. 2001a. Commission Staff Working Paper, "Completing the internal energy market." SEC(2001) 438. Brussels, March 12.

Commission of the European Communities. 2001b. "Interpretative Communication of the Commission on the Community law applicable to public procurement and the possibilities for integrating social considerations into public procurement," COM(2001) 566 final, November 28.

Commission of the European Communities. 2002. European Commission staff working document, "European competitiveness report 2002." SEC(2002) 528. Luxembourg: Office for Official Publications of the European Communities.

Commission of the European Communities. 2004a. "A Report on the Functioning of Public Procurement Markets in the EU: Benefits from the Application of EU Directives and Challenges for the Future." February 3, 2004.

Commission of the European Communities. 2004b. Communication from the Commission, "Fostering structural change: an industrial policy for an enlarged Europe," Brussels, 20.4.2004; COM(2004) 274 final.

Commission of the European Communities. 2005. "Communication from the Commission to the Council, the European Parliament, the European Economic and Social Committee, and the Committee of the Regions: Second Implementation Report of the Internal Market Strategy 2003-2006," Brussels, COM(2005) final, p. 9.

Conant, Lisa. 2002. *Justice Contained: Law and Politics in the European Union.* Ithaca: Cornell University Press.

Court of First Instance. 1995. Judgement of 28 September, Case T-95/94, Sytraval and Brink's France v. Commission. ECR II-2651.

Court of First Instance. 1998. Decision of 15 September, Case T-95/96, Gestevisión Telecinco S.A. v. Commission, ECR II-3407.

Court of First Instance. 2003. Judgement of 6 March, Joined Cases T-228/99 and T- 233/99, Westdeutsche Landesbank Girozentrale and Land Nordrhein Westfalen, supported by Federal Republic of Germany v Commission of the European Communities, supported by Bundesverband deutscher Banken eV.

Cowles, Maria Green. 1995. "Setting the Agenda for a New Europe: The ERT and EC 1992," *Journal of Common Market Studies,* 33, 4, December 1995: 501-526.

Cowles, Maria Green, James Caporaso, and Thomas Risse, eds. 2001. *Transforming Europe*. Ithaca: Cornell University Press.

Cram, Laura. 1997. *Policy-making in the EU*. London and New York: Routledge.

Crauser, Guy. 1993. "Public Tenders in 1993" in *EC Public Contract Law: Public Procurement in Theory and Practice*, Volume 1, 2.

Deeg, Richard. 1996. "Economic Globalization and the Shifting Boundaries of German Federalism," *Publius* 26, 1: 27–52.

Deeg, Richard. 1999. *Finance Capitalism Unveiled: Banks and the German Political Economy*. Ann Arbor: University of Michigan Press.

Dehousse, Renaud. 1992. "Integration v. Regulation? On the Dynamics of Regulation in the European Community," *Journal of Common Market Studies* 30, 4: 383–402.

Della Sala, Vincent. 1997. "Hollowing Out and Hardening the State: European Integration and the Italian Economy," *West European Politics* 20, 1: 14–33.

Deutsche Sparkassen-und Giroverband (DSGV). 2000. "Public-Law Credit Institutions in Germany." Berlin.

Dommering, E. J. 1993. "Article 90 of the EEC Treaty and the Telecommunications, Broadcasting and Postal Services Sectors," in J. H. V. Stuyk and A. J. Vossestein, eds., *State Entrepreneurship, National Monopolies and European Community Law*. Deventer, Netherlands: Kluwer Law and Taxation Publishers.

Drahos, Michaela. 1999. "Convergence of national competition laws: The cases of Germany, Austria, and the Netherlands." Paper prepared for panel on "National Policy Adaptation," Sixth Biennial International Conference of the European Community Studies Association. Pittsburgh, PA, June.

Dyson, Kenneth. 1999. "The Franco-German Relationship and Economic and Monetary Union: Using Europe to 'Bind Leviathan.'" *West European Politics* 22, 1: pp. 25–44.

Eberlein, Burkard. 2000. "German Infrastructure Management: The Case of Electricity Reform," *German Politics*, 9, 3: 81-104.

Edwards, Jeremy, and Klaus Fischer. 1994. *Banks, Finance and Investment in Germany*. Cambridge, Cambridge University Press.

Ehlermann, Claus-Dieter. 1992. "The Contribution of EC Competition Policy to the Single Market," *Common Market Law Review* 29: 257–282.

Ehlermann, Claus-Dieter. 1995. "State Aid Control in the European Union: Success or Failure?" *Fordham International Law Journal*, pp. 1212-1229.

Eising, Rainer, and Nicolas Jabko. 2000. "Moving Targets: Institutional Embeddedness and Domestic Politics in the Liberalization of EU Electricity Markets," European University Institute Working Paper RSC No. 2000/6.

European Council. 2000. Presidency Conclusions, Lisbon European Council, 23 and 24 March 2000.

European Court of Justice. 1988. Case 45/87, Commission v. Ireland. ECR 4929.

European Court of Justice. 1990. Case C-21/88, Dupont de Nemours Italiana SpA v. Unitá Sanitaria Locale No. 2 di Carrara. ECR I-889.

European Court of Justice. 1992. Judgment of 12 February in joined cases C-48/90 and C-66/90, Kingdom of the Netherlands and Koninklijke PTT Nederland NV and PTT-Post BV v Commission of the European Communities, ECR I-627.

European Court of Justice. 1994. Judgment of 27 April, Case C-393/92, Municipality of Almelo and Others v Energiebedrijf IJsselmij NV, ECR I-1508.

European Court of Justice. 1995. *Commission of the European Communities v Federal Republic of Germany*. Case C-433/93, ECJ 1995–8: I-2303–2320.

European Court of Justice. 1996. *Commission of the European Communities v Kingdom of Belgium*. Case C-87/94, ECJ 1996–4/5: I-2043–2096.

European Express Association. 1999. EEA Position Paper on the Implementation of the Postal Service Directive (97/67/EC), October.

European Express Association. 2000. "EEA Position Paper on Postal Liberalisation." October.

European Report No. 2384. 1999. "Days Numbered for Postal Monopolies as Commissioner Sets His Sights on Legislation." European Information Service, February 20.

European Report No. 2482. 2000a. "UPS Urges Commission to Finalize Deutsche Post Cross-Subsidy Case." European Information Service, March 11.

European Report No. 2505. 2000b. "Commission Opens Formal Proceedings Against Deutsche Post." European Information Service, June 1.

European Report No. 2508. 2000c. "Electricity: Commission Launches Infringement Proceedings Against France." European Information Service, June 14.

European Report No. 2510. 2000d. "Postal Services: MEPs Clash With Bolkestein Over Liberalisation Plans." European Information Service, June 21.

European Report No. 2516. 2000e. "Commission Acts Over Deutsche Post Tariffs Complaint." European Information Service, July 12.

European Report No. 2591. 2001. "Commission Orders Germany to Restructure Landesbank Credit System." European Information Service, May 9.

European Report No. 2701. 2002. "Industrial Policy: Commission Fails to Reach Consensus at Seminar." European Information Service, July 17.

Fernandez Martin, José Maria. 1996. *The EC Public Procurement Rules: A Critical Analysis*. Oxford: Clarendon Press.

Fernandez Martin, José Maria, and Oliver Stehmann. 1991. "Product Market Integration versus Regional Cohesion in the European Community," *European Law Review* 16: 216–243.

Gardner, Anthony. 1995. "The Velvet Revolution: Article 90 and the Triumph of the Free Market in Europe's Regulated Sectors," *European Competition Law Review* 16, 2: 78–86.

Garret, Geoffrey, R. Daniel Kelemen, and Heiner Schulz. 1998. "The European Court of Justice, National Governments and the Dynamics of Legal Integration in the European Union," *International Organization* 52: 149–176.

Gerber, David J. 1994. "The Transformation of European Community Competition Law?" *Harvard International Law Journal* 35, 1: 97–147.

German Savings Bank and Giro Association (DSGV) and Federal Association of Public Banks (VOeB), "Public-Law Credit Institutions," a briefing paper.

German Savings Bank and Giro Association (DSGV). 2000. "Public-Law Credit Institutions in Germany," Berlin (January).

Goyder, D. G. 1998. *EC Competition Law,* Third Edition. Oxford: Clarendon Press.

Greenwood, Justin. 1997. *Representing Interests in the European Union.* Basingstoke: Macmillan.

Greenwood, Justin and Karsten Ronit. 1994. "Interest Groups in the European Polity: Newly Emerging Dyanmics and Forms," *West European Politics* 17, 1: 31-56.

Hancher, Leigh. 1993. "Competition, State Monopolies and the Internal Energy Market," in J. H. V. Stuyk and A. J. Vossestein, eds., *State Entrepreneurship, National Monopolies and European Community Law.* Deventer, Netherlands: Kluwer Law and Taxation Publishers.

Haverland, Markus. 2000. "National Adaptation to European Integration: The Importance of Institutional Veto Points." *Journal of Public Policy* 20 (1): 83–103.

Hix, Simon, and Klaus H. Goetz. 2000. "Introduction: European Integration and National Political Systems," special issue on "Europeanised Politics? European Integration and National Political Systems," *West European Politics* 23, 4: 1–26.

Hollingsworth, J. Rogers, and Robert Boyer. 1997. "The Variety of Institutional Arrangements and Their Complementarity in Modern Economies," in Hollingsworth and Boyer, eds., *Contemporary Capitalism: The Embeddedness of Institutions.* Cambridge and New York: Cambridge University Press: 49–54.

Hollingsworth, J. Rogers. 1997. "Continuities and Change in Social Systems of Production: The Cases of Japan, Germany, and the United States," in Hollingsworth and Boyer, eds., *Contemporary Capitalism: The Embeddedness of Institutions.* Cambridge and New York: Cambridge University Press: 265–310.

Huber, Peter M. 2001. "The Europeanization of Public Procurement in Germany," *European Public Law* 7, 1: 33–49.

Jacoby, Wade. 2000. *Imitation and Politics.* Ithaca: Cornell University Press.

Johnson, Peter A. 1998. *The Government of Money: Monetarism in Germany and the United States.* Ithaca: Cornell University Press.

Knill, Christoph, and Dirk Lehmkuhl. 1999. "How Europe Matters. Different Mechanisms of Europeanization," *European Integration online papers* (EioP) 3, No. 7; http://eiop.or.at/eiop/texte/1999–007a.htm.

Kurzer, Paulette. 1993. *Business and Banking: Political Change and Economic Integration in Western Europe.* Ithaca: Cornell University Press.

Kurzer, Paulette. 2001. *Markets and Moral Regulation.* Cambridge: Cambridge University Press.

Lauk, Kurt J. 1994. "Germany at the Crossroads: on the efficiency of the German economy," *Daedalus* 123, 1: 57–83.

Lodge, Martin. 2000. "Isomorphism of National Policies? The 'Europeanisation' of German Competition and Public Procurement Law," *West European Politics* 23, 1: 89-107.

Mahoney, Christine. 2004. "The Power of Institutions: State and Interest Group Activity in the European Union," *European Union Politics* 5, 4: 441-466.

Majone, Giandomenico. 1993. "The European Community: Between Social Policy and Social Regulation," *Journal of Common Market Studies* 31, 2: 153–169.

Majone, Giandomenico. 1994. "The Rise of the Regulatory State in Europe," *West European Politics* 17, 3: 77–101.

Majone, Giandomenico. 1996. *Regulating Europe*. London: Routledge.

Marks, Gary, Liesbet Hooghe, and Kermit Blank. 1996. "European Integration from the 1980s: State-Centric v. Multi-level Governance," *Journal of Common Market Studies* 34, 3: 341–378.

Maselis, Ignace, and Hans M. Gilliams. 1997. "Rights of Complainants in Community Law," *European Law Review* 22, 2: 103–124.

Mazey, Sonia, and Jeremy Richardson, eds. 1993. *Lobbying in the European Community*. Oxford: Oxford University Press.

Mazey, Sonia, and Jeremy Richardson. 1996. "Interest Groups and the 1996 Inter-Governmental Conference." *West European Politics* 20: 111–133.

McGowan, Francis, and Helen Wallace. 1996. "Towards a European Regulatory State," *Journal of European Public Policy* 3, 4: 560–576.

McGowan, Lee, and Stephen Wilks. 1996. "Competition Policy in the European Union: Creating a Federal Agency," in G. B. Doern and Stephen Wilks, eds., *Comparative Competition Policy: National Institutions in a Global Market*. Oxford: Oxford University Press, pp. 225–267.

Millett, Timothy. 1992. "The Role of the European Court of Justice in relation to Public Procurement," *Public Procurement Law Review* 1992, No. 1.

Milward, Alan S. 1992. *The European Rescue of the Nation State*. London: Routledge.

Milward, Alan S., and Vibeke Sørensen. 1993. "Interdependence or Integration? A National Choice," in *The Frontier of National Sovereignty*. London: Routledge: 1–32.

Moravcsik, Andrew. 1994. "Why the European Community Strengthens the State: Domestic Politics and International Cooperation." Paper presented to the Ninth International Conference of Europeanists, Chicago, March 31–April 2.

Moravcsik, Andrew. 1998. *The Choice for Europe*. Ithaca: Cornell University Press.

Moser, Stefan, Nicola Pesaresi, and Karl Soukup. 2002. "State Guarantees to German Public Banks." Competition Directorate-General of the European Commission, *Competition Policy Newsletter*, Number 2 (June): 1–11.

Nugent, Neill. 1995. "The Leadership Capacity of the European Commission," *Journal of European Public Policy* 2, 4: 603–623.

Ottervanger, T. R. 1993. "Transparency in Relations between Member States and Public Undertakings: State Aids," in J. H. V. Stuyk and A. J. Vossestein, eds,

State Entrepreneurship, National Monopolies and European Community Law. Deventer, Netherlands: Kluwer Law and Taxation Publishers.

Page, Alan C. 1982. "Member States, Public Undertakings and Article 90," *European Law Review* 7: 19–35.

Pagoulatos, George. 1999. "European Banking: Five Modes of Governance," *West European Politics* 22, 1: 68–94.

Pappalardo, Aurelio. 1991. "State Measures and Public Undertakings: Article 90 of the EEC Treaty Revisited," *European Competition Law Review* 12, 1: 28–39.

Patterson, Dennis, and Dick Beason. 2001. "Politics, Pressure, and Economic Policy: Explaining Japan's Use of Economic Stimulus Policies," *World Politics* 53, 4: 499–523.

Peterson, John. 1995. "Decision-Making in the European Union: Towards a Framework for Analysis," *Journal of European Public Policy* 2, 1: 69–93.

Pierson, Paul. 1993. "When Effect Becomes Cause: Policy Feedback and Political Change," *World Politics* 45: 595–628.

Pohl, Manfred, and Sabine Freitag, eds (for European Association for Banking History). 1994. *Handbook on the History of European Banks.* Aldershot, England: Edward Elgar.

Pollack, Mark A. 1997. "Delegation, Agency and Agenda-Setting in the European Community," *International Organization* 51, 1: 99–134.

PriceWaterhouseCoopers. 1998. "Study on the Impacts of Liberalisation in the Postal Sector: Liberalisation of Incoming and Outgoing Intra-Community Cross-Border Mail."

Richardson, Jeremy. 1998. "The EU as an Alternative Venue for Interest Groups," paper presented to the 94th annual meeting of the American Political Science Association, Boston, September 3–6.

Risse, Thomas, Maria Green Cowles, and James Caporaso. 2001. "Europeanization and Domestic Change: Introduction," in Cowles, Caporaso, and Risse, *Transforming Europe.* Ithaca: Cornell University Press: 1–20.

Sandholtz, Wayne. 1993a. "Choosing Union: Monetary Politics and Maastricht," *World Politics* 47, 1: 1–39.

Sandholtz, Wayne. 1993b. "Institutions and Collective Action: The New Telecommunications in Western Europe," *World Politics* 45: 242–270.

Sandholtz, Wayne. 1996. "Membership Matters: Limits of the Functional Approach to European Institutions," *Journal of Common Market Studies* 34, 3: 403–429.

Sbragia, Alberta. 1998a. "Italy Pays for Europe: Political Leadership, Political Choice and Institutional Adaptation," paper presented at Third Project Workshop on Europeanization and Domestic Political Change, Robert Schuman Centre, European University Institute, June 19 and 20.

Sbragia, Alberta. 1998b. "The European Union as Coxswain: Governance by Steering," European University Institute, Workshop on Governance in the European Union, June.

Scharpf, Fritz. 1991. *Crisis and Choice in European Social Democracy.* Ithaca: Cornell University Press.

Scharpf, Fritz. 1999. *Governing in Europe: Effective and Democratic?* Oxford: Oxford University Press.

Schmidt, Susanne K. 1996a. "Sterile Debates and Dubious Generalisations: An Empirical Critique of European Integration Theory Based on the Integration Processes in Telecommunications and Electricity," Max-Planck-Institut für Gesellschaftsforschung Discussion Paper 96/5 (June).

Schmidt, Susanne K. 1996b. "The European Commission's Ability to Act under European Competition Law. The Example of Telecommunications and Electricity Policy." Paper presented at the HCM Conference on The European Policy Process, Brussels, October 17–18.

Schmidt, Susanne K. 1998. "Commission Activism: Subsuming Telecommunications and Electricity under European Competition Law," *Journal of European Public Policy* 5 (1): 169–184.

Schmidt, Susanne K. 2000. "Only an Agenda Setter? The European Commission's Power over the Council of Ministers," *European Union Politics* 1 (1): 37–61.

Schmidt, Vivien A. 1998. "National Patterns of Governance under Siege: the Impact of European Integration." European University Institute, Workshop on Governance in the European Union, Robert Schuman Centre, June 18.

Schmidt, Vivien A. 2002. *The Futures of European Capitalism*. Oxford: Oxford University Press.

Schmitter, Philippe C. 1997. "The Emerging Europolity and Its Impact Upon National Systems of Production," in J. Rogers Hollingsworth and Robert Boyer, eds., *The Embeddedness of Institutions*. Cambridge: Cambridge University Press: 395–430.

Schneider, Volker, Godefroy Dang-Nguyen, and Raymund Werle. 1994. "Corporate Actor Networks in European Policy-Making: Harmonizing Telecommunications Policy," *Journal of Common Market Studies* 32 (4): 473–498.

Schneider, Volker. 2001. "Institutional Reform in Telecommunications: The European Union in Transnational Policy Diffusion," in Maria Green Cowles, James Caporaso, and Thomas Risse, eds., *Transforming Europe*. Ithaca: Cornell University Press: 60–78.

Schoppa, Leonard J. 1993. "Two-Level Games and Bargaining Outcomes: Why Gaiatsu Succeeds in Japan in Some Cases But Not Others." *International Organization* 47 (3): 353–386.

Sinn, Hans-Werner. 1999. *The German State Banks*. Cheltenham, UK: Edward Elgar.

Smith, Mitchell P. 1997. "The Commission Made Me Do It: The European Commission as a Strategic Asset in Domestic Politics," in Neill Nugent, ed., *At the Heart of the Union*. London: Macmillan: 167–186.

Smith, Mitchell P. 1998. "Autonomy by the Rules: The European Commission and the Development of State Aid Policy," *Journal of Common Market Studies* 36, 1: 55–78.

Smith, Mitchell P. 2001a. "In Pursuit of Selective Liberalization: The Impact of European Integration on State Capacities," *Journal of European Public Policy* 8, 4: 519–40.

Smith, Mitchell P. 2001b. "Europe and the German Model: Growing Tension or Symbiosis?" *German Politics* 10, 3: 119–140.

Söder, Marie Moberius. 1995. "European Public Procurement in the Single Market—A Question of National Shaping Factors?" College of Europe, Economics Department, Bruges: Academic year 1994/1995.

Strange, Susan. 1996. *The Retreat of the State.* Cambridge: Cambridge University Press.

Streeck, Wolfgang. 1997. "German Capitalism: Does it Exist? Can it Survive?" in Colin Crouch and Wolfgang Streeck, eds., *Political Economy of Modern Capitalism: Mapping Convergence & Diversity.* London and Thousand Oaks: Sage: 33–54.

Sturm, Roland, and Stephen Wilks. 1997. "Competition policy and the regulation of the electricity supply industry in Britain and Germany." London: Anglo-German Foundation.

Swann, Dennis. 1992. "Standards, Procurement, Mergers and State Aids," in Dennis Swann, ed., *The Single European Market and Beyond.* London: Routledge: 53–80.

Tilly, Richard. 1994. "A Short History of the German Banking System," in Manfred Pohl and Sabine Freitag, eds., *Handbook on the History of European Banks,* published for European Association for Banking History E.V., Frankfurt am Main. Aldershot, England: Edward Elgar.

Union of Industrial and Employers' Confederations of Europe (UNICE). 1997. "UNICE Comments on the European Commission's *Green Paper on Public Procurement in the European Union: Exploring the Way Forward,*" March 27.

Wade, Robert. 1996. "Globalization and Its Limits: Reports of the Death of the National Economy Are Greatly Exaggerated," in Suzanne Berger and Ronald Dore, eds., *National Diversity and Global Capitalism.* Ithaca: Cornell University Press: 60–88.

Weiss, Friedl. 1993. *Public Procurement in European Community Law.* London and Atlantic Highlands, NJ: The Athlone Press.

Winter, Jan A. 1991. "Public Procurement in the EEC," *Common Market Law Review* 28: 741–782.

Woolcock, Stephen. 1991. "Public Procurement" in Leon Hurwitz and Christian Lequesne, eds., *The State of the European Community: Policies, Institutions & Debates in the Transition Years.* Boulder: Lynne Rienner: 127–136.

Newspapers, Magazines, and News Services

Agence France Press
The Daily Telegraph
Les Echos
European Report
The Economist
Financial Times

Frankfurter Allgemeine Zeitung
Handelsblatt
Official Journal of the European Communities
Der Spiegel
Süddeutsche Zeitung
die tageszeitung
La Tribune
Vereinigte Wirtschaftsdienste
Die Welt
Wirtschaftsblatt

Websites

EU and Member State Institutions:

European Commission Online: www.europa.eu.int/rapid/start/cgi
European Commission, Public Procurement infringements web site: www.europa.eu.int/comm/internal_market/en/publproc/infr
Postcomm (Britain's postal services regulator): www.postcomm.gov.uk
UK Department of Trade and Industry: www.DTI.gov.uk
Land Nordrhein Westfalen: www.NRW.de

Individual Firms or Business Associations:

European Express Association (association of private sector express carriers): www.euroexpress.org
PostEurop (organization of national postal services operators): www.posteurop.org
Westdeutsche Landesbank: www.westlb.com

INDEX

SUNY Series in Global Politics

James N. Rosenau, Editor

LIST OF TITLES

American Patriotism in a Global Society—Betty Jean Craige

The Political Discourse of Anarchy: A Disciplinary History of International Relations—Brian C. Schmidt

Power and Ideas: North-South Politics of Intellectual Property and Antitrust—Susan K. Sell

From Pirates to Drug Lords: The Post-Cold War Caribbean Security Environment—Michael C. Desch, Jorge I. Dominguez, and Andres Serbin (eds.)

Collective Conflict Management and Changing World Politics—Joseph Lepgold and Thomas G. Weiss (eds.)

Zones of Peace in the Third World: South America and West Africa in Comparative Perspective—Arie M. Kacowicz

Private Authority and International Affairs—A. Claire Cutler, Virginia Haufler, and Tony Porter (eds.)

Harmonizing Europe: Nation-States within the Common Market—Francesco G. Duina

Economic Interdependence in Ukrainian-Russian Relations—Paul J. D'Anieri

Leapfrogging Development? The Political Economy of Telecommunications Restructuring—J. P. Singh

States, Firms, and Power: Successful Sanctions in United States Foreign Policy—George E. Shambaugh

Approaches to Global Governance Theory—Martin Hewson and Timothy J. Sinclair (eds.)

After Authority: War, Peace, and Global Politics in the Twenty-First Century—Ronnie D. Lipschutz

Pondering Postinternationalism: A Paradigm for the Twenty-First Century?—Heidi H. Hobbs (ed.)

Beyond Boundaries? Disciplines, Paradigms, and Theoretical Integration in International Studies—Rudra Sil and Eileen M. Doherty (eds.)

International Relations—Still an American Social Science? Toward Diversity in International Thought—Robert M. A. Crawford and Darryl S. L. Jarvis (eds.)

Which Lessons Matter? American Foreign Policy Decision Making in the Middle East, 1979–1987—Christopher Hemmer (ed.)

Hierarchy Amidst Anarchy: Transaction Costs and Institutional Choice—Katja Weber

Counter-Hegemony and Foreign Policy: The Dialectics of Marginalized and Global Forces in Jamaica—Randolph B. Persaud

Global Limits: Immanuel Kant, International Relations, and Critique of World Politics—Mark F. N. Franke

Money and Power in Europe: The Political Economy of European Monetary Cooperation—Matthias Kaelberer

Why Movements Matter: The West German Peace Movement and U.S. Arms Control Policy—Steve Breyman

Agency and Ethics: The Politics of Military Intervention—Anthony F. Lang Jr.

Life After the Soviet Union: The Newly Independent Republics of the Transcaucasus and Central Asia—Nozar Alaolmolki

Information Technologies and Global Politics: The Changing Scope of Power and Governance—James N. Rosenau and J. P. Singh (eds.)

Theories of International Cooperation and the Primacy of Anarchy: Explaining U.S. International Monetary Policy-Making After Bretton Woods—Jennifer Sterling-Folker

Technology, Democracy, and Development: International Conflict and Cooperation in the Information Age—Juliann Emmons Allison (ed.)

Systems of Violence: The Political Economy of War and Peace in Colombia—Nazih Richani

The Arab-Israeli Conflict Transformed: Fifty Years of Interstate and Ethnic Crises—Hemda Ben-Yehuda and Shmuel Sandler

Debating the Global Financial Architecture—Leslie Elliot Armijo

Political Space: Frontiers of Change and Governance in a Globalizing World—Yale Ferguson and R. J. Barry Jones (eds.)

Crisis Theory and World Order: Heideggerian Reflections—Norman K. Swazo

Political Identity and Social Change: The Remaking of the South African Social Order—Jamie Frueh

Social Construction and the Logic of Money: Financial Predominance and International Economic Leadership—J. Samuel Barkin

What Moves Man: The Realist Theory of International Relations and Its Judgment of Human Nature—Annette Freyberg-Inan

Democratizing Global Politics: Discourse Norms, International Regimes, and Political Community—Rodger A. Payne and Nayef H. Samhat

Landmines and Human Security: International Politics and War's Hidden Legacy—Richard A. Matthew, Bryan McDonald, and Kenneth R. Rutherford (eds.)

Collective Preventative Diplomacy: A Study of International Management—Barry H. Steiner

International Relations Under Risk: Framing State Choice—Jeffrey D. Berejikian

Globalization and the Environment: Greening Global Political Economy—Gabriela Kütting

Sovereignty, Democracy, and Global Civil Society—Elisabeth Jay Friedman, Kathryn Hochstetler, and Ann Marie Clark

United We Stand? Divide and Conquer Politics and the Logic of International Hostility—Aaron Belkin

Imperialism and Nationalism in the Discipline of International Relations—David Long and Brian C. Schmidt (eds.)

Globalization, Security, and the Nation State: Paradigms in Transition—Ersel Aydinli and James N. Rosenau (eds.)

Identity and Institutions: Conflict Reduction in Divided Societies—Neal G. Jesse and Kristen P. Williams

Globalizing Interests: Pressure Groups and Denationalization—Michael Zürn (ed., with assistance from Gregor Walter)

International Regimes for the Final Frontier—M. J. Peterson

Ozone Depletion and Climate Change: Constructing A Global Response—Matthew J. Hoffmann